ALISON INGLEBY

Defenders

The Wall Series Book 3

First published by Windswept Writing in 2018

First edition

This book was professionally typeset on Reedsy.
Find out more at reedsy.com

Dedication

For Grannie D, who loved to write, and Granny I, who loves to dream. These may not be the stories you want to read, but they're the stories you helped inspire me to write.

A Note on Language

This story is set in a future London and is written in British English. For my readers who are more accustomed to U.S. English spellings and terms, I hope you don't find this too distracting.

1

Aleesha

They're burning bodies in Rose Square.

The stench hangs in the air and catches at the back of my throat, coating my tongue with an acrid, slightly earthy, metallic taste. Smoke rises lazily to hang over the surrounding streets. For once, I long for rain and wind to clear the air. Even though it's not yet midday, I'm sweating under my light jacket. Summer's on its way.

People move around the pyre, dressed in white suits and masks. They're from the government and flew in by pod this morning, just when people were wondering what to do with all those who died fighting the Metz. Some of the bodies were removed by friends and family to be taken to the official crematorium, or more likely the river. But not everyone has a family to look after them.

I wonder how many of the dead were illegal citizens like me. People who, in the eyes of our government, never existed in the first place.

A solitary priest stands at one end of the pyre, mumbling prayers for the dead. I don't know what religion he claims to be from, and I've never really had much time for priests, but he's been standing there for hours surrounded by the smell and the heat of the flames, and that demands respect.

At the other end of the square, the large screens set into the surrounding buildings blare out the usual news and propaganda. They're largely ignored by the crowd, who are gathered around a smaller screen displaying a series of images: the faces of the dead.

I hover at the back of the crowd, not really sure why I've come. It's not as if I need reminding of all those who died in the Battle of Rose Square. That's what people are calling it, as if it was some noble fight rather than a mad chaotic scramble of people trying to stay alive.

A young girl smiles down on me, her toothy grin lighting up her face. The image must have been taken from the government's Personax database. She's followed by an old man whose face is unrecognizable, his skull caved in and his skin dark with blood. I guess the government didn't have a record of him.

The faces blur together until one catches my eye. The man stares straight into the camera and while his face is hard, kindness lingers in his eyes. His dark hair is shaved down the right side, and his remaining hair is braided tightly to his skull.

Jonas.

My stomach clenches as a familiar wave of guilt washes over me. He had stood over me, defending me with his body as I tried to deactivate the officers surrounding us. His shield had been practically useless against the Metz bullets. I hadn't been fast enough to save him.

I turn and walk away.

At the base of the monument where we'd fought, someone's placed a misshapen wire heart with a strip of blue fabric woven through it.

So many deaths. You'd have thought I'd have got used to people dying by now. It happens a lot in Area Four. But never on this scale, not even in the worst of Cleanings, when we could barely get the warning out before the Metz rampaged through the streets, destroying everything as they went.

I just want it all to end.

Sometimes I wonder if we should just give up and stop fighting the government, but even if we do, the killing won't stop. There will still be Cleanings. And slower deaths from starvation and tronk.

Tronk.

For a moment, I can taste it on my tongue, the slight bitterness overwhelming the taste of smoke and death. I close my eyes as the world spins and my mouth goes dry.

Then I shake my head and snap my eyes open. *How can I still want it, still crave it, even now?*

And for that reason, if no other, I know we have to keep fighting.

I arrive at the back entrance to the Snakes' headquarters to find Katya and Samson engaged in a heated discussion. Samson looms over her, his bulk making her seem all the smaller, but she holds her own, a tinge of pink on her pale cheeks the only sign of her agitation.

They break off as I approach and Katya's eyes drop to the bulge in my jacket. "You still have it?"

"Of course." I rest one hand protectively over the device that hangs around my neck, my heart beating a little faster than normal. I still don't trust either of them not to try and take it from me.

"I see you've deactivated one of the Metz already," Samson

says, jerking his head toward the old warehouse behind us.

I nod. "Is he … okay?"

Samson shrugs. "Who knows? He's refusing to talk to anyone but you." He cocks his head. "You've landed yourself in quite a position."

His eyes appraise me and a shiver runs down my spine. For all he seems to want to help, he's still bloody intimidating.

But as always, his words cut right to the point. And that's the reason I've spent the past four hours wandering the streets.

What do I do now?

The black box that Giles had entrusted to me hangs like a lead weight around my neck. It saved us in the battle, making it possible for me to take control of the communications to the Metz officers' implants and order them to stop fighting. Giles had said it could also be used to deactivate their implants, so they could no longer be controlled by their captains or by me.

I wasn't sure whether to believe him. I wasn't sure how much human was left in the officers or whether deactivating them would just let loose an army of uncontrollable cyborgs on the people of Area Four.

That was why I'd snuck out of Abby's in the middle of the night to test it alone on the one officer who I knew had something of the old person left inside him.

Rogue. Or Kian Eamon Anderson, as he seems to be called.

I think I prefer Rogue.

I nod to the doorway, where a pair of gang members are cobbling together a makeshift door from some pieces of scrap metal. The old door had been blown apart when the Metz had broken into the headquarters, and the brick around the entrance is blackened from the firebomb. "Shall we go in?"

The two gang members eye Samson and Katya warily as we

walk past them into the building, but they don't stop us.

Inside the vast main hall, the rows of Metz officers stand motionless in lines, like an army of soldiers awaiting their orders. The atmosphere is hushed. People creep around them warily, as if afraid they might suddenly wake up. It's a far cry from the clamour, the scuffles and jeers – some friendly, some goading – that's usually part and parcel of gang life.

Even for these people, there has been too much fighting recently. I cast my eye around the hall, searching for familiar faces. There are so many missing. A tightness grips my stomach and I bite my lip.

How many died protecting me? How many fell at the hands of the Metz just so we could bring their killers into their home?

Footsteps approach and I turn to see a young woman with large blue eyes and brown hair. She smiles at Samson and gives Katya an uncertain nod. I look down at my feet. Beth is the last person I want to see right now.

"Jay wants to see you. He's in his office – first door on the right." She points to an open doorway.

"Thanks, Beth." Samson smiles warmly at her. Katya's eyes narrow as they flick from the girl to the leader of the Brotherhood. I wonder if she's figured out that Beth works for him, first and foremost. I suspect so – Katya's nothing if not sharp.

I move to follow them, but Beth grabs my arm.

"Aleesha, I just wanted to say I'm sorry."

I yank my arm from her grip and wince as the movement causes a flash of pain in my shoulder. The bullet had taken a chunk of flesh out, nothing worse, but it stings all the same.

Sorry about what, I wonder. Taking Jay from me? Inadvertently contributing to Lily's death? Or just generally about everything that's happened? But I'm not really in the mood for a confrontation, and so much has happened in the past few weeks that Jay's betrayal feels like a lifetime ago.

"It's fine," I mumble, turning to leave.

She stops me again and her clear blue eyes search mine. "I know we'll probably never be friends. But if you need anything, let me know."

I don't reply, and she shrugs awkwardly and nods to the back of the room. "I've been trying to talk to the officer you woke up. But he won't talk to anyone. He just keeps asking for you."

The Metz officers in front of me hide the raised platform at the end of the room where I'd left Rogue after running back out into the night to get away from ... from everything.

I take a deep breath. "Tell Jay I'll be a few minutes."

Rogue looks like he hasn't moved a muscle since I left him. His huge frame – almost as big as Samson's – dwarfs the chair he sits on. His body is rigid, his hands braced on his thighs, and his eyes flick constantly around the room.

I pull up a chair and sit down opposite him.

"Aleesha." The relief in his voice is almost overwhelming.

I force a weak smile onto my face. "How are you feeling?" I glance down at the bottle of Chaz and the protein bar on the floor beside him, both untouched. "You should eat."

Uncertainty clouds his eyes. I reach out and rest my hand on his knee. "It's safe. They're not trying to poison you. Probably not as good as the food you're used to, but food's food."

He hesitates for a second then reaches down and flicks open the bottle. His face twists at the sickly sweetness of the drink.

"Most people out here drink Chaz, especially in the summer when the rains don't come. Water's in short supply."

He nods and continues to drink until the bottle is almost

empty.

I look down at my hands twisted in my lap. "Sorry for running off earlier."

There's a pause.

"What do you remember?" I force myself to look up into his eyes. They're so blue. Not the sky blue of Trey's eyes, but a darker, richer blue, like the brightly coloured clothing Insiders wear.

Thinking of Trey makes my chest ache and I swallow, trying to push him from my mind.

Rogue frowns. "I remember being a kid, going to school, wanting to join the Metz. The day I joined the Metz was hot and sunny. My mother wore a flower-print dress and my little sister nearly fainted in the heat. They were proud of me ..." His eyes mist over as he stares into the distance. "I remember the recruits training but after that, I struggle to remember anything at all." He looks back at me. "You look familiar, like we've met before?"

I nod.

He shakes his head, the furrows on his brow deepening. "I don't really remember where. I just have fragments ... flashbacks. But they don't seem real, as if I wasn't really there, really involved ..."

"What sort of flashbacks?" I ask softly.

A pained expression crosses his face. "Killing," he whispers. "Fighting, blood and violence." A shudder wracks his body. "People screaming, homes being burned, people being executed ... criminals?"

He looks to me, wanting reassurance that yes, they were criminals. I bite my lip and look away. Perhaps some of them had been, but many of those rounded up and shot during Metz raids or Cleanings were innocent citizens. Or people like Lily, whose only crime was being alive.

Rogue leans forward and clutches his head in his hands. "They're memories, aren't they? I did that. *We* did that ..."

My chest tightens and Giles's words come back to me. *Perhaps it is best that they don't know what they've done.*

The officers weren't supposed to remember anything of the missions they went on. Their implants controlled their movements and wiped their memories when they returned to the Metz compound. At least, that's what we think. But Rogue had been, well, rogue. His implant hadn't worked properly, or perhaps he was too strong for it. That strength had made him remember enough about me to be curious about what really went on Outside. It had made him care enough to risk his own life to help Trey and me break into the Metz compound.

I kneel down in front of him and rest my hands on his knees. "You weren't to blame. *They* were using you, messing with your mind to make you do what they wanted. You didn't have a choice." I hesitate. "Do you remember the last few days? What happened in Rose Square?"

He nods, still not looking at me. My heart sinks. I had hoped he would be spared that.

I rock back on my heels and chew my bottom lip. I don't know if Rogue is the only one who'll remember things or if the other officers will experience the same horror and realization when we deactivate their implants.

Can we put them through that? What choice do we have?

"We're discussing what to do with the rest of them. I think you should be involved."

He glances up, his eyes glistening with tears. "What can I do?"

I stand and look out over the rows of black statues. "You can speak for them."

Rogue stares out across the hall. Then he seems to pull himself together, nods and stands. "You're right," he says, and his voice has lost its uncertainty. "I may be able to help."

He looms over me and it takes a conscious effort not to flinch away. "Great," I manage. "Follow me."

Jay, Samson and Katya are waiting in what Beth called Jay's "office". In reality, it's just a room with a table, a handful of chairs and a fold-up bed pushed against one wall.

They look up when we enter and Katya frowns at Rogue trailing behind me. "Who's this?"

"He's the officer who helped us get into the compound. Figured he should be in on this discussion."

Her eyes narrow but she doesn't reply. Samson stands and moves to intercept Rogue. The two men are both tall and muscular, but there the similarities end. Rogue's brown hair is cropped short, and though his skin is lightly tanned, he seems pale and wan next to Samson, whose skin is so dark he makes the shadows thrown by the single light in the room look like ghosts.

Rogue is the first to break their stare, averting his gaze to look around the room. Samson gives a faint nod of satisfaction and returns to his seat.

I look around the table. Each of us bears the scars of the fighting. Blood leaks through the dressings plastered over Jay's body and I suspect the reason he's sitting so still is that he doesn't want to show how painful it is to move. The outline of a wide bandage bulges from underneath Samson's t-shirt. Even Katya didn't escape unscathed, though she wears her bandage on her arm like a fashion accessory. Everyone is wounded. Everyone except Rogue.

Jay coughs. "Let's get started. What's yer name?"

The question's aimed at Rogue. He sits down next to Jay and I take the remaining chair between him and Katya. "Aleesha has named me Rogue."

"But that's not your real name?" Katya leans forward.

"No."

Katya looks about to press further, but Jay gets in first, directing his next question at me. "How long's it goin' to take you to get them lot out of here?"

"We need to decide what to do with them first," Katya says before I can speak. "They are weapons."

Beside me, Rogue stiffens.

Samson's expression is placid. "Technically, they are government property."

Katya snorts. "So you want to send them back?"

"It's one option."

Katya sits back in her chair. "Look, we brought the Commander's pod down. We ended the battle. And we need *them* to carry out the next part of our plan."

Samson raises an eyebrow. "And that is?"

"Bringing down the government." She smiles across the table at Jay, who shifts uncomfortably in his seat.

Katya's used to making men uncomfortable. Her beauty is her power, but she's trying to convince the wrong person. Jay may be in charge of this building, but I'm the one who has control of the Metz.

I finger the strap around my neck. Giles trusted me to do the right thing, to protect the people inside those black suits.

But what is the right thing?

I turn to Rogue. "If we gave you a choice now, between going back to the compound and staying here, what would you do?"

He looks surprised. "I would stay."

"Why?"

He hesitates for a second. "What I have seen … What I remember. It makes me think that perhaps we've not been told the full story about our missions. I would like to learn more about what is real before making a decision on who is right and who is wrong."

Jay snorts. "Well, that won't take long. There's nothin' right about what you lot do out here. All you do is kill and destroy!" He glares at Rogue, who flinches under the onslaught.

I give Jay a look and he subsides. "What about the others? What do you think they would decide?"

"I don't know. It might depend on what they remember. I suspect many may choose to return to the safety of the compound." Rogue pauses. "It would be a big step to betray the family. But some may stay if they feel safe out here."

"The family?" Katya frowns.

"The Metz family. We take a vow to work together to keep order and protect our society. At least, that's what we were told we were doing." He looks down at his hands.

I take a deep breath and look at Samson, then Katya. "I'm the only one who can deactivate their implants. Which means I decide what happens to them." Katya's eyes narrow but she waits for me to continue. "I'll wake them up, and we'll look after them and tell them what's happened. Then give them a choice: stay here and live by our rules or return to the Metz compound."

"But that's madness!" Katya stands and leans forward over the table. "You'd just set a hundred trained killers loose on the streets so they can attack us again?"

Samson rubs his jaw. "It is a risk. We don't have the resources to keep them here against their will, but we need to make sure they don't go on a rampage out here. Perhaps we should execute a couple of them. Show people that they bleed like us."

Rogue's face blanches.

"What, and start another battle? Do you not think we've had enough fighting?"

"We could make them fight for us." Katya's fists are clenched on the table. "There's an army out there. With them, we'd have a chance at getting to the President. We may never get an opportunity like this again."

"No!" I stand and force myself to meet Katya's eye across the table. "That's not an option. They are people. Not machines."

Her green eyes flash with anger, but after a moment she sits back down.

"You may regret that decision."

Like you said I'd regret not killing Andrew Goldsmith?

I take a deep breath, trying to control the anger rising inside me.

"You may not want to stick around either." I turn to Samson. "If they see you here and then decide to return to the Metz, the government will know you're involved."

Katya presses her lips together. "I'll send Murdoch down. He'll keep out of sight but observe what happens with the first few you deactivate. We might learn something."

Samson nods agreement. "Beth will be here. There's no need for me to be here too. Besides, I have other matters to see to."

"Wait a minute. What about us Snakes? There's barely enough for us to eat and drink at the moment, and what with all the raids, there ain't much in the shops around here." Jay glowers at Samson. "People are goin' hungry, even hungrier than usual. And if we're takin' the risk of havin' 'em here, in *our* headquarters, we need payment."

Samson shrugs. "I'll see what I can do, but there's not much food anywhere. These riots have been going on all over the city."

I look pointedly at Katya. "Have you got some contacts inside the factories? You or Mil—"

"I'll see what I can do," Katya snaps, shooting me a look that quite clearly says "shut up". A smile twitches the corner of my lips.

It feels good to have some control at last. To not just be a pawn in their games.

But a thread of fear tightens my gut all the same. I know Samson and Katya too well to risk underestimating them. If they feel threatened, they won't hesitate to attack.

And it may not just be me who suffers the consequences.

2

Trey

"Please eat something, Trey." Abby looks pointedly at the bowl in front of me. "You need to keep your strength up."

I stare listlessly down at the bowl of soup and give it another stir. A chunk of unidentifiable protein rises to the surface, disturbing the pattern of green leaves that float on top of the thin liquid. My stomach churns. I really don't feel hungry.

"Trey …" Abby's voice carries a warning.

I lift the spoon to my lips and take a sip.

Who is she to nag at me? She's not even my mother.

I immediately berate myself for the thought. Abby risked her life to take me in and nurse me back to health. She's gone hungry to feed me, given me a room in her home and never asked for anything in return.

I force myself to take another mouthful. A chair scrapes on the floor and Abby sits down next to me.

"You'll go and see them today?"

She doesn't have to say who. I nod. "As soon as Bryn lets me out." I bite my lip at the bitterness in my voice, but Abby just rests a hand on my arm.

"He'll be back soon, I'm sure. Now, please finish that bowl? I don't want your mother thinking I don't feed you."

I nod and swallow down another mouthful. I know Abby has made an effort to make something I'll like but everything tastes of cardboard today.

"How's your head?" I ask, turning to look at her.

Abby makes a face. "Sore. I've got a good lump." She raises a hand to her head and winces. Her hair is pulled back into an untidy braid and I wonder if it's too painful for her to brush. "Good job I've got a good head of hair and a thick skull. But I'm alive at least, and they knocked me out before they could do any other damage."

Warmth blossoms in my chest and I squeeze her hand, managing a small smile. "Thank you, Abby. For everything."

For a moment I think she's going to pull me into a hug, but she settles for just squeezing my hand back. "It's my pleasure. It's nice having someone young around."

There's a bang from the yard, and footsteps outside the back door. It opens and Bryn limps in. He moves awkwardly, one arm still in a sling to protect the wound on his shoulder. The wound from the bullet that was supposed to have been for me.

He sinks into a chair with a sigh and sniffs the air. "Something smells good."

Abby smiles and moves stiffly over to the hotplate. "Soup again, I'm afraid."

"You know I love nothing more than your soup, Abby."

She places a bowl down in front of him and he takes a gulp. His eyes widen and he opens his mouth like a fish, wafting his hand in front of it. "Hot!"

Abby rolls her eyes then looks pointedly at me. I sigh and concentrate on finishing my own bowl.

When we've both finished, Bryn turns to me, his face serious. "Your father's body is still at the Chain headquarters. They didn't have time to return it to your mother before the fight started yesterday. Do ... do you want to see him?"

I hesitate, then nod.

Abby looks worried. "You don't have to, Trey."

"No, it's okay. I want to."

The sequence that's kept me awake for the past two nights replays in my mind again. My father kneeling in front of the statue in Rose Square, surrounded by a mob baying for his blood. The moment his eyes meet mine, his lips moving as he tries to say something. Then the shot fires, he falls forward and is hidden from sight by the crowd.

"We can go now, if you're ready?" Bryn's voice is gentle.

I look down at my fist, clenched on my thigh, knuckles white. "I'm ready."

We walk in silence through Area Five, up to the Chain's headquarters in Area Six. The ache in my muscles is almost painful enough to distract me from what's to come and I appreciate the slow pace that Bryn sets. Two men stand guard at the bottom of the steps that lead up to the front door. One of them – a guy a few years older than me with warm copper skin and tightly braided black hair – gives me a sympathetic nod. Zane, I think his name is.

Once inside, Bryn directs me into a small room. It's empty save for a hover, on which a man lies, encased in a clear dome.

My footsteps falter. A shiver runs through me and I find myself averting my gaze, not wanting to look at the body of the man I have called Father for the past seventeen years. The man who risked everything for me, even though I was not his flesh and blood.

The air feels close and stale around me and I have a sudden urge to run from the room, back to the comfort and warmth of Abby's home.

And what kind of son would that make you?

Taking a deep breath, I force myself forward until I'm looking down on him. He's dressed in his work shirt and trousers, though his tie and jacket are missing. Someone has cleaned the dirt and blood from his face, smoothed his hair back and tied a piece of cloth around his jaw, I guess to keep his mouth closed. I wish they could have done the same with his eyes. They stare vacantly up, sunken into his skull.

I swallow and look away. His hands rest on his chest, the wedding band still on the ring finger of his left hand. His skin is pale, almost wax-like. My fingers trace the Plexiglas dome that encases him.

"I can remove it, if you like?" Bryn says, moving forward. "It's just to control the temperature and keep him cool. Matthews laid him out before ..." His voice trails off.

Before she died.

Her body jerks as the bullets thud into her chest and she slumps down the wall. Jameson's terrified eyes meet mine. I blink and push the images from my mind. Matthews had been kind to me too, even though she'd lost her partner when Aleesha and I had broken into the government building. Perhaps they were together now, in death.

So much death ...

"No, leave it."

Bryn nods. "I'll leave you for a minute then."

The door clicks shut behind him.

I stare down at my father and wonder for the millionth time if I could have stopped the chain of events that led to his death.

Why did I not see what was staring me in the face? Beneath the shame, a deeper guilt crushes my stomach until I'm bent almost double, my cheek pressed to the cool dome.

I try to push the memory away but faced with him, it returns. The final time we'd spoken I had been angry. Angry that he'd authorized the Metz operation that had led to Aleesha's mother's death all those years ago. Angry about the unjustness of our society. I had blamed him for that, as if he had the power and opportunity to single-handedly change the system.

And that would have been his final memory of me.

I'm sorry, Father. I didn't mean it.

But it's too late. It's all too late.

The door clicks open behind me and light footsteps tap on the floor.

"How are you, Trey?"

My body tenses at the cultured voice. "How do you think I am?" I mutter.

Milicent doesn't answer but walks around the other side of the hover to look down on my father. Her face is smooth, belying her age, but for some reason she doesn't dye her grey hair. "He was a good man. One of the few in government who truly wanted to do the right thing." She pauses. "I tried to recruit him once, you know, to help the Chain. But he was too loyal to the government then. He still believed they were trying to do the right thing even if they didn't always succeed."

Tears prick at my eyes, my father's words coming back to me.

I've always tried to do my best for everyone.

"I've made arrangements for him to be taken to the crematorium. He will be there this evening so your mother can make the necessary arrangements."

She waits for an acknowledgement but my mouth is empty

of words. She waits a moment, then sighs and turns, her shoes clicking over the tiled floor. As she reaches the door, I find my voice.

"Milicent?"

She turns to look back at me. "Yes?"

"Have you tried to recruit other government ministers?"

She nods silently.

"And did any of them agree to help you?"

A small smile twists her mouth. "Perhaps."

I turn back to my father as the door closes behind her. He had always been the one to direct me, to answer my questions and tell me what to do with my life.

"What do I do now?" I whisper.

But this time, my father can't give me an answer.

* * *

I stand in front of the Wall, staring up at it. A swirling mass of colour, it stretches high into the sky, as tall as the tallest towers Outside. Today it's shades of red. Fitting, given the bloodshed of the past few days. The light casts a deathly glow on the windows of the apartment blocks that back onto it and I wonder if the people living inside them have heavy curtains or shutters to block out the ever-changing kaleidoscope.

The wide street is deserted. My hand tingles as it passes through the barrier. Even after all these weeks, adrenaline flushes through me. Until I know the reason why Aleesha and I can pass through the Wall when everyone else who tries it dies, I don't think I'll ever feel comfortable about touching it.

I take a deep breath and plunge through, emerging onto a wide strip of empty space that separates the barrier from the office blocks Inside. I cross the distance at a run, wondering if workers look down on me from the windows above. I've lost track of what day it is, what week it is.

No one stops me as I climb over a low wall and jump down into a narrow alley that leads between the tall buildings, but as I emerge onto a busy street, passers-by cast curious glances in my direction. I look down at my clothes. Grey and black. Very Outsider.

On a smaller side street outside a gleaming apartment block, I come across a clothes chute. A brightly coloured image wraps around it, depicting a smiling family of four holding bags of garish fabric. The text above reads: *Finished with last year's fashions? Outsiders don't mind being behind. Donate today!*

A chirpy voice trills the same message as I yank open the chute. For a moment I think it's empty, and I nearly slam the lid down in frustration, but a flash of red catches my eye. I bury my arm to the shoulder in the chute and my fingers brush across soft cloth. It's caught on something, but with a tug it comes free.

A red t-shirt. On the large size for me – I'm pretty skinny for an Insider – but it'll help me blend in. I pull it over my head and set off through the streets.

It takes me a couple of hours wandering the streets and asking for directions to find the address Ella had given me. It's in one of the less wealthy parts of the city, though homes here are still modern and luxurious compared to the apartments Outside. But my heart sinks as I compare it to the home I'd known growing up, and I know how much it would have hurt my parents to have to move here.

A woman emerges from the tall glass entrance to the white-washed block, and I run to grab the door before it closes. She gives me a surprised look but doesn't challenge me. I walk up the four flights of stairs rather than take the elevator. Apartment 14 faces onto the street.

I hesitate outside the orange door, my mouth suddenly dry.

What do I say? How do I tell them he's dead?

But when the door opens and Ella stands in front of me, I realize they already know.

"Trey."

She tries a smile, but it fails to materialize. Her face is blotchy from crying and dark bags hang under her red-rimmed eyes.

"C-can I come in?"

She shakes herself and steps back. "Sure, you better had."

No smiles. No hugs or teasing of her little brother.

Does she know what happened? Does she blame me?

I follow her down a narrow hallway into the living room. Plexiglas doors lead to a small balcony, and an opening on the far side of the room reveals a small kitchenette. The room is larger than any in Abby's house, but it feels cramped. Furniture that had been chosen to fit our old apartment feels oversized and it's packed so tight together that there's barely room to move. But it's the absence of familiar things I notice more: the ancient grandfather clock that had belonged to my great-grandmother and the huge dresser that my mother had been so proud of.

Anabel is the first to look up when I enter the room. Anger flashes in her eyes and she gives my mother a squeeze before removing her arm from around her shoulders.

"Trey. You came." My mother's voice is dull and lifeless. She pats the sofa beside her and I sink down on it and reach for her hand. Her slim fit clothes hang loose and her face is lined. She's a ghost of the vibrant woman I knew who took such pains over her appearance.

"How did you find out?"

"The President himself came to see us. He … he said …"

"He said that Father had been killed," Anabel intervenes as my mother begins to sob. "Murdered by an Outsider mob."

I look down at my hands. "It's true."

"But he didn't know what Father was doing Outside," Anabel continues, her voice steady. "There was footage of him in a pod with a dark-haired girl, and a record of him leaving through the East Gate. But I think *you* know why he went Outside, don't you, Trey? Why he would risk going to Area Four alone, without protection?"

"Yes," I whisper. I can feel their eyes on me and my chest tightens, making it hard to breathe. I look up at her – the sister I never knew I had until a few weeks ago.

Her dark hair is pulled back into a tight bun and she's dressed in her work uniform, the dark grey of the palace guard. Unlike my mother and Ella, her eyes aren't red from weeping but are tight and angry.

I force myself to take a deep breath. "I think I need to start from the beginning."

I tell them everything. Well, almost everything. I skim over the details of how we found out about Operation Nightshade – I figure admitting to the deputy head of the palace guard that we broke into the Metz compound isn't the smartest idea, even if she is my sister – but I tell them how I confronted Father about it, how Aleesha had drawn him Outside by pretending I was badly wounded, how, despite wanting to kill him, she'd let him go, only for him to fall into the waiting arms of the Chain, who had executed him on behalf of their leader.

I don't mention why the Leader wanted him executed, or that he's Aleesha's father. It doesn't seem important.

Except Anabel seems to want to know every detail. Who in the Chain had pulled the trigger, who had held him down. She throws question after question my way, probing me as if I were a criminal on trial.

Finally, my mother has had enough. "Stop, Anabel!" She throws off her daughter's arm. "It doesn't matter anymore. Nothing matters anymore."

There's an awkward silence. Ella, ever the peacemaker, gets up from her chair. "I'll make some coffee."

A few minutes later, she returns with four steaming cups.

"I don't understand why Bryn didn't stop it …" My mother trails off as Ella hands her a cup. "I thought he was better than that."

Anabel snorts. "Really, Mother? He's a *spy.* Killing people is his job."

Anger flares in me. "What do you know? You don't know him at all!"

"Well, I hardly think you're a good judge of character. How many times have you fallen for their lies?" She gives me a withering look and I stare down at the cup in my hand.

Too many times.

"Can we not argue, please? It's not going to bring him back." Ella's voice is strained.

"Sorry. It's just … Everyone hides things, Trey. Everyone." Anabel massages her temples, her eyes drooping with tiredness. "I thought you'd have realized that by now. You can't trust anyone."

"That's ridiculous, Anabel," Mother snaps. "If you live your whole life not trusting anyone, you'll never get anywhere."

"Mother …" Ella gives me a frustrated look.

"The Chain is going to take his body to the crematorium this evening," I say, trying to change the topic of conversation. But at the mention of my father's body, Mother descends into a fresh bout of sobbing and Anabel has to take the cup from her hand before coffee spills everywhere.

I lift my own cup to my lips, but the strong bitter smell makes my stomach churn. I never liked coffee.

"And where ... are we going to find the money ... for the funeral?" My mother hiccups through her sobs.

"We'll find the money," Ella replies grimly. "You'll help, Anabel, won't you?"

"Of course." Anabel sighs and pats Mother's hand. "I'm sorry. I just want to bring those who killed him to justice."

Justice. That's what brought about his death in the first place: Aleesha's misplaced sense of justice.

"Well that's sorted, then," Ella says.

She doesn't ask me for money. She knows I haven't got any.

My hands tighten around my coffee cup, the heat burning my skin through the thin china. *My father is dead and I can't even help pay for the funeral. What kind of son am I?*

My mother sits up and wipes her eyes. "I'll speak to the President. See if we can get permission for you to attend the funeral, Trey. Perhaps now Andrew's gone ..." She pauses and closes her eyes briefly before continuing, "He'll reconsider his decision to banish you and give you your rights back."

Make me a legal citizen? The thought hadn't crossed my mind. But we're a family of four again. A sacrifice has been made.

A life for a life.

The thought doesn't make me feel any better.

3

Aleesha

It takes two days to deactivate all the Metz officers, and by the end of it I'm exhausted. Exhausted at having to explain the same thing over and over again. My throat is hoarse from talking and I feel an overwhelming urge to get as far away as possible from the headquarters building and just spend some time alone.

At night, I sleep fitfully, my arms hugging the box to me like a stuffed toy. Rogue often stays up to keep watch, but even with him there, I'm afraid that someone will attack me and try to steal the device.

Finally, the day after the last officer has been woken up, I go and find Jay.

"I'm going out for a bit."

He looks alarmed. "How long for?" He glances over my shoulder at the freed officers, huddled in groups on the opposite side of the hall to the remaining gang members, and lowers his voice. "People aren't happy at them being here."

"Well, *you're* their leader. Talk to them."

He lets out a frustrated sigh and runs his hand over his close-cropped hair. "Yeah, but I need to know what yer plannin' on doing with them. When they'll be gone."

I shrug. "I told you, it's their decision." I raise my hands as he scowls at me. "Okay, look, I just need a break. I've been doing this non-stop for days, my brain is frazzled. I'll be back this evening."

Jay nods reluctantly. "You'd better be."

I roll my eyes and leave, my feet racing to get out of the building.

Out in the street, I pause and lean against a wall, closing my eyes and breathing in deeply. The air is fresh – it must have rained overnight – but the familiar stench of Area Four carries a smoky taint. Or perhaps I'm just imagining it.

I don't think Jay would have set a tail on me but I'd bet a chit or two that Samson and the Chain are having me followed, so I take to the rooftops. If someone follows me up here, they'll be easy to spot. I mix up my route, sometimes dropping down into buildings or edging around the outside of a parapet, my feet testing the stone with each step to make sure it won't crumble under my weight.

There's a row of old, low-rise apartments that line the open space between the main part of Four and the concrete jungle. The streets below look empty, but as I pull back to make my way down, a movement catches my eye. A kid sticks his head out of a doorway below and turns his face toward the jungle.

One of Samson's runners.

It's twenty paces across the flat open area to the pile of concrete and rubble. There's no way I can get across without him spotting me, and the last thing I want to do is lead Samson to Giles. Better to wait until it gets dark.

I nap for a few hours, then do some stretching and exercises. My body is stiff and sore from the fighting a few days ago, but it feels good to be moving after sitting down for two days. The bullet wound on my shoulder still leaks blood into the dressing, but my bruises have mostly turned from purple to yellow.

Thick clouds make night come early and block the light of the moon. I slip down to street level and run across the open space. To anyone watching, I'd just be a dark shadow. I take my time climbing up the rubble, using my hands as much as my feet. Even so, a few shifting blocks catch me out, sending pebbles scattering down. I wince. The sound is loud in the still night, and people more dangerous than Giles live here.

Like the Boots Brothers.

An icy chill ripples through me. I don't want to run into *them* if I can help it.

After what feels like an hour, I come across a low, uneven opening I think is the entrance to Giles's home. I duck inside and whisper his name. There's no answer. I crawl further down the tunnel.

"Giles? Are you there?"

A faint noise – the scraping of a pebble perhaps – makes my ears prick up. A moment later, the hairs on the back of my neck tingle.

"Giles?" I whisper.

"Aleesha."

His breath is warm on my arm and I have to fight the urge to pull away. I didn't think he was *that* close.

"It worked. Your box … it worked, it st—"

"Shhhhhh!" he hisses in my ear. This time, I do flinch. "Not here," he whispers.

He tugs on my arm and I follow him down the tunnel, one hand stretched out in front of me, feeling for the point where the floor drops away. I find it and twist my body to drop down feet first, then walk forward blindly until my hand catches on a fold of fabric.

I step inside the chamber, wondering why it's so dark. There's a click and suddenly I'm blinking, my eyes watering from the bright light.

Giles motions for me to sit down but I shake my head. Opening my jacket, I pull out the black box and lift the strap over my neck.

"Here." I hold it out to him.

He folds his arms and looks at me, his head cocked to one side. "You don't want it anymore?" His pale eyes bore into me and I look down, unable to meet his gaze.

"It's served its purpose. The Metz have been deactivated." I gesture again with the box. "Don't you want it back?"

Giles doesn't answer but moves over to a low table piled high with techy bits and pieces. I follow him and set the box down carefully on top of a metal lock box that's precariously balanced on the edge of the table, before turning to leave.

"Wait."

I pause and look back. Giles is staring down and twisting something in his fingers. A piece of wire. He's an odd guy. Looks like a ghost and acts like one too sometimes, with all his hissing and refusing to be touched. It's like there are two sides to his personality – the technical genius and the crazy recluse. Though perhaps the two go together.

"What happened?" he asks eventually.

"You don't know?"

He shrugs. "I know some of it."

I take a deep breath and sit down on an upturned barrel. This is going to take some time.

I tell Giles everything that had happened, from when I'd left with his box to the moment Katya and Samson had brought down the Metz Commander's pod, ending the battle between the Metz and Outsiders. I tell him how I'd ordered the Metz to march to the Snakes' headquarters and line up, and how, one by one, I'd used the box to deactivate their implants.

Giles doesn't look at me while I speak. He moves around the room, occasionally adjusting some book or ornament, or brushing a surface that, to my eye at least, is clean. If it were anyone else, I'd think they weren't listening, but with Giles … Well, I think he's taking in everything I'm saying and analyzing it in that big brain of his.

As my voice trails off, he picks up the black box from the table and crouches down in front of me. "Do they …" He pauses, turning the box over and over in his hands. "Do they remember?"

This was what Giles was worried about. I still don't know the full story of how he escaped the Metz compound, or even how he ended up there in the first place, but I think he was important to them somehow. And I get an odd feeling that there's someone he's protecting.

"They remember their lives before the Metz," I say carefully. "Most remember their time training as new recruits."

"And their time as officers? Do they remember what they were made to do?"

"Flashbacks or images mostly. Many don't remember anything at all. A few …" I pause and swallow. "A few remember everything."

I haven't been able to face them yet. The expressions of horror and disbelief on their faces when I'd deactivated their chips had been bad enough. I'd made Rogue take them away. I think Beth has been looking after them. Seems she's a natural comforter.

I swallow down the bitter taste in my mouth and look at Giles. He's staring at the black box.

"What … what do we do now?"

"We?" He glances at me sharply. His eyes are tight and his shoulders are hunched, as if he's trying to curl in on himself.

I stand and flick my long braid back over my shoulder. "I said I'd give them the choice. To go back Inside, to the compound, or stay here and help us. But I don't know how they can help us or *who* they should help. The Chain wants them. The Brotherhood wants them. The Snakes are scared of them and just want them out of their headquarters, but there's nowhere else for them to go." I begin to pace, feeling the tension and frustration of the past few days building inside me. "I don't know what's *right*, Giles. What's best for them."

I hesitate, then say it anyway. "This shouldn't be my decision."

He doesn't answer but stands, straightening his shoulders, and holds the box out to me. For once, he stares straight at me. "Why don't you want this, Aleesha?"

"Because I don't need it anymore. They're all deactivated. You said we can't switch them back on."

"You don't want the responsibility. With this box you had power. People listened to you because you had control. And you want to give that up now? When things become difficult?"

"It's not my job to look after them. I'm not a gang leader or a politician. I'm a nobody."

"But you know what's right and wrong."

"Really? Do I really?" I lean forward. "I got a man murdered because I couldn't see what was right or wrong!" Tears prick at my eyes and I turn away from him. "Look, it's your box. I'm just returning it to you now we don't need it anymore."

"One mistake doesn't make you a bad person," Giles says as I walk toward the door. “I thought you wanted to stop the killing? Stop Outsiders dying?”

“I do!” My fists clench at my sides. “I do,” I repeat quietly, more to myself than Giles.

“Well, what are you prepared to sacrifice?”

I turn to him. “What do you mean?”

An odd smile twists his face as he holds the black control device up. “You don’t need this box to make people listen to you anymore than you need someone to give you orders to do the right thing. Sometimes it’s not about choosing the right side to follow, but forging your own path.”

And what’s that supposed to mean?

But before I can question him further, Giles turns and walks over to the small bed at the far side of the cavern. He lies down and pulls a blanket over his shoulders. If that’s not a signal to go, I don’t know what is.

I sigh and pull back the curtain hanging over the doorway. As I step out into the tunnel, there’s a click and the lights behind me go out, plunging me into darkness.

* * *

I hear the sound of fighting from fifty paces away. I run into the Snakes’ headquarters and through to the main hall.

It’s chaos.

A mass of writhing bodies takes up half the space. People scream in anger and pain. Fists thump against flesh and feet trample those who have fallen to the floor.

I don’t know who started the fight, but the former Metz officers have the upper hand now. They may not have armour or weapons, but they’re bigger, stronger and faster than any

Outsider.

Above the din, a familiar accent catches my ear. "Stop fighting! We're on the same side!"

Murdoch explodes out of the crush. His dark hair is a mess and a scratch on his forehead trickles blood. He catches sight of me and strides over.

"What the hell's going on?" *And where is Jay?*

A movement up high catches my eye. A young boy of about twelve runs toward us along a metal walkway. Jay follows him, pulling on a t-shirt as he walks. Behind him, I catch a glimpse of Beth.

"One of those idiots started goading the officers," Murdoch growls in his thick Irish accent. "A minute later, they started jumping all over them. The officers fought back and we ended up with this." He slices his hand through the air in frustration. "I'd like to know where the hell Jay is."

"Here." Jay jogs over to join us.

He surveys the carnage in front of him. "Stop fighting!"

He cups his hands around his mouth to amplify his voice but no one can hear him over the racket. We need something to jolt them out of this. My eyes dart around the hall, lingering on the skylights high above us.

This building is old, from the time before the Great Flood, I think. Which means the skylights may be glass rather than unbreakable Plexiglas.

"Jay, give me your knife."

He doesn't respond, so I poke him and repeat the request, then just pull it from his pocket.

I take a couple of steps forward and pull my arm back, judging the distance. Light dances over the blade as it spins through the air.

The skylight shatters with a crack. There's a moment of deathly silence, then a mad scramble as the fighters try to get out the way of the falling shards of glass. Most of them fall on empty space – I'd picked the other end of the hall to the fighting – but a few unlucky people curse as fragments cut into their exposed flesh.

I dig Jay in the ribs. "Now!"

He starts, then steps forward. "Snakes, get yer backsides over here this minute. That is an order!" He glowers at the nearest Metz officer as if the woman was personally responsible for this mess. "And you lot, get over there." He jerks a thumb toward the back of the room.

The two factions begin to pull apart. Jay turns to me and scowls. "Why didn't you use your blade?"

I shrug. "Didn't want to lose it."

He huffs and turns away.

"Who started it?" I ask Murdoch in a low voice as Jay begins to shout at the gang members crowded in front of him.

He nods in the direction of a man in his early twenties who's muttering something to a slim, dark-haired girl. "Him. Seems to be a bit of a troublemaker?"

My heart sinks. "Yup."

I recognize the guy, though it takes me a minute to remember his name. *Vihaan*. He was some relative of Dane's. They look similar: greasy, limp hair, light brown sallow skin and a wide, flat nose. The snake tattoo that shows his allegiance to the gang winds like a collar around his neck.

After Dane's death, Vihaan had supported Rich, Jay's rival, to be the leader of the Snakes. And when Jay killed Rich in the leadership challenge, Vihaan immediately got pushed down the gang ranking system. I wonder if he's looking for an opportunity to challenge Jay's leadership.

The fact that he's talking to Megan – Rich's girlfriend – suggests that he's doing just that. I watch their body language, wondering if they're together. But Megan pulls slightly away from Vihaan and everything in her posture suggests that while she may look on him as an ally, that's all he is to her.

"Aleesha?"

My head snaps around. Jay looks at me expectantly. Everyone's eyes are on me.

Heat rises to my cheeks. "What?"

"Weren't you listening? I was telling them that we won't have to put up with the Metz being here much longer. Give 'em an update on what's going to happen."

He nudges me forward. My pulse quickens and I take a deep breath, fighting to hold back my rising panic. Some of the guys are already elbowing each other and muttering under their breath.

Damn you, Jay.

I push my shoulders back and pull over a chair to stand on, so they can at least see me. The group is pathetically small compared to when Jay had taken charge and my breath catches in my throat as it hits me how many have died.

"Hi everyone ..." My voice is small and frail. "I-I know it's not easy, having the officers around. But they ... they've also had a shock. They are not the killing machines they were. They're people – like you and me."

Out the corner of my eye, I catch Megan's frown. She whispers something to Vihaan, her eyes never leaving me.

"Some of them may choose to go back Inside. But some of them may choose to stay here, to fight with us, if we treat them right."

There's a hoarse laugh from the back of the crowd. "You want *them* fighting with us?"

A murmur of support follows.

"Over my dead body," a baby-faced guy in the front row mutters.

Jay steps forward to intervene but I wave him back.

I have to deal with this.

But I just wish I could crawl away, back to the peace and quiet of my rooftop. I'm starting to understand the appeal of Giles's reclusive lifestyle.

"And what if we don't have them fight with us. What if they go and fight against us? Perhaps the Shanksters will take them in? Or the Bigland Boys? Is *that* what you want?"

More murmurings. People shift uneasily.

"Look, we'll ... have a vote on it. *If* any of them want to stay. Which right at this moment, I doubt." I fold my arms and glare down at them. "So lay off the violence. Enough people have died this week."

Jeers follow me as I step down, my cheeks burning. It takes Jay another five minutes and the mention of dinner to calm them down. As they drift away, he turns to me.

"What d'ya think you were talkin' about, voting?"

I duck my head. "Well, I just figured it might help if they felt they had some say."

Jay leans in. "This ain't some gov'ment. It's a gang. That's not how we work and you know it."

The adrenaline seeps from my muscles, leaving me feeling weak. "Well, maybe we should change how things work." I glance up at him. "Anyway, you put me up there with no warning."

He sighs and pulls back. "Yeah, well, you did alright. Apart from the voting thing. But you need to do somethin' with that lot before the gang falls apart completely."

He walks away, leaving me standing alone. My eyes move over the officers, looking for Rogue. I don't find him.

But another man catches my eye. Even sat down he stands out as a giant. He stares at me unblinkingly in a way that makes me very uncomfortable. Even more so because I've seen him before.

He was the officer we ran into when Trey and I broke into the Metz compound.

Rogue's captain.

4

Trey

The crematorium is packed. We stand at the front as my father's coffin is carried down the aisle. Traditionally, we would have walked in with it, but Mother thought that would draw attention to me and spark the rumours again. So we stand, shoulder to shoulder, as the pall-bearers complete their slow march and lower the coffin onto the stand at the front of the chapel.

I rub my damp palms down my new suit, bought for the occasion. The fabric is expensive and it fits me perfectly. Even now, my mother has to keep up appearances. She wears a skirt, blouse and high heels, and her makeup is flawless. I know she visited the rejuvenation clinic yesterday and I dread to think about how much she spent.

Money that she needs to live off now Father is gone.

I swallow and look down at the floor. My aunt stands between me and Ella. Unable to admit that they had a third child, my parents had passed me off as her son. Despite the fact that my face and real identity has been paraded across screens all over the city, it seems Mother still wants to keep up the illusion.

The celebrant begins his opening speech. We aren't a religious family, but Mother had opted for the standard Christian service. He thanks everyone, on our behalf, for attending the funeral of "our dedicated public servant and friend, Andrew Goldsmith". Music starts up as he finishes. It's a classical piece by Beethoven – one of Dad's favourites.

We sit and I take the opportunity to look around. It's the first time I've been in a crematorium and it's not quite how I imagined it. I thought it would be grander, more like the few ornate Christian churches that still exist in the city. But it's remarkably plain. Wood-panelled walls, a cream carpet and a stand for the coffin, covered in a purple cloth. The only nod to religion is the cross at the head of the coffin.

The music dies away and the celebrant invites Anabel to speak. I guess she was the obvious choice of family representative – both my mother and Ella are already in tears, and of course, I couldn't have spoken – but I wonder how much she can talk about our father given she hasn't seen him for the best part of seventeen years.

Is she still bitter at having been sent out of the country because of me?

Probably.

To give her credit, she does a good job. Her voice is steady and although she sounds a little robotic, she doesn't break down. Her hand trembles as she steps down from the stand, and when she bows her head I see tears glisten in her eyes.

More music, then, to my surprise, the celebrant announces that the President will say a few words. There's a murmur from the people behind me and my head snaps up as he walks forward.

He's not a tall man, or as stocky as most Insiders. Thick hair, dyed black, is slicked back from his forehead and his dark brown skin is taut, but not from rejuvenation treatments.

He's not as old as I'd thought. Younger than Dad, anyway.

He looks around the room and I duck my head, not wanting to meet his eye. As he begins to speak, I glance up and see that he's not using notes. His voice carries across the room, undulating and soothing, as he tells us about the man he worked with for years, the dedicated minister who always put others first. He doesn't mention my father's demotion or how he'd spent the last few weeks of his life doing work that any low-level administrative official could have done.

I clench my jaw and blink back tears. If it wasn't for me, he wouldn't have been demoted. If it wasn't for me, perhaps he would still be here today.

I glance over at my mother, but her grief is too much for me to bear. Instead, I focus my gaze straight ahead and tune out the President's words and the words of the celebrant as he commits my father's body to the flames.

Ashes to ashes, dust to dust.

I will not cry. I will stay strong, as he would have wanted me to.

This, at least, I can do for him.

* * *

After the ceremony, people spill out into the gardens surrounding the crematorium. I hang back and slip out in my family's wake, moving toward a corner of the garden where I can stand undisturbed. Waiter bots offer guests coffee, glasses of juice and wine.

The outside of the building is as bland as the inside. Black marble pillars flank the entrance, the rest of the façade undecorated apart from a Latin inscription above the door.

Quam bene vivas refert, non quam diu.

It is how well you live that matters, not how long.

Emotion constricts my throat and I turn to the carved yew tree hedge that towers above me. I wonder idly how they keep it trimmed – it must be thirty foot tall. The hedge separates the two sides of the crematorium. We're on the smaller side, where funerals are held for the few people who die unexpectedly or of natural causes. The larger part of the building is used to process those people making the sacrifice. I guess the hedge is for their benefit. Seeing weeping mourners must make it harder to go willingly to your own death.

A sea of people in black crowd around my mother. It's odd to see Insiders in such dark clothing. The government regulation blue suits are about as sombre as people get with everyday wear.

The mourners seem to be my mother's friends and my father's ex-colleagues. I recognize a couple of government ministers from the holo screens and wonder if my father had any friends outside of work. I never spent enough time in London to know – my parents preferred to keep me hidden away at our house in Wales.

"You okay?"

I start, then smile at Ella. "I didn't hear you sneak up."

She makes a face and hands me a glass of juice. "I wasn't trying to sneak. You looked lost in your own world."

"Maybe I was."

"What did you think of the service?"

"It was fine." Across a flower bed, the crowd parts and I catch sight of my mother talking to the President. "I didn't know *he* was going to speak."

"Neither did I. It must have been a last-minute decision."

We stand in silence for a minute.

"Ella ..." I hesitate.

"Yes?"

"How much did this all cost?"

"Didn't Mother tell you? It's all paid for." She stares out at the crowd. There's a trace of tension in her voice.

"*He* paid for it?"

"The President?" She shakes her head. "No. Someone else. We're not sure who. When we turned up at the crematorium, they said everything had been paid for in advance. It appears we have a mysterious benefactor."

I frown. "Who would do that?"

Ella shrugs. "Some old friend, perhaps. At least it took one bill off our plate."

I bite my lip and look over at her. Grief still lines her face, but there's worry there too. "What's the money situation?"

"Well, we can't live off my salary. Anabel has said she'll help out, but she has to pay for her own accommodation. I can cover our rent but not M—" She checks herself and turns away. "We'll figure something out."

"Can Mother not get a job?" I ask, hating myself for it.

I should be helping them. But who would employ me? I didn't even finish school. Not to mention, I'm still a wanted criminal.

Ella casts me a searching look. "No. She can't."

My chest tightens. She's keeping something from me. But before I can question her further, she reaches out and gives my arm a squeeze. "I'd better go and mingle. Chat to you later."

I down the juice and hand the glass to a bot, who shoots over with a replacement. It offers me a selection of canapés, but I shake my head. I wonder if I should go and talk to people too, though I'm not sure what I'd say.

A murmur of conversation catches my ear. The voices are coming from behind me, through the tall hedge. I find myself straining to listen.

"I'm scared, Robert. I know it's weak of me, but I don't *want* to die." A woman's voice, cracked with emotion.

"Hush now." The man makes soothing noises, and the woman's sobs become muffled as if he's pulled her into an embrace. "You know it's the only way. They've waited long enough to start a family."

The woman hiccups. "I-I know. And I know we're old, but I don't *feel* old. I don't feel ready to go."

The couple fall silent.

"Do you think it will hurt?"

The man sighs. "They say it's just a prick. And they can put you to sleep first so you don't feel a thing. You can go first. I'll be with you, holding you tight, just like on our wedding night."

"Well, maybe not *quite* like our wedding night." The woman sounds coy, almost girlish.

"There you go, that's the smile I like to see. Let's wipe those tears from your eyes."

There's a pause, broken by a sniffing.

"Ready for our final journey? Hand in hand, together all the way – that's what I promised you."

"You did, Robert. And I promised you." Her voice is stronger now. "Together all the way."

I stare at the evergreen fronds as their footsteps fade. I'd never really thought to question the laws that govern population control. When we'd been taught about it, I'd thought it had made sense. After all, who would want to go through the frustration and pain of ageing and dying a natural death? It made sense to conserve resources and keep the population at a steady level.

At least, it had made sense then. Now, I'm not so sure about the government's allocation of resources.

Do we really not have enough for everyone?

My skin prickles, my shoulders tensing as I sense someone approach.

"Darwin."

I take a deep breath and force myself to turn around. "President, sir."

I feel him appraising me.

Is he here to arrest me? Surely he wouldn't do that, not at my father's funeral.

As if he can read my mind, he barks a laugh. "Don't worry, boy. I'm not going to be upsetting your mother any further today. She's had about as much as she can take." His eyes soften as he glances back to where my mother is standing, talking to a group of men. Her posture is strained, a small smile pencilled onto her face.

"What do you put first, Darwin Trey Goldsmith, loyalty to your family or loyalty to your cause?" He places a sardonic emphasis on the final word.

"I-I don't know what you mean, sir."

He fixes those piercing eyes on me again. "I think you do. Sometimes life gives us a second chance. You'd be wise to take it."

"Sir?"

But he just nods and walks away. I uncurl my fists and stretch my neck from side to side, wondering what the President meant. Part of me wishes I'd given in to the urge to punch him. It had only been the knowledge that Father wouldn't have wanted that, that I'd have disappointed him by letting my anger show, that stopped me.

The President gives a small nod to Anabel, who takes a step toward him, almost instinctively. But that's her job, of course, protecting him. The President places a hand on her shoulder and says something to her. Anabel nods, her eyes tracking to a man and woman in grey uniforms who stand to one side. Her shoulders relax and she turns back to talk to a familiar, grey-haired woman.

Milicent. What's she doing here?

As Anabel turns to greet another mourner, Milicent looks at me and winks before turning and walking away.

I stare after her retreating back, things finally clicking into place. A mysterious benefactor …

I wonder if she wanted to pay for the funeral or if it was an order from the Chain.

I take a sip of juice. It turns sour in my mouth.

Blood money. And my mother accepted it, without knowing.

* * *

"Thank God that's over." My mother sinks down onto the sofa. "Get me a whisky, would you, Ella?"

I frown as Ella walks over to the sideboard and pours a measure of amber liquid into a tumbler. My mother hates whisky. In fact, she rarely drinks at all.

Ella hands the glass to my mother, who throws it back in one gulp. She shakes her head and grimaces, then closes her eyes. "I needed that."

Anabel had helped us into the black pod, giving Mother and Ella hugs and me a tight smile before saying she had to go back to work. Once inside the pod, away from everyone's eyes, Mother had half collapsed onto me, as if the rod that had been holding her up all day had suddenly broken.

"Would you like anything to eat?" Ella asks.

My mother shakes her head.

This time, it's Ella's turn to frown. "I'm making coq au vin."

Mother's favourite.

Ella moves to the kitchen and pulls a packet from the cupboard, shoving it into the food heater. Making a meal is rather different here than in Abby's kitchen. A rich smell wafts out and my mouth starts to water.

"Dar— Trey, come and sit down." My mother pats the sofa next to her. I obey, wondering if Ella has put enough in for all three of us, and let her take my hand. "I was talking with the President. He ... In light of what's happened, he's agreed to offer you a full pardon. You can come back Inside, live with us, get a job. Have your old life back." She smiles weakly. "If you want to, that is."

I pull my hand away. "You need the money."

A wounded look crosses her eyes. "No! I mean, that's not what this is about. I want you to come home." She cups my cheek. "Thinking of you out there, in danger, it's driving me crazy. I ... I can't lose you too."

Her eyes shine with sorrow and love, and guilt gnaws at my stomach. Money has always mattered to my mother, but I shouldn't have assumed that was all she was after.

How hard it must have been for her, to give birth to me alone and in secret. She could have given me up as a baby, but she didn't.

"I'd be chipped again?"

She nods. "Of course. You'd have access to your bank account, healthcare, everything you had before."

Everything I gave up.

The air in the room feels suddenly suffocating. It all feels too much. I need to leave this tiny apartment and this pristine part of the city and go back to Abby's, to her cosy, comforting kitchen that feels more like home than this place ever will.

"I-I'll think about it, okay?"

My mother's face drops in disappointment.

I stand and kiss her on the forehead. "I have to go. I'll come back in a day or two to see how you are."

Her eyes search my face. "And you'll let me know then?"

"Yes, I promise."

Ella catches me at the front door. "Please come back, Trey. She needs you … we both do. And she won't admit it, but if you can get a job, it would really help." She scans my face anxiously and drops her voice to a whisper. "I know you want to help Outsiders, but you can do that living here. Some of us want things to change, and you can do more to help in here than out there."

"What do you mean?"

"I … we've started a group. I never realized how deeply our society was divided until you told me what it was like Outside and Father told me about his work. Anyway, I'm not the only one who thinks that change would be a good thing."

She reaches out and pulls me into a hug. "Think about it, okay?"

"Sure." I pull back to look at her. "But, be careful, Ella. Talking about that kind of thing can get you arrested."

She smiles impishly. "Oh, don't worry, we're careful."

But are you careful enough?

I bite my lip and turn to leave, knowing that whatever I say won't be enough to dissuade Ella once she's decided on something.

Like Aleesha, my sister is stubborn. And I get a bad feeling that'll land both of them in trouble at some point.

5

Aleesha

I force Vihaan's arm further up his back. "Yield!"

He's hurting. Tension radiates from his body as he lies face down on the mat, my knee in his back. Clearly, he doesn't want to accept the fact he's been beaten by a girl.

I lean forward to whisper in his ear. "Look, we both know I could break your arm. If that happens you won't be fighting again for months. Just tap the bloody mat."

The sour smell of stale sweat hits my nostrils and I pull back. *Come on, Vihaan. Don't be such a stubborn idiot.*

His right hand rises a fraction from the floor, then falls back. I glance over at Jay, who's refereeing the fight. He shrugs. I roll my eyes and apply a fraction more pressure to the armbar. "Again."

This time his hand clearly taps the mat. Jay nods. "Aleesha wins."

Finally.

There's a scatter of applause as I push myself up off the mat, but the crowd quickly falls silent. It's the first time a girl has won a fight since I've been with the Snakes. Actually, it's the first time I remember a girl even being challenged. We've always just been hangers-on, tolerated as long as the guys find us useful.

And now, a girl has beaten one of them in a fair fight. No wonder there are murmurings of uncertainty rather than the good-natured back slaps for the winner and jibes at the loser. It just adds to the tense atmosphere in the hall.

Jay catches my eye and gives a slight shake of his head. *Don't push it.*

I push through the crowd and head to a quiet corner to stretch in peace. I wrenched my shoulder when Vihaan nearly floored me, and the wound on my other shoulder has opened up again. I could really have done without that fight.

But you won.

I allow myself a small smile. Vihaan had not been expecting that when he challenged me to a brawl. He wanted to put me down and exert his authority. Never mind that he'd been in the wrong, bullying that kid, and no one else would stand up to him about it. He just couldn't let a woman answer back to him in any way.

And now he'd be even more pissed *and* after revenge.

I sigh and drop into a crouch, stretching the muscles on the back of my leg. Perhaps I should take some time away from here.

"Where did you learn to fight like that?"

Megan's slouched against the wall, her arms folded. She's wearing a tight low-cut jumpsuit that emphasizes her curves, and her dark hair curls over her shoulder. Her tone is accusatory, but she doesn't look upset about the outcome of the fight. Quite the opposite, in fact.

I switch legs and drop down to stretch the other. "Just picked up a few things over the years."

"More than a few things, I'd say."

"What do you want, Megan?"

"Just came to offer a bit of friendly advice. Jay may have ditched you, but it's clear you're still siding with him. That may not be the best place to be over the next few weeks, if you get what I mean."

The last thing Megan would offer me is friendly advice. Her expression may be sweet, but I've no doubt she'd stick a knife in my back if she could.

I straighten and look her in the eye. "Vihaan's going to challenge Jay's leadership?"

She smiles. "I didn't say that."

No, but you meant it.

"I think Jay can look after himself just fine."

Megan raises one eyebrow. "Given he's managed to get half the gang killed in the past week, I wouldn't be so sure about that." She straightens and turns to leave, then pauses. "Oh, but I forgot. Most of them died protecting *you*, didn't they?"

And with that parting shot, she saunters across the hall, her hips swinging from side to side. Half the eyes in the room follow her.

I drop to the floor, the satisfaction I'd felt from beating Vihaan replaced by the guilt that's been my constant companion over the past few days.

Most of them died protecting you.

I close my eyes and rest my forehead on my knee. I know she only said it to needle me, but in my heart, I know she's right.

The Snakes was the biggest and most powerful gang in Area Four. Now? I'm not so sure. I didn't notice so many of the Shanksters or the Bigland Boys in the fight at Rose Square. But then, they might have been involved in their own fights, on their own territory.

"How are you feeling?"

I look up at Rogue. "Sore."

His lips twitch and he crouches down beside me. "I can imagine. Have you got any first aid supplies? Looks like you need to replace that dressing." He nods to my shoulder.

"It's fine, I'll sort it later. How ... How are they all doing?"

Rogue blows out a breath. "Some better than others. I've been keeping a tally. There were two hundred and twenty-three of us, to begin with. About half shot straight back to the compound as soon as they'd been deactivated. They didn't even want to listen, just wanted to get out of here." He shakes his head. "A handful more left later on, so we're down to about ninety-five. I'm not sure they'll all stay though."

"Do they all remember?"

"Some of them. Others are still confused about what happened. I think perhaps if we can show them what it's really like out here, we may be able to persuade them to stay."

I glance sideways at him. He's staring at the far side of the hall, a frown creasing his forehead.

"What's wrong? You don't want them to stay?"

His eyes flick to mine. "I do. If they're staying for the right reason. That one over there, talking to Vihaan, he was my captain."

I follow his gaze to the giant of a man I'd noticed staring at me. His white-blond hair is cut short to his scalp and he towers over Vihaan, who he's talking to in a low voice. I can't read the expression on Vihaan's face, but every now and then he shoots a look in my direction.

"I thought he'd be the first to go back Inside but he seems to have chosen to stay." Rogue's voice is taut.

"You don't trust him?"

"I don't know." Rogue falls silent. "He must have been a good officer to have been made a captain."

"But if he was a captain, that means he'd have had access to the confidential files. He would have known the truth about what the Metz do."

"Yes."

"What's his name?"

"He's calling himself Primo."

There's something about the way Rogue says this that makes me look at him. "You don't think that's his real name?"

Rogue shrugs. "I just knew him as X4 – that was his number. We were all just numbers in there."

There's a pause. Eventually, Rogue sighs and gets to his feet. "Just, maybe keep an eye on him. There's something about him that unnerves me."

A shiver runs down my back as Primo turns in our direction. His eyes bore into me. "I know what you mean."

I finish stretching, then skirt around the edge of the hall to find Tommy, the kid I'd been defending when Vihaan challenged me. He's with a couple of the younger members of the gang, studiously practising baton drills under the supervision of Jax, an older man with steel-grey hair whose lean body is covered with scars. He's the unofficial trainer for the Snakes, and one of our best artists. The huge blue snake whose head looks down on the entrance to the headquarters was his work.

I lean against the wall next to Jax and watch as Tommy dodges a strike and catches his opponent on the arm. The kid squeals.

"That was good fightin', back there," Jax says in a low voice. "But I'd be careful. Vihaan doesn't like to lose."

A flicker of irritation rises in my belly. *Does everyone feel like they need to warn me?*

But I nod as we both continue watching the boys fight. Jax could be a good ally, though he's known for not taking sides. Probably how he's survived so long in the gang; that, and the fact he's unbeaten in a fight. Never challenged for leadership though – that's not a role he wants.

"Thanks. And I know. But *he* challenged me."

"Aye, and I know you was standin' up for Tommy, an' I approve of that. He was gettin' a bit high-handed. But mebbe take a bit of a time away from here. You've been stirrin' things up a lot recently, bringin' *them* here. People are feeling threatened."

It's the longest speech I've ever heard Jax make. He's a surly man, not known for being chatty.

"Sometimes change is necessary."

He shrugs, then pushes himself off the wall. "Watch that left side, Tommy. Yer letting him take you for granted."

I watch him as he stands behind the boy and demonstrates how he should defend himself. He's a good teacher. I suspect I could learn a lot from him if he'd teach me. Which he won't. I'm only a girl, after all.

Jay catches me as I walk back out into the main hall. I can see from the worry lines on his forehead what he's about to say. "It's okay, I'm going." I stifle a yawn. It's getting late. "I'll come back tomorrow afternoon to talk to the officers."

Jay's face clears and he nods. "Good. Everyone's a bit on edge still."

He turns to leave but I grab his arm. "Look, Jay, watch out for Vihaan, okay?"

He scowls. "I think if *you* can beat him, I won't have any problem."

I swallow down my irritation at the comment. I've never fought Jay, and he's a pretty good fighter, but still …

"He's been talking with that blond officer – the big one called Primo. He was a captain. I think ..." My voice trails off because I don't know what I think, other than I get a bad feeling about that man. A really bad feeling. "Just be careful, okay?"

Jay puffs out his chest. "I'll be fine. Or at least, I will be once you get *them* out of my headquarters. Then we can get back to normal."

I sigh as Jay strides out into the hall. That's just the problem. I don't think things can ever go back to the way they were. Too much has changed.

* * *

I spend the night on my rooftop, sleeping fitfully as a strong wind batters the corrugated iron roof above my head. Come morning, I feel more tired and bruised than ever before and the skin around the blood-stained dressing on my shoulder feels hot. I haven't been able to clean it properly for days.

Perhaps Abby will have something I can put on it.

It's early morning and even the hobies are curled up asleep, or trying to sleep, so few eyes follow me as I make my way up to Area Five and along the narrow alleyway that leads to Abby's backyard.

I peer in through the kitchen window. It's dark and empty. They must still be asleep. I wander around the yard, wondering how on earth Abby manages to get anything to grow out here. A lot of the beds are empty – it's still the tail-end of winter, after all – but some bushier plants give off a fragrant scent. Along one side, a clear plastic tunnel covers rows of tiny green seedlings that peek up through the soil.

The kitchen door opens. "You're up early." Abby gives me a

tired smile.

I return it. "So are you."

"Come in, it's good to see you. I've been worried about you."

Abby worries about everyone, but her words cause a faint warmth to spread in my chest. It feels good to be back in this kitchen. The bright colours and pictures pasted haphazardly on the wall make it feel warm and welcoming. It's what I imagine having a home feels like.

Abby clicks her tongue. "Electricity's off. We may have to wait a bit for the panels to start working." She puts the kettle she was holding down on the worktop and peers out the window at the lightening sky. "Looks like it's going to be a fine day."

"Can you have a look at this?" I strip down to my cropped bra and begin to peel off the dressing on my shoulder, wincing as it tugs at my skin. "I think it might be getting infected."

The skin under the dressing is red and swollen. Abby walks over and frowns. "It should have healed better than that. I'll give it another clean when we have hot water and give you something for it." Her eyes flick to the fresh bruises on my arms and side, purple against my golden skin. "You've been fighting."

"One of the Snakes was bullying a young kid. I intervened and he challenged me to a fight." I shrug and wince. "He lost."

"Was that wise?"

I sigh. "Probably not."

Abby potters around the kitchen until a ping from the hotplate indicates the electricity's back on. "Tea?"

I nod.

She adds a spoonful of dried herbs to two mugs and fills them with boiling water. Fetching a small jar down from the cupboard, she sets it on the table along with a bowl of hot water and a bottle containing a yellowish liquid. "This may sting a bit."

I take a sip of the tea as she pulls on a pair of gloves. The hot liquid scalds the top of my mouth but that's nothing compared to the pain that shoots from my shoulder when Abby dabs a warm, damp cloth on my skin.

"Sorry, the vinegar does sting but it'll help."

I grit my teeth and eye the black paste in the jar. "What's in that?"

"Honey and charcoal. It should help draw the infection out. I'm afraid I'm out of anti-infection pills."

I tense as she smears a spoonful of the paste onto my shoulder, but it doesn't sting like the vinegar.

Footsteps sound on the stairs as she presses a fresh dressing down. "There you go. If you're around this afternoon, I'll change it again."

The door opens and Trey walks in. "Morning, Ab—" He stops when he sees me and a red flush rushes to his cheeks. He drops his gaze to the floor. "Uh, sorry, I didn't …" He turns to leave.

"It's okay, we were just finished." I pull my top back over my head to cover my bruised body.

There's an awkward silence and I wonder if I should leave.

His words haunt me: *I don't know if I can forgive you yet. Not completely.*

"Come and sit down, Trey." Abby pours another mug of tea. "Did you manage to sleep?"

He shrugs but sinks into a chair on the opposite side of the table. "A little. How are things going with the officers?" His eyes flick to my chest. "You don't have the box?" There's a trace of worry in his voice.

"I gave it back now they're all deactivated. Half of them have gone back Inside, to the compound, but there are plenty still around the headquarters. It's getting a little ... tense over there."

"They went back to the compound? After you told them what they'd done?"

I swirl the mug in front of me. "Many of them don't remember. The implants wiped the memories of what they did as officers. All they remember is their lives before the Metz."

"And most of the Metz officers are recruited Inside." Abby takes a sip of her tea. "You know how scared you were, Trey, when you ended up Outside. Is it any wonder they ran off back to what they know?"

"What about the others? Will they help us?"

"Who's us? The Chain? The Brotherhood? The Snakes?" I'm surprised by the sharpness of my words.

Trey drops his eyes to the table.

"Sorry." I take a sip of the hot liquid. "I just don't know what's best for them at the moment. Rogue suggested we show them what life's really like out here to help persuade them to stay, but that would take time, and I'm not sure how long Jay can keep the Snakes off their backs."

"Is there anywhere else they can go?" Abby asks.

I spread my hands. "I'm sure the Chain would find somewhere for them. Or the Brotherhood. But what would they want in return?"

Trey looks as if he's about to say something but stops.

"What?"

He hesitates. "If Bryn was right and your father is coming to London, you could ask him."

The mug nearly slips from my hands. *Ricus Meyer. My father. The father who doesn't know I exist.*

"Has Bryn said any more? About when he might be here?" My voice breaks.

"No," Abby replies. "Just that he'll get here when he gets here."

"Okay." I search for another topic of conversation. "How's your family, Trey?"

Trey's eyes tighten and he looks away. "Father's funeral was yesterday. They want me to go back Inside. Without his wage, they'll struggle to afford their apartment. And Mother …" He swallows and looks down at his clenched hands. "Mother wants me back with them."

My throat constricts and I tug at the high collar of my top, suddenly finding it hard to breathe.

"But would you be allowed back Inside?" Abby asks.

Trey nods. "The President has agreed to give me a pardon."

I try and swallow but it feels like I have a hard lump in my throat.

A pardon. But what about all the Outsiders who are illegal? There's no pardon for them. No pardon for me.

I had thought Trey was different. That he really believed our system was wrong and we should do something about it. That he cared for me.

And you still think that after what you did to him?

Guilt sours my mouth.

"Do you want to go back?"

My tone is cold and he glances up in surprise. I see hurt in his eyes. I didn't mean it to come out like that. I want him to stay.

But Inside, he would be safe. He'd have money and a proper life. He could be happy.

I take a sip of my tea so he can't see my flushed cheeks.

"I don't know," he says eventually. "But they're my family, and if it wasn't for me, Father would still be alive."

"Not because of you. Because of me."

Abby reaches out a hand to each of us. "Neither of you is

responsible for what happened," she says gently. "Your father knew the risks of his position and keeping your identity a secret, Trey. And Aleesha, you weren't to know what the Chain was planning. Please don't blame yourselves. You're both too young to have this hanging over you."

How can she say that? How can she say I'm not to blame when I held a gun to his head?

The kitchen feels suddenly suffocating. I push my chair back and pull my hand from Abby's grasp. "Maybe it is better if you go back Inside. Safer there than out here." I turn away and head for the door.

"Aleesha, wait!" Abby calls after me. But I don't answer.

I make it to the end of the yard before the tears fall from my eyes.

6

Trey

I stare at the kitchen door as Aleesha storms out. Abby lets out a sigh. "Breakfast?"

She makes some porridge and watches me while I eat it. I turn the empty bowl toward her. "Happy?"

Her face tightens and I instantly feel bad. "I'm sorry."

"It's okay." There's a bang from upstairs and footsteps thunder down the stairs. "It must be a tough decision."

"What's a tough decision?" Bryn asks, walking into the kitchen. The wound on his shoulder has healed enough that he no longer needs the sling. He yawns. "You let me sleep in."

"You obviously needed it." Abby shoves a bowl of porridge over the table to him.

"Thanks." He sits down and digs his spoon into the thin mush. "I saw Aleesha leave."

My hands grip the mug in front of me a little tighter.

Bryn stops eating and looks from me to Abby. "What's going on?" He frowns. "What was she doing here?"

"She came to get her wound checked out." Abby sits down at the table. "That's all."

"That's not all." Bryn licks the back of the spoon and his eyes turn to me. "What did you say to her to make her run out like that?"

I stare down at the herbs bound to the sides of the mug.

"Trey?" A trace of irritation enters his voice.

"I don't know. I just said that my mother had asked me to come back Inside. She wants me to go back and get a job. The President's agreed to grant me a pardon."

Bryn places his spoon carefully back in the bowl. "And do you want to go back?"

I shrug. "I'm not sure what I want." The porridge feels like concrete in my stomach. I lean forward and rest my head in my hands. "I want to help Outsiders, but what good can I do out here? I've got no skills, I hate the sight of blood so I'm useless to Abby, and when it comes to fighting I'm a total wuss."

"No, you're not," Bryn says quietly.

I glance at him in surprise.

Bryn twists his hands together awkwardly. "You went into the heart of the fighting, despite me telling you not to, and you stood in front of that Metz officer who was holding a gun to you. You're *not* a wuss." He clears his throat and looks down at his bowl, his cheeks reddening slightly. "I ... I'm proud of you, Trey. You did well."

My chest swells.

I catch Abby smiling out the corner of my eye. "He's right, Trey. You're not the scared Insider boy who came into my kitchen, terrified of his own shadow."

Heat rises to my cheeks. I still feel scared of everything even if I manage not to show it.

I clear my throat. "Well, I also don't want to outstay my welcome. You've been so good about looking after me, but at some point I need to figure out how to look after myself."

"Nonsense, I love having you here." Abby stands and, grabbing Bryn's bowl off the table, turns her back. "This house is too big for one person."

But now you have Bryn.

"Truth be told, I quite like having you around," Bryn says gruffly. "And if you want to be useful, well, we need someone who's good with tech. Now Jameson's ..."

Now Jameson's dead.

My hand trembles as I push my mug away. Bryn's only saying that to make me feel better. Like he feels obliged to look after me now the man I thought was my father is dead. But how can someone I've known a few months take the place of the father I've known for seventeen years?

I meet his blue eyes, the same as mine. "But my mother needs me. What would you have me do?"

He turns away. "Whatever you think is right. But don't feel like you can't stay out here. This can be your home too." He pushes his chair back from the table and gets to his feet, wincing slightly. "I feel old. I never used to take so long to heal."

"Well, maybe you should start taking it easy at some point?" Abby gives him a pointed look.

"Maybe I should." He gives her a sheepish grin. "Need anything while I'm out?"

Abby shakes her head.

"See you both later."

The door bangs shut behind him. I get to my feet. "You need a hand with anything?"

"No, thanks. I'm going to head out to see Amber in a few minutes. Will you be okay here by yourself?"

"I'll be fine. I'm not a kid, you know."

She ruffles my hair, then catches the expression on my face

and smiles ruefully, letting her hand drop. "I know, sorry."

I stay sitting at the kitchen table after Abby's gone, thinking about what I should do, but my head is thick and making any kind of decision feels impossible. I trail a finger listlessly in circles, resting my head on my hand. If I'm honest with myself, I don't really belong out here. I wanted to help, wanted to be a hero, but it's not what I thought it would be like.

My eyelids begin to close, and it's only when my head slips from my hand that I'm jerked awake. I feel sick with exhaustion, but my sleep is so crowded with nightmares filled with fighting and death that I try and stay awake at night.

I can't do this anymore.

I'm not brave and strong like Aleesha. She may not be right all the time, but there's something about her conviction and certainty that pulls people along with her. I don't think she realizes she's doing it half the time. Whereas when they see me, they just see a weedy Insider boy and dismiss me out of hand.

At least if I went back Inside, I'd be helping my mother and Ella. Besides, I'm not a boy anymore. I can't keep relying on other people to look after me.

I get to my feet and walk upstairs, realizing as I enter my bedroom that I have nothing to pack. Everything in this room belongs to Abby or was bought for me by Bryn. I turn around and return to the kitchen.

I came with nothing and I'll leave with nothing.

* * *

It's only when I reach the Wall that the consequences of my decision really hit me. I glance down at the thin pink scar on my right forearm. It brings back memories of my escape from school, having to slice through my skin and dig into my flesh with a broken piece of glass to get to the tiny gold microchip embedded in my arm. The blood … there had been so much blood.

I lean back against a crumbling concrete wall and close my eyes, swallowing hard.

Going back to my family will mean getting chipped again. I'll get a bank account, access to food and healthcare, and all the other benefits of being a citizen. But they'll also be watching me. Tracking me. If I go to see Abby and Bryn or meet Aleesha, they'll know. Insiders don't go wandering around in Area Four. *Shouldn't* be wandering around in Area Four.

In front of me, the Wall shimmers. Swirls of jade and turquoise merge and diverge, like eddies and currents in a stream.

Aleesha's words come back to me. *Maybe it is better if you go back Inside.*

Does she want rid of me that easily?

She doesn't need me anymore.

Tears prick at my eyes. She cares for me, I know she does.

Why did she say that then? Why did she run off as if she had somewhere more important to be instead of trying to persuade me to stay?

A sharp pain cuts through my thoughts. Spots of blood dance on my knuckles where I've scraped them on the wall. Dammit. Perhaps the nagging voice in my head is right. But when we kissed … I *know* she felt what I felt then.

But that was before my father's death. Before Rose Square. That changed her. She stood her ground with Katya and Samson in Rose Square and was ordering Jay around like *she* was the leader of the Snakes.

I can't help the sharp twist of jealousy that turns my insides. *A leader. Just like my father wanted me to be.*

And if that's the path she's going down, she'd be better off with someone like Jay, or Rogue. Someone her equal, who can fight with her and protect her. I saw the way Rogue looked at her when we were in the Metz compound, saw the blush in her cheeks as she pulled away from him.

The knot in my stomach tightens.

They would be a good pair: both rebels, both fighters. He's not a weedy, skinny Insider who's average at best.

My knuckles crack as I slam my fist into the concrete behind me. I take a step toward the Wall and stretch out my hand, ghostly green in the reflected light.

There's no going back.

I swallow down the lump in my throat and step through the shimmering barrier to the Inside.

* * *

Ella answers the door when I knock. Her eyes scan mine and her face relaxes into a smile of relief.

"Thank you," she whispers, stepping to one side to let me through.

Am I that transparent?

My mother is lying listlessly on the sofa in the main room. She jerks upright when I walk into the room. "Darwin!"

"Trey." I walk over and sit down beside her. "It's Trey now, Mother."

She brushes my comment aside. "We've been waiting for you to come back. Have you ... have you decided?"

The rejuvenation treatments she'd had for the funeral already seem to be wearing off and her eyes are red-rimmed from crying.

No going back.

"Yes. I'll come back. I'll take the President's offer and try to get a job Inside."

Her face sags in relief and she throws her arms around my neck. "Thank you," she whispers. "It's good to have you home."

I glance around at the cluttered room and wonder if it will ever feel like home. Mother's perfume chokes my nostrils and I pull back slightly. "It's great to be here. Though I'm not sure what sort of job I'll be able to get, given I haven't got any qualifications. Maybe one of the other schools would let me in to take my final exams?"

"Oh don't worry about that." She sits upright and waves a hand. "I've got something lined up for you. A favour from a friend."

Her eyes sparkle and colour returns to her pale cheeks. She looks more like her old self again.

There's a ping from the kitchen and Ella comes out balancing three mugs of coffee on a tray. I add spoonfuls of powdered milk and sugar to my mug and take a sip. Better. My taste buds must have got used to the subtle tastes of Abby's herbal teas.

"So what's the job?" I ask.

"Production manager at Coleman's," my mother replies. She smiles brightly. "It's a great opportunity! We really owe Brad for offering it to you, especially considering, well, you know …"

Considering my face has been publicized as a thief and criminal, you mean.

I frown. "Coleman's the food company?"

"Yes, they're the second biggest in the country, though Brad has plans to change that soon. He's very ambitious. Always was.

We were at school together. I do believe he had a crush on me once, though of course he has the most *wonderful* wife now." Her cheeks turn pink.

The coffee sours in my mouth as my father's words come back to me: *There are two companies who deal with the production of factory food ... They are more powerful than anyone.*

I try and remember what else he'd said, but I'd been angry at the time, demanding to know about the tronk in the government food rations.

"That sounds great, Mum." My words sound forced, but she doesn't appear to notice.

"You'll start on Monday. After we've got you chipped and your bank account set up." She looks me up and down. "And got you some proper clothes."

I roll my eyes at Ella, who takes a sip of her coffee to hide her smile.

"Well, I might just go and freshen up a bit. Then we can go and see about getting your chip sorted. No point wasting time." She bounces up off the sofa and heads in the direction of the bathroom.

"What's got into her?" I ask.

"I think she's just happy to have you home. Something's going right for a change." She lets out a heavy sigh.

I step around the table and join her on the smaller sofa. "Ella, you remember what Dad said about the food companies? I can't work for them!"

"Shhh!" She glances anxiously over my shoulder. "Don't you see? This is an opportunity!"

I stare at her. Now it's her turn to roll her eyes. "Come on, Trey, you're not that daft," she says in a low voice. "If you're an employee, then you can spy on them, find out what's really going on in there. Maybe you can even make them change."

"I'm a production manager, not a director! What does a production manager even do?"

"I'm sure they'll train you up. Look, you'll be paid decently *and* you can feed information back to us that might help."

"To us?"

"My group. Well, it's Dexter's group really, but that doesn't matter. They can't wait to meet you."

"Wait, who's Dexter?"

Ella flicks her hand impatiently. "My boyfriend. Just give it a go, Trey. You may even enjoy the work, and if not, it'll still give you some experience and you can apply for something else."

My heart sinks but I know she's right. Even so, it feels like the ultimate betrayal. A few weeks ago, I'd been arguing about how we needed to make the information about the government cover-up public. Because it was wrong that they had poisoned citizens with tronk, that that had led to the divide in our society. It wasn't the Outsiders' fault they weren't as smart or strong or healthy as Insiders. It was the system – the system the government and the food companies had created.

And now I was going to be part of that system.

I pull my arm from Ella's grip and rake my fingers through my hair. "I can't do it, Ella. I just can't."

"You have to, Trey." She stands and collects up the empty coffee cups. Her voice is oddly cold, unlike the Ella I know. "We all have to do things we don't want to sometimes. All of us."

7

Aleesha

I flit in and out of the Snakes' headquarters for the next few days, trying to stay inconspicuous. Summer is on its way, so the nights spent on my roof aren't as cold as they were a few months ago. In many ways, it's better than sleeping at headquarters. At least up there, I feel safe.

The downside is, it gives me time to think. And somehow, my thoughts always seem to turn to Trey.

I haven't been back to Abby's, not wanting to know if he's gone back Inside, to *them*. But if the President has given him a pardon, I guess it makes sense for him to go back to his old life. Who wouldn't want to be an Insider? It was what I always wanted.

My stomach grumbles. I need food.

Or tronk. Tronk takes away the hunger. You can forget everything …

I realize I'm clenching my fists and force myself to relax. "Not tronk, food."

I find a back-alley shop that I know accepts chits. The shelves are almost bare, but there are boxes scattered along the aisles. The shopkeeper's at the back, unloading packets of instant noodles onto the shelves.

"What you got in, McGinty?"

He starts and turns, his face relaxing when he sees me. "Oh, it's you. Just got fresh supplies in today." He stretches his back out. "First time in a week. What are you after?"

I eye the boxes of meals enviously. I could probably afford one but I've no way of heating and hydrating it. Protein bars are tasteless and dull, but they give maximum calories for cost. "Protein bars. And water, if you have any?"

"Just Chaz, I'm afraid." He points. "The boxes are over there. Help yourself."

I dig around until I find the right boxes and pull out four protein bars and a couple of bottles of the fizzy orange drink. McGinty comes over to the counter to take my chits. "Not seen you around much lately. Or that little girl you were 'ere with last time."

My breath catches in my throat at the mention of Lily. "Didn't you hear? The Metz got her."

His face darkens. "I didn't. Those bastards. There's been too much fightin' goin' on around here." He jabs his finger into the counter. "Not to mention your lot clearing my shelves out. I can't live off nothin' you know."

"I'll mention it to Jay," I mumble, backing toward the door.

I clutch the bottles to my chest and keep my head down as I wind through the streets and duck into a narrow alley. I've dropped the bottles and the protein bars through the empty window and am about to pull myself up when a patter of footsteps causes me to turn.

"Aleesha!"

I let my arms fall back to my sides. "Tommy? What is it?"

The boy skids to a halt in front of me, his face flushed. "Jay …

the Metz officer … fight," he pants.

I grip his shoulders gently. "Calm down. Take a few breaths, you're not making sense."

He nods vigorously, his unruly brown hair falling over his freckled face. He opens his mouth to speak but I shake my head. "Uh-uh, wait until you can report properly."

He manages to restrain himself for ten seconds. "Primo, the big Metz guy. He challenged Jay to a fight."

My blood runs cold. "A fight?"

The boy's face twists in pain and I realize I've tightened my grip on his shoulders. I force my fingers to relax. "Sorry. What do you mean a fight?"

"A-a leadership contest. They're goin' down to the square now. Beth sent me to find you." His face pales. "What 'appens if he beats him? Will the Metz take us all in?" His thin body begins to tremble.

I straighten and put a hand out to the wall to steady myself. *I'd thought Vihaan would challenge him. And Jay could easily take him down. But a challenge from outside the gang? That's unheard of.*

"Aleesha?"

I pat Tommy's shoulder. "Jay will be fine. He's a good fighter. Have they got the jury ready?"

"I-I think Vihaan is sorting it out."

Damn.

But with Jonas dead, Jay's short a second. Of course Vihaan would press his advantage.

"And Danny."

Well, that's something. An image of the stocky young man with a snake tattooed on his shaved head appears in my mind. Danny's no leader, but at least he's loyal to Jay.

Tommy looks scared.

"Look, just go back to headquarters and wait to see what happens. It can be a bit rough around the challenge arena."

"But I want to see what happens."

"If you can find a way up to the rooftops, you might be able to look down from there. But stay off the streets, okay?"

He nods and I give him a gentle push. As he runs away, I slump against the wall and close my eyes. This is bad. Really frickin' bad.

There's got to be some way to fix it. Some way Jay can win.

But try as I might, I can't think of anything as I sprint down toward the river.

* * *

There's already a crowd gathering as I run into the large square where leadership contests are held. A couple of guys with the double knife tattoos of the Shanksters are roping off an area in the centre, about twenty metres square. The square is the largest in this part of the city and is ringed on three sides by old, six-storey buildings. The buildings extend out into the river, which laps up to form the fourth side of the square.

I scan the crowd for Jay, but he doesn't seem to be here yet. Neither does Primo. My eye falls on Vihaan, talking in a low voice to a group of people gathered around a set of tables. The jury. I wander over to them and listen in on the conversation. There are twelve altogether: seven members of the Snakes and five representatives from other gangs. None of them look happy to be here.

"We can't have a fuckin' Metz officer taking over," the Bigland Boys rep mutters angrily. "It's against the rules. What the hell are you lot playin' at anyway? Going to get 'em to do yer dirty work?" He steps toward Vihaan, who glares up at him.

"Shut yer face. And it's not against the rules. Anyone can challenge – you know that."

"But a Metz officer?"

Vihaan shrugs. "He's decided to leave the Metz behind. Says he wants to help us."

The man's eyes narrow and he reaches out and grips Vihaan's t-shirt, pulling him forward. "Help who?"

"Cool it," a female voice snaps. A hard-faced woman pushes them apart. I recognize her from Jay's leadership contest. She's unofficially in charge of setting up and running leadership contests. No one messes with her. I allow myself a small smile.

"I know this isn't usual, but Vihaan's right. Technically, anyone can challenge for leadership of a gang. And as much as I don't approve of the suddenness of this contest *or* the contestants, it will go ahead. Understand?" She glares at them. The Bigland Boys rep – their leader, I think – seems about to protest, but the woman shoots him a look and he subsides, picking at the acne that covers his cheek.

The smile falls from my face.

"Given how much fightin' there's been lately, I think it's best just to get this over and done with as quickly as possible," the woman continues. "Jury, you've had your briefing." She jerks her thumb. "Vihaan, get out of here, you're not part of the group."

I turn my back as Vihaan walks away in a huff and down toward the river. A commotion at one of the entrances to the square catches my attention. Primo is striding purposefully toward one corner of the roped-off ring. A handful of other officers trail after him, easily distinguishable from the Outsiders by their size and black suits, along with a couple of members of the Snakes. I take care to memorize those faces. It pays to know who your enemies are.

Jay enters the square a few minutes later. He has more supporters around him, but they're all Snakes. Obviously, none of the Metz are prepared to declare their allegiance against the captain.

Is that because they support Primo or because they think he'll win?

Jay spots me and gives a slight nod. He murmurs something to Beth, then pushes through the crowd around him and heads in my direction. Beth's gaze follows him, her face lined with worry. Jay walks with a slight limp, still not fully healed from the fighting at Rose Square.

"What happened?" I hiss as he gets closer.

"You were right." Jay's face is dark. "Bastard challenged me. Vihaan put him up to it, I think. Knows he won't win himself, so gets someone else to do his dirty work for him."

"And you accepted?"

"What else could I do?"

I fall silent and bite my lip. He's right. Gang leaders can't refuse a challenge. It's the rules. And besides, refusing would only show everyone that he was too scared to fight and that would prove he wasn't fit to be in charge of the Snakes. That was why Dane had been leader for so long. He'd commanded such fear and respect that no one dared challenge his authority. Until Samson had killed him, of course.

I grab Jay's arm. "Does Samson know? Maybe he can help, like last t—"

"Shut up." Jay looks around alarmed, but there's no one close enough to hear. He lowers his voice. "No. Beth's sent a message but she doesn't think it'll get to him in time. It's all happened so quickly. I … I don't know if I can win this, Aleesha."

It's the first time I've ever heard Jay admit that he might be weaker than anyone. His brown eyes are wide with fear and for once he looks young and vulnerable. Fear laces my stomach in knots. Jay may be arrogant and cocky but he needs that confidence if he's to have any chance against Primo.

"Primo can't win, Jay. This isn't just about the Snakes. A Metz officer in charge of a gang? It can't happen." I grip his arms. "You *have* to beat him."

For a moment we stare into each other's eyes, then Jay looks away.

"Look, I know I haven't been the best leader for the Snakes, but there's no one else." He pauses, then turns to look at me. "You're the smartest person in the gang by far. And one of the best fighters. The way you put Vihaan down? Not many people could have done that. You're the one who should be leadin' them, Aleesha."

"Are you mad?" The words are out of my mouth before my brain has fully processed what he's said. They're louder than I'd intended and people nearby turn to look at us. I lower my voice to a whisper. "Don't be an idiot. I don't want to be a leader, and even if I did there's no way the Snakes would accept me. Most of them don't like me."

"They don't 'ave to like you. They just need to respect you." Jay pulls me toward him. "Look at me, Aleesha."

Reluctantly, I drag my eyes up to meet his.

"I dunno if I can win against Primo." His eyes cut across the square to where the huge Metz officer is stretching and warming up. "But you're smart enough to figure out a way to beat him. If I go down—"

"You're not going down, Jay."

You can't go down.

He glares at me. "If I go down, promise me you'll look after the Snakes. Swear you'll do whatever it takes to get rid of *him.*"

I feel sick to my stomach. He really doesn't believe he can win. *He's going to throw away his life and expect me to pick up the pieces.*

Jay grips my shoulders and gives me a shake. "Promise me, Aleesha." His voice is fierce.

I snap out of my daze and stare into his eyes. They're harder now – the vulnerability is gone. That's good.

"I won't promise, Jay. Because I don't need to promise." I reach up and remove his hands from my shoulders. "You are going to go out there and give that Metz officer the ass-kicking he's never had." Now it's my turn to grip Jay's shoulders. "Focus. Look for his weak spot. He has to have one. *Everyone* has one. The Metz are used to fighting with guns, not clubs and knives. You can do this. You *will* do this."

Jay's muscles tense under my grip as he straightens his shoulders and looks pointedly at my hands. I release my grip and give him a light punch on his arm. "Go get him."

As he strides off to his corner of the ring, I turn and freeze. Primo's looking straight at me, and even from this distance I can see the calculating expression on his face.

Does he remember me? From the compound?

I rack my brain for anything that could help Jay get some advantage over him, but nothing comes to mind. Jay's going to have to win this one for himself.

A bell rings out and Jay and Primo step into the roped-off arena and walk toward the head official, who's waiting in the centre. Jay swaggers with his shoulders back, but it's clear for everyone to see that his bravado is a show.

Primo moves slowly, lazily, like a man who's already won.

The official says something to them, then the bell rings out again. The fight has begun.

I push through the growing crowd to Jay's corner. The Snakes part to let me through and I go to stand by Beth. She stares at the two men circling each other in the ring, her face strained.

"How long until Samson can get here?"

"An hour, maybe more. It depends if he's at headquarters."

Which means Jay has to get through the first two rounds at least.

"Why didn't Jay insist on more time to prepare?"

This time it's Danny, standing on the other side of Beth, who answers. "Vihaan had already run off to make the arrangements. If Jay had tried to put it off, it would have made him look bad."

"Bloody Vihaan," I mutter under my breath.

"He's a sly worm, that one."

I turn at Jax's voice. "What do you mean?"

He shrugs, somehow managing to give the impression of being slouched against a wall, even though the nearest building is fifty feet away. "He's been bidin' his time ever since Dane got himself killed. Knew he couldn't beat Jay in a fair fight so he's got someone to do it for him. Wants the number two spot."

I turn back to the arena. Neither man has made a move yet. Both are stripped to the waist and my eyes can't help but be drawn to Primo's chest.

Is it actually possible for a man to have that much muscle?

That must make him heavy, though. I wonder if Jay can figure out some way to use that to his advantage.

The first round is wrestling. It's usually a warm-up round, each fighter trying to tire their opponent out before weapons come into play. Jay's good at wrestling, but he's never fought anyone the size of Primo.

The former Metz captain stands lightly on the balls of his feet. His arms hang relaxed at his sides and his eyes never leave Jay's. Everything I'd tried to teach Trey about how to fight when we'd sparred on my rooftop.

My fingers tighten on the rope cordoning off the arena. Of course he's a fighter. They all are. That's all they've been trained to do – fight and kill.

And you set them free.

Primo makes the first move, lunging forward in a blur of movement. Jay backs away, nearly stumbling over his own feet. He gathers himself and runs at Primo. I wince as his shoulder slams into the bigger man's chest. It's like hitting a brick wall. Primo barely sways as Jay staggers away, clutching at his shoulder.

I bite my lip. Jay's used to being the biggest and strongest. That's how he's won his fights in the past. But he won't win that way against Primo. He needs to come up with something else.

The crowd is silent at first, but as the clock counts down the minutes and seconds, an uneasy murmur swells around us. Usually, leadership fights are a pretty even match. But this is different.

Primo is stronger, bigger, faster.

He bounds in and out, landing blows before Jay can even register the movement, then dancing away, fists raised in front of him like a boxer. Jay changes tactics, trying to keep away from the larger man as much as possible. But Primo's just so damn *fast*.

He's like a crow pecking at his prey, weakening it slowly just to show he's completely in control of its pathetic little life as he drags out the inevitable.

It would take a miracle for Jay to win this fight.

I close my eyes and try to swallow but there's no moisture left in my mouth.

"Two minutes," Danny mutters.

The two men draw apart and I wonder if that's it, if they're going to just waste the remaining time circling each other and resting for the next round.

But Primo's not done.

He strikes, knocking Jay clean off his feet. Jay slams onto the hard ground and I can almost feel the impact of the concrete knocking the breath from his lungs. He lies motionless.

A murmur of unease ripples through the crowd.

Primo walks slowly toward him, the crow finally ready to end the fight. But as he gets closer, Jay kicks out and a cloud of dust rises in the air, sending Primo reeling back, coughing.

Clever, Jay.

Perhaps I've underestimated him.

The bell rings and my shoulders sag. The end of the first round.

Jay stumbles over to us. He's breathing heavily and a sheen of sweat covers his skin. A dark bruise is already rising on his jaw and blood trickles from some of his old wounds, which have reopened. He grabs the bottle of Chaz Beth holds out to him and gulps it down.

"You're doing great," Beth says to him, gripping his arm as if by doing so she can somehow transfer her energy to him.

"He's a big guy."

"But you know the ring. You know the weapons," she says encouragingly.

I glance over at Primo's corner. A towel, heavy with sweat, hangs around his shoulders and he's downed two bottles of water in the space of a minute. As he lifts a third to his lips, I catch sight of a tattoo on his right arm. X4.

"He's not used to fighting in these conditions."

"What?" Jay stops stretching and turns to look at me.

"The Metz suits control their body temperature. He's not used to fighting in this heat." It's cooler today than it has been, but still much warmer than the air-conditioned Metz compound. I turn to Jay. "He's sweating buckets. Keep him moving. He may tire more quickly."

Jay nods. "Aleesha, what I said before, about you—"

"It doesn't matter." *He can't go in thinking he'll lose.* I place a hand on his arm. He's trembling. "We can talk later, once you've beaten him."

Beth gives us a questioning look, wrapping one arm around Jay as if she still sees me as a threat. My eyes are drawn to a set of curved indentations on the back of her hand. *Fingernail marks?*

She catches me looking and pulls her hand back, turning Jay's face toward her for a kiss.

I turn away.

There's a movement in the arena. The official walks in dragging two wooden clubs behind her.

"Time to go." Jay pulls back from Beth, then places a final kiss on her forehead. He drops his voice to a whisper, but I'm close enough to hear the words meant only for her. "I love you, Beth." The clamour of the bell drowns out the rest.

Round two.

Jay goes immediately on the offensive, swinging his club at Primo's legs, chest and shoulders. He lands a few blows, but Primo just shrugs them off. He hefts his own club in his hand as if he's trying to get a feel for its weight and balance.

Then he strikes.

The weighted wooden baton whirls through the air. Jay ducks out the way of the first blow, but he's too slow to miss the second. Primo's club slams down on his shoulder and Jay staggers away, his left arm hanging limply by his side.

There's a sharp intake of breath beside me but I don't dare look away, even for a second.

Primo gives him a moment to recover, but it's clear Jay's injured. He still holds his club in his right hand but his face twists in pain as he tries to lift his left arm to the handle.

I lick my lips as my stomach works itself into knots. Has Samson got the message yet? Is he on his way? Surely if anyone can save Jay, he can.

"Come on, Jay," Beth murmurs, a tremor in her voice.

Jay tries to rally, holding his club up as Primo approaches. They're closer to us now, and I can smell their sweat on the breeze. Jay goes for the dust trick again, but Primo's expecting it this time and backs away, covering his mouth. Jay skirts around him, back toward the centre of the ring.

That's it, keep him moving.

My heart hammers in my ears, in contrast to the silence of the crowd. They know this fight is different, but I wonder if they really understand the consequences if Primo wins.

Primo attacks again. Jay dodges, but the club glances off his right side. In a move almost too quick for me to catch, Primo follows it up with a second blow and Jay falls to the floor, a cry of pain escaping his lips.

"No!"

As if he can hear Beth, Jay raises his club above his head, just in time to deflect Primo's next blow. The force reverberates down the wooden club and through his arm.

Where are you, Samson?

I feel a hand on my arm, pulling me back, and realize I've lifted the rope cordoning off the arena to duck underneath it. Jax shakes his head at me.

"You can't go in. You know the rules." His eyes are tight, but he's right. If I go in now, the contest will be forfeit. Primo would automatically win.

But Jay would survive.

"It's his fight, Aleesha," Jax warns.

And what could I do anyway, against that mountain of a man?

I step back. Jay is bent over, clutching his side. If a miracle's going to happen, now is the time.

"Get up Jay," Beth murmurs beside me. Her knuckles are white on the rope. "Get up."

But before he can move, Primo brings his club down on Jay's knee. There's a horrible crack and Jay falls onto his back, screaming in pain. He drops his club and twists his body, clawing at the ground as he tries to pull himself out of Primo's way. His face is contorted in pain, the whites of his eyes showing his fear.

Come on, Samson.

The square is so quiet, you could hear a chit drop.

Primo steps forward and raises his club.

Jay turns his head toward us and his mouth moves, but I can't make out what he's trying to say or if his words are meant for me or Beth.

The club falls through the air to land with a sickening thud on Jay's head.

8

Trey

Coleman's food factory is the largest building in Area Six. From the outside, it looks like a giant white cube, devoid of windows or decoration. But looking down from above, through the transparent slit of the pod, I see it's divided into sections: long lengths that criss-cross each other so the overall effect is rather like one of those mind-boggling pictures that trick your brain into seeing something that isn't there.

The pod lands on one of the four corners of the building's roof and I wait for the rest of the occupants to exit before stepping out. In the distance, pods land and depart from the other three corners. The whole roof is encircled with a tall white wall that hides the view of the city. Gardens stretch between the pod stations and, about a hundred metres in from the white wall, a transparent barrier rings the central part of the factory.

I walk over to it. It's head height and too slick to climb. When I look through it, I realize why.

The building drops away below me. A few floors below, a clear tube cuts across the void. Every few seconds a pod rushes through it. Further down, another tube cuts across, perpendicular to the first. The void is a few hundred metres wide. On the far side, different levels of the building are stacked, like gigantic blocks, on top of one another. A few have gardens on top of them, but most have black solar panels, a stark contrast to the blinding whiteness of the rest of the building.

I take a step back from the edge, feeling suddenly dizzy.

"Quite something, isn't it?"

I turn to see a lithe, dark-skinned woman watching me. Corkscrew hair surrounds a smiling, round face. She looks young, perhaps a few years older than me, and wears a geometrically-patterned jumpsuit of bright green and yellow.

"First day?"

I blush and look down at my new, polished shoes. "That obvious?"

"Everyone has that expression on their face when they see it for the first time." Her voice is warm. "I'm Emilie."

I take her proffered hand. "Trey … I mean, Darwin. Darwin Goldsmith."

Emilie raises an eyebrow. "Well, Trey-I-mean-Darwin, it's nice to meet you." She hesitates for a second then drops my hand. "I recognized you from your holo. You're my new boss." She points to a bank of glass elevators set into the wall. "Reception is one floor down. You'd better get going." She flashes me a shy smile. "Look forward to seeing you later."

"Yeah, you too!" I call as she walks away. I wince inwardly.

If I'm supposed to be her boss, I'm not sure I've made the best first impression.

I glance once more down into the void, then push back my shoulders, take a deep breath and walk toward the elevator.

Inside, I press the button marked "Reception" and a few seconds later, step out into a vast room. To my right is a polished wood reception desk; to my left, screened off by pot plants, seems to be a café or informal meeting area. In front of me, a tiered fountain stands in front of the floor-to-ceiling windows that span the far wall. At least, I think they're windows until I look closer and realize that the panoramic cityscape I see through them can't possibly be real.

I walk over to the reception desk and give the man behind it a warm smile. The reception area is small. I guess they don't get many visitors to the factory.

"Hi, I'm Darwin Goldsmith. I start work here today."

The man's megawatt smile drops slightly, but he turns and reaches for a scanner. "Your arm, please?"

I proffer my right arm and he runs the scanner down it, then gives a small nod of satisfaction. "Thank you, Mr Goldsmith. Please take a seat, someone will come up for you shortly."

He waves to a group of chairs set around a low table and I sit down. The chairs smell new, like my suit – which I glance down at. It feels too bright and gaudy, but at least the sky blue isn't as bad as the tangerine or crimson suits Mother had tried to force on me. Given a choice, I'd have worn the black suit she bought me for Father's funeral, but she's hidden it away somewhere. I guess she's right – I'd stand out more here wearing black than blending in with the bright colours.

At least the suit fits well and the shirt underneath regulates my body temperature so I don't have to worry about sweat patches. But I find myself longing for the loose, simple Outsider clothing Bryn had given me.

I run my fingers up my right sleeve. Giving me a new chip had taken seconds and was almost painless. The technician had frowned at the long pink scar, stark against my pale skin.

"Do you want me to heal that for you?" she'd asked.

"No," I had answered.

I keep it as a badge of pride. And as a reminder of what lies outside this perfect bubble.

"Darwin Goldsmith, good to have you here," a cheerful voice rings out.

I look up to see a golden-haired young man in an impeccably tailored teal suit holding out his hand. I stand and take it.

"Nice to meet you …"

"Louis Coleman. My proper name is Aloysius but it's a mouthful so I go by Louis." He makes a face. "It's Darwin, isn't it?"

"Actually, I prefer T—" I change my mind and snap my mouth shut.

Trey is for Outside. Here I will be Darwin. Another reminder that I'm here to do a job.

"Yes. Darwin." I straighten my jacket unnecessarily, my fingers curling for something to do.

"Good stuff. Well, come this way – I'll give you the grand tour. As you've probably guessed, this is the main entrance and there's a staff café up here. The main restaurant is through those doors."

Louis continues chatting as we walk over to the elevators. I'm glad. It saves me having to think of something polite to say. The elevator's empty, but Louis's finger pauses over the keypad.

"Look, Darwin, I know this is your first day, but you're going to have to buck up a bit." He looks me up and down. "Phillips was glad enough to get rid of me, but he's not happy about *you* replacing me. He had someone else lined up for the job. A top graduate and daughter of one of his tennis partners. Then my F—" He stops himself. "Coleman himself came down and told him he'd already hired you. You look fresh out of school. This your first job?"

"Yes." I hesitate, then add. "You're Coleman's son?"

Louis's face twists. "Yeah, not that it does me any favours." There's a trace of bitterness in his words.

I search for a different topic of conversation. "So, er, where are you working now?"

Louis types a code into the keypad and leans back against the glass wall as the lift rushes down, inspecting his fingernails. "Got headhunted by another department. I'm Head of London Distribution, and somehow got lumbered with responsibility for Outsider welfare in the factory too." He rolls his eyes. "But that was a small price to pay to get out of here."

He mistakes my look of irritation for one of fear. "I'm sure you'll fare better. Phillips and I just clashed. Don't let him walk all over you, though. I doubt he'll give you much support but I'll give you my comm link, so any questions or issues, just ask."

The lift pings and the doors open. Louis motions for me to go first. "Welcome to Level 31 – your new home."

I step out into a long corridor. Glass windows stretch along the top half of the wall. I walk over and look down onto a hive of activity. Rows of machinery line one half of the vast room, stretching away into the distance. There are production lines of robotic arms that move in a blur, so fast I can't make out what they're actually doing. The other half of the room is filled with rows of huge sealed vats. The sides of the vats are transparent, but I can't make out what's inside. People dressed in white tunics walk between the lines.

Louis joins me at the window. "Did they tell you anything about this job?" he asks quietly.

I hesitate, wondering if I can trust him. But I don't really have a choice. If I'm to last two minutes in this place, it's obvious I'm going to need his help. "No," I admit.

"Thought as much." He gives me a curious glance, obviously wanting to know why I've been given this role. I just stare down at the machines. "Okay, well you're in charge of the production lines for meat products. Fake meat products, of course." He laughs. "There are three grades that cover food at different qualities and price points: lower, mid and premium. Generally speaking, the higher quality stuff is at this end, and the cheap burgers we ship to the Outsiders are at the other end. It's your job to keep things running."

My stomach clenches and I clasp my hands tightly in front of me.

"Don't worry, you don't need to know how it all works," Louis says, as if reading my mind. "The scientists have set everything up and Barnes keeps the production line running and oversees the workers."

"Barnes?"

"The foreman." Louis's voice is tight. "Come on, we'll go down and I'll introduce you."

We return to the elevator and Louis presses the back of his hand to a panel above the keypad. "We'll get your authorization sorted later."

The elevator spits us out in a small circular room encased by clear walls. "Cleaning chamber," Louis comments. There's a hiss and it feels like the air is being sucked from the room, my hair rising as every molecule of dust is removed. There's a ping and the red light above the exit door changes to green.

As soon as the doors open, the noise hits me. Layers upon layers of noise. A deep constant hum from the tanks on the left side of the room, and a dull pounding interspersed with rhythmic clacking from the rows to the right. But cutting through it all is a high-pitched screech that makes the hairs on the back of my neck stand.

I glance at Louis. His face is twisted in a grimace and his eyes scan the room, looking for someone – Barnes presumably. One of the white-suited women spots us and nods, disappearing up a row.

"Is it always this noisy?" I ask.

"Yes, and no. That screeching isn't normal." Louis strides off toward the back of the room. The screeching gets louder and then abruptly stops. I jog to catch up and am panting when he finally slows his pace. Ahead of us, the rows of machinery and robots end and there's an open space separating the production lines from a set of metal towers that seem to fill the back part of the factory floor. A group of people stand arguing.

"Ah, Barnes," Louis mutters.

I look around, confused. Surely Barnes, as foreman, would be wearing something different to distinguish himself from the rest of the workers. But perhaps not. I look over the group and pinpoint an elderly man talking to a young woman as the most likely candidate. The woman catches my eye, or rather, her hair does as she's standing with her back to us. It's a rich copper, drawn up into a loose ponytail that hangs to her shoulder blades. Her white suit is as shapeless as everyone else's but it doesn't fully disguise her curves.

"Barnes!" Louis yells as we approach. The elderly man glances at us over the woman's shoulder and his eyes widen a fraction. He mutters something to her.

The woman turns slowly. She's not quite as young as I'd thought from the back – perhaps mid to late thirties. She carries a holo pad and faint wrinkles line her forehead, suggesting that the frown she wears now isn't unusual.

"Now is not a good time, Louis," she snaps, turning away and giving an order to a young woman, who nods and hurries off.

This is Barnes? I had expected ...

A man. I chide myself for the assumption and force a smile onto my face.

"What was that noise?" Louis demands.

The woman sighs and turns back around to face us. "Problem with one of the dehydrators." She motions to the towers behind us. "Second time today I've had to shut it down. We'll have to take it apart to figure out what's wrong. We're ahead on today's quota so it shouldn't affect delivery, but if we can't get it fixed today, we'll be behind on tomorrow's."

"Noted," Louis says stiffly. He seems uncomfortable but I can't figure out why. "Barnes, this is the new production manager, Darwin Goldsmith."

Barnes glances at me as if it's the first time she's noticed my presence. "You look young. Fresh out of university? Welcome to the real world."

I step forward and hold out my hand. She takes it, reluctantly. Her skin is rough and calloused. "Nice to meet you. Louis has spoken highly of your work."

She snorts and pulls her hand away, giving Louis a look I can't read. He frowns and takes her to one side, speaking to her in a low urgent voice. Whatever he's saying, she's not happy about it. But she inclines her head and nods in acquiescence.

"I'll give you a tour tomorrow morning. I hope you're a quick learner," she says to me. Louis shoots her a look and she forces a smile onto her face. "*Lovely* to meet you, Mr Goldsmith. Now, if you'll excuse me, I need to go and get this dehydrator fixed."

She doesn't wait for me to reply but stalks off in the direction of the towers. The other workers look at each other, unsure whether they're supposed to follow their boss or stay with us.

I give them what I hope is a reassuring smile. "I'm sure you've all got more important things to do than stand around chatting to me. I look forward to meeting you properly tomorrow."

I turn and stride back down between the rows of robots, leaving Louis to follow. We walk in silence back to the elevator. Louis presses his hand to the panel and punches in a code before turning to me.

"Barnes is ..."

"Difficult?" I supply.

He sighs. "Touchy. She doesn't really like people and she *definitely* doesn't like authority. The only reason she keeps her job is because she's a genius with the machines. No one else understands the manufacturing process like she does, or can fix things as quickly. And the workers like her," he adds as an afterthought.

"So if she keeps everything running down there, what's my job?"

Louis gives me a sly smile. "Keeping *her* under control."

The elevator doors open and he steps out, leading the way along the long corridor. I glance through the windows at the factory floor and my heart sinks. If that really is the main part of my job, I'm not sure how well I'm going to succeed.

Louis stops by a door. "This is your office."

He presses the back of his hand to the panel, using his Coleman Corporation chip to unlock the door, and walks inside. I follow him into a modest room. Windows line one wall, looking out over the factory. There's a large desk next to the window, with three chairs set around a low table in front of it. On the other side of the room, two smaller desks face each other, divided by a low screen, though only one is in use. There's a black cabinet in one corner and a couple of pot plants that look like they've seen better days.

"Darwin, this is Emilie, your assistant."

The lithe woman with corkscrew hair smiles and gets up from one of the smaller desks. She walks over and holds out her hand. "Nice to meet you again, Mr Goldsmith."

"Again?" Louis raises an eyebrow.

Emilie shrugs. "We arrived at the pod point at the same time this morning."

"Great." Louis turns to me and spreads his hands. "Well, I must be going – have to get back to my real job. I'll swing by this afternoon to get your authorization sorted and talk you through the reports you're responsible for. I think there's a Production Board meeting this week …?" He glances at Emilie, who nods. "So you'll need to get that done by close of play Wednesday."

He turns to leave.

"When will I be meeting Phillips?"

"Oh, he'll call for you when he's ready." Louis sighs and turns back to me. "Look, just to warn you, he can be a beast. Whatever he says, don't take it personally – we've all been on the wrong side of his temper at one point or another." The serious expression on his face breaks into a wide grin. "But what am I thinking? We should go for drinks! I'll introduce you to the *fun* people in this place." He gives me a wink. "Later."

The door clicks shut behind him.

Emilie rolls her eyes. "Yes, he's always like that," she says, answering my unspoken question. "He thinks everything is a big game, like he's still at university or something."

"Still, he must have been good at his job to get promoted."

She shoots me an odd look, reminding me that Louis is the

boss's son. I walk over to the window and look out over the factory floor. It feels like my first day at school. No, worse than that. At least then, there were lots of other boys in the same position.

"How long have you been here, Emilie?"

"Just over a year," she replies, coming to stand next to me. "I ... I didn't go to university, my parents couldn't afford it. Oh, we're Insiders," she says hurriedly as I turn to look at her. "But it cost enough to get me to a good school, and you know what the price of housing is like at the moment." She makes a face. "I'm hoping I can save enough to help my sister go to university. She's really smart."

"Do you enjoy it here?"

There's a fraction of a pause. "It's not bad. The work is okay, especially as Louis let me take on some of the more interesting bits."

I wonder if Louis had been doing her a favour or off-loading his work onto her.

I force a smile onto my face. "Well, I'm going to need your help. This is all new to me. Where do we start?"

A smile lights up her face and her eyes twinkle. "We start by getting a coffee – you're going to need it. Then we'll talk numbers."

I sigh. *This is going to be a long day.*

9

Aleesha

For a full ten seconds, there's silence. Primo raises his arms in triumph, but if he's waiting for applause, he doesn't get it. A low murmur of anger and fear runs through the crowd but no one's brave enough to shout out loud. There's a ragged cheer from Primo's supporters but it stops as the official walks into the ring.

She holds up a hand and the crowd fall silent. "The judges have agreed. Primo wins."

At her feet, Jay lies still, his head crushed by Primo's final blow.

"This isn't right. It's not how the gangs work." Beth is pale and her body is rigid, her hands still gripping the rope ringing the area. Her eyes are fixed on Jay's body.

"It's exactly how the gangs work," I say bitterly. "The biggest and strongest wins. That's why no one's challenging him. How can any Outsider win against someone like that?"

"And you brought them in. Asked the Snakes to look after them." She spits the words. "You brought them in!"

I turn to her. "I-I'm sorry, Beth." My voice chokes. "I didn't—"

"Didn't what? Think?" She turns to me, fire flashing in her

eyes. "You wanted to save *them* but what about your own people? What's going to happen to them now?"

Guilt fills my belly, a lead weight dragging me down.

Why, whenever I try and do the right thing, does it turn out wrong?

Tension and fear thicken the air around me. A change in gang leader isn't unusual, and even if you supported the losing side you still had a place in the gang. But this has never happened before. An Insider taking over. A Metz officer.

On the other side of the ring, Primo is celebrating at the centre of a small crowd of people. Vihaan is there, looking smug as he talks to Megan.

Primo turns and catches my eye. His lips twist into a cold smile that makes my limbs go weak. Suddenly, the day doesn't feel warm at all.

His eyes move from me to Beth and the corner of his mouth twitches.

"Beth, we have to go. Now."

She pulls her arm from my grip. "Let go of me!"

"I'm serious." I lower my voice. "He'll come for us, for you. You do *not* want to be here. Winner's spoils?"

Her eyes widen as she catches my meaning.

"But Jay ..."

"You can't do anything for 'im now," Danny says. "Aleesha's right. You need to get out of here. Go back to those other people of yours. Mebbe they can protect you."

Beth looks back to where a team of medical volunteers are rolling Jay onto a makeshift stretcher. None of them have opened their bags of supplies. They know there's no point trying to treat him.

"He wouldn't want you to risk yourself." Part of me wonders why I'm even trying to protect her, given what she did to me.

But I saw that look Primo gave her. The look he gave me. And I wouldn't wish that on any woman.

There's a commotion behind us. Samson pushes through the crowd, accompanied by a lean man with a thin, sharp face. Danny melts back as they approach. Samson's long dreadlocks swing behind him and his face is stern.

He takes in the scene at a glance and turns to Beth. "I came as soon as I could. You need to get away."

She pulls back from his grasp, tears welling in her eyes. "Why didn't you stop this? This shouldn't have happened!" She points angrily behind her to where Jay is being carted off.

"Later, Beth!"

She flinches back under his gaze and drops her arm.

"Come." He takes her arm in an almost brotherly fashion and gently pulls her forward.

I make a move to follow, but he shakes his head. "Stay away from the Snakes. Don't do anything stupid."

"Me don't do anything stupid? What are *you* going to do?" I say in a low voice. "You need to challenge him, now, while he's tired. There's no one else who can beat him."

Samson stops and bends his head to mine. His scent is heavy and the air feels thick around him. I may not feel the same level of fear I once had for him, but he's still the most intimidating person I know.

Which is exactly why he's the one to sort this out.

"Leave it, Aleesha. We need to think this through. No more hasty decisions."

His voice is low and controlled but there's something in his eyes that makes me catch my breath.

Fear?

But Samson doesn't fear anyone.

As he pushes Beth through the crowd, I turn back to look at Primo. An elite member of the Metz. A captain who knows exactly what the Metz have done. A trained killer, with enhanced genetics for strength and speed.

No wonder Samson's afraid.

We all should be.

* * *

I watch as Jay's body is carried to a floating raft. The tide is in, but the water's still too shallow for boats to come in. I climb up to the roof of a building that extends out into the river and get as far out as I can before it becomes impassable. Below me, Jay is transferred from raft to boat. It's not big enough to take the stretcher, so they just roll him off it and he lands with a thud in the bottom of the dinghy. A few chits change hands and the man in the boat picks up his oars.

A wind is coming up from the south. It whips around my face, tugging at my tightly braided hair and making the hairs on the back of my arms rise. But I don't duck down behind the shelter of a parapet. I stand sentinel for Jay, the only attendee at his funeral.

That's what happens if you die out here and your family don't have enough money to take you to the crematorium, or if you have no family at all. There's no funeral, no words spoken by a minister who pretends to care about your grief. There is only the river.

The boat makes its way slowly out between the buildings, the oarsman carefully steering around hidden obstacles under the water. It goes past me, further up the drowned street toward the river. But there are still remnants of buildings between it and the main expanse of water when the boat stops.

I strain my eyes. Water rushes through an open space between buildings. It tugs at the small boat, pulling it around, but the man throws a loop of rope around a post. The rope tightens but doesn't break.

He bends over Jay's body, looping his arms through what looks to be a rough sack filled with stones. To weigh him down I guess. Then, without ceremony, he heaves Jay over the edge of the boat and into the water.

Jay sinks immediately, head first, the rushing water closing over his feet. The boat rocks violently, and for a minute I think it's going to overturn, but the man braces himself and steadies it. He nods in satisfaction of a job well done, then pulls on the rope, picks up his oars and disappears into the drowned city.

I climb slowly back over the roofs and down to the square. The crowd has dispersed, the rope and tables have been carried away. The only sign that the fight took place is a dark stain in the dirt.

"He fought well."

I turn to find Rogue standing behind me. I scan his face, trying to figure out whose side he's on now but his expression is wooden.

"He meant something to you?"

I nod. "We …" But I let my voice trail off. "You watched the fight?"

"Yes. A few of us took the risk of leaving the headquarters. We watched from up there." He points to the roof of one of the buildings.

Smart. Even out of their black armour and helmets, it's clear that the officers are not Outsiders.

"What happens now?"

"Well, traditionally, there'd be a party at headquarters. Gang members who backed the losing side would do a bit of grovelling to the new leader and that would be that. Now? I don't know. This has never happened before. It *shouldn't* have happened."

I turn and glare at him, feeling my fists tighten. "Why didn't you stop it?"

He flinches back at my words. "How could I have stopped it?"

"You said he was going to be trouble."

"But I didn't know he'd do *this*." He pauses. "So he's in charge now?"

"Yes."

Rogue presses a hand to his chest and frowns. "When you shouted at me, I felt … hurt. An emotion thing?"

"Sorry," I mutter, looking down at the ground. His hand grazes my arm, sending electricity shooting across my skin. I look up to find him staring at me, confusion in his blue eyes.

I swallow hard. "Yes, it's an emotion. I'm sorry, I shouldn't have snapped at you."

"I feel a lot of emotions around you. But they're mostly good ones."

I want to step away, but my legs feel oddly weak. He reaches a hand up to stroke my hair.

I jerk away. "Don't do that!"

He looks hurt. "What did I do?"

I put another step between us. The air helps me breathe. "Touching my hair. You don't do that to a friend." Confusion flashes across his face. "Look, didn't you have a girlfriend in that compound? Or before you joined the Metz?"

"No. I …" His face clears and his cheeks flush red. He stiffens and his hand falls to his side. "I'm sorry. I didn't realize. And there wasn't any of that in the compound. We are – were – all officers. There was no emotion. No … relationships."

I feel a twist of guilt. Even more so because, despite everything, part of me hadn't wanted to pull away from him.

An image of Trey appears in my head. So different from Rogue in almost every way. But the image makes my chest feel uncomfortably tight and I push it away.

Why does it feel like I'm betraying him when we're not even together?

And never will be together. Any possibility of that flew out the window the day I dragged his father to his death.

I rub my forehead. "Look, it's fine, okay? But Primo being in charge? That's not fine. He was your captain – what do you know about him?"

"Not much. My memories come and go." He looks shamefaced. "I think he was one of the more senior captains, which means he'll have been in the position for years, decades maybe."

"Is that what his number relates to? X4?"

Rogue shakes his head. "No, that's his unit." He pulls up the sleeve of his skin-tight black suit to reveal an inked code on his forearm. ML486. "I was the eighty-sixth officer in unit four. The X designates he's a captain." He pulls the sleeve back down hurriedly, as if ashamed of the tattoo. "He's the only captain you captured who stayed."

I jerk my head up. "The only one?" I try and remember how many we'd captured. Three perhaps?

"Yes. I kept an eye on them. They met together, the first night they were all awake. They all remembered." His jaw tightens. "Two left that night, but Primo stayed."

"Why?"

"I don't know. Maybe as a spy? Or maybe …" He looks thoughtful.

"Maybe what?"

"Maybe he just wanted a new start. A place where he could be in charge. He … he always wanted us to be the best unit, pushed us the hardest. Maybe that's why he's called himself Primo. He wants to be number one."

"Number one in the Metz?"

Rogue tugs the sleeve of his suit down further over his wrist. "Or outside the Metz," he says quietly.

"Are the other Metz officers following him?" I turn to him. "Are *you* following him?"

"No." Indecision crosses his face. "There are a few of us who remember … things. We don't trust him, but what other option do we have?" He spreads his hands. "Where else can we go out here?"

He looks to me for an answer, but I don't have one.

"And those who don't remember?"

"They feel lost. They're looking for a leader – someone to tell them what to do. Some sense of normality."

"And Primo would provide that. They're used to being ordered around like … like Outsiders. So they'll follow Primo, eat up whatever lies he tells them." I feel sick.

How could you have let yourself get killed, Jay?

But I know it's not his fault. It's mine. I was the one who screwed up.

"I have to go and see some people. I'll try and find a safe place for you and the others to stay." I look up at him. "Can you get them all together, maybe up on the rooftops?"

"I can try." Rogue takes my hand. This time, I don't pull away. "I'm sorry. I never meant for this to happen."

"I know."

* * *

I barrel into Abby's kitchen without bothering to knock. It's empty. *Dammit.*

"Abby? Bryn?"

I hear a movement upstairs, and a moment later Abby walks in carrying a pile of sheets. "Aleesha? What's wrong?"

"Is Bryn around?"

"I think he's at the Chain's headquarters." She frowns. "What's going on?"

My heart sinks. I don't want to go to the Chain's headquarters. Not after what they did.

But do I have any choice? I've got no way of getting in touch with Samson, who's the only other person who may be able to help.

"Here he is." There's a bang from outside and I turn to see Bryn walk into the yard.

His brow furrows when he sees me. "Something wrong?"

"Yes …" I slump onto a chair and lean forward on the table, pressing my palms against my forehead, trying to stem the emotion welling up inside me. "Everything is wrong."

There's a click as Bryn closes the back door. His heavy footsteps cross the floor and he sits down next to me and places a hand on my shoulder. "What's happened?"

I've never heard him speak so gently and that in itself is enough to bring tears to my eyes. "The Metz have taken over the Snakes. Primo – one of the captains – challenged Jay to a leadership fight and won."

There's a sharp intake of breath from Abby, but Bryn just sits in silence while I tell them the full story.

When I finish, he sighs. "We wondered if this would happen."

I raise my head. "Then why didn't you say something? Why didn't you stop it?"

"Well, you weren't exactly keen for us to take charge. And we didn't think it would happen so soon."

"How do we get rid of him?"

"Right now, we can't," Bryn says flatly. "We could surround the Snakes' headquarters, cut them off, possibly attack using grenades. But I'd bet he puts the gang members on the front line. Do you want to see them die to get to him?"

I grind my knuckles into the table.

"You could challenge him. Someone could challenge him – he'd have to accept."

Bryn snorts. "And who's going to beat him? I can't. Any one of those Metz officers would swat us in a one-to-one fight. And that would just consolidate his power. We're not throwing anyone's life away." He softens his voice. "We'll think of something, Aleesha. But right now, we have to let it go."

"I will *not* let it go." I push back my chair. "If you can't help me, I'll go to someone who can."

Bryn grabs my arm. "Aleesha, wait. Don't go rushing off – it didn't help last time."

I lock eyes with him, then reluctantly sit down.

"I'm sure Samson won't be rushing into anything, either. He's too smart for that." There's a trace of respect in Bryn's voice.

I remember the fear in Samson's eyes and how fast he'd been to pull Beth away, and know that Bryn is right.

"The first thing we need to do is get anyone who doesn't want to follow him to safety." He frowns. "I'm not sure we have anywhere big enough. But I do have another idea."

He shakes his head at my enquiring glance. "No, I'm not going to tell you. They may not agree to it." He gets up and points a finger at me. "You stay here. I don't want to get back with a solution to find you've run off again."

"Yes, *sir*."

He smiles wickedly. "That's my girl."

"I am *not* y—"

The kitchen door slams, cutting me off. I turn to Abby, who's trying to contain her laughter, and glare at her instead.

"Oh come on, he was only winding you up. Now, let me have a look at your shoulder."

Abby removes the dressing and reapplies some of the strange-smelling paste.

"Where's Trey?"

Her hand freezes. "He's gone."

She finishes with the paste and reaches for a dressing. "He left a note saying he'd decided to go back to his family."

My stomach twists. "I shouldn't have said that to him, about going back Inside."

"It wasn't you, Aleesha. It's not all about *you*, you know." There's an unexpected bitterness in Abby's words. Her hand drops from my shoulder and she sighs. "I'm sorry, that was uncalled for. I just hope it is the right decision for him. That it makes him happy."

"But if he goes back, he'll be chipped, won't he? Which means he won't be able to come out here and see us. They'll be following him."

Abby walks over to the sink and washes her hands. "Yes. But we have to think about what's best for him. He'll have money, access to health care, proper food. Things I— we can't give him."

I stare down at the table, feeling strangely lost. Abby's right. It is the best thing for Trey. He deserves all those things.

Does that mean he'll forget all about us now?

"Abby, will you play some music for me?"

She glances around in surprise, then smiles. "Sure. It would be good to take our minds off things."

She lifts the guitar off the wall and, sitting down, begins to strum. I rest my head on my arms and close my eyes, remembering the night the four of us had sat here. Remembering Trey playing, his fingers not quite as practised as Abby's but producing beautiful music all the same.

I try and lose myself in the music and focus on that happy night. Before everything went wrong.

10

Trey

I stumble up the stairs to the apartment, pausing on each floor to catch my breath. Wave after wave of dizziness washes over me. My vision blurs and there are suddenly two staircases in front of me. I blink and they coalesce into one.

Good thing Emilie warned me about Louis's idea of fun. At least I ate something before the drinking started.

My stomach churns and I wonder if I'm about to regret that preparation. I've never really drunk alcohol before. I'm not even old enough to, legally, not until I'm eighteen. But Louis must have assumed I was older. Either that, or he didn't care.

I tug at my tie to loosen it, take a deep breath and launch myself across the landing to the next set of stairs. I pull myself up using the rail. *Why do people do this to themselves?*

As soon as the clock reached six, Louis had arrived at my office to drag me away. We'd taken a pod Inside and headed to a bar in Soho with neon lighting and scantily clad waitresses. Louis had introduced me to his friends, some of whom also worked at the factory.

I'd sipped at my drink, despite Louis's protestations that I should "drink up", but even though I must have drunk barely half of what he did, it wasn't long before I felt the alcohol take effect.

The guys were friendly and I tried to make conversation and answer their questions, but it was tough when I couldn't really talk about me. I didn't want to let on that I hadn't been to university, hadn't even graduated school, so I dodged the questions and turned the conversation back to them. At every moment, I expected someone to recognize me as the criminal who'd been on the big screens and call me out. But no one did.

I'd made my excuses after a couple of hours and stumbled from the bar to find a pod station. The fresh air perked me up a bit, but the effects of the alcohol seemed to have got worse, not lessened.

At least it made me forget the numbers. Reams of data and reports and responsibilities that Louis and Emilie had talked to me about. I'm not sure if I'd taken any of it in. I still don't really understand what my job *is*. I just have this gnawing sensation in my stomach and a little voice in my head telling me I'm a fraud, that this was all a mistake.

I close my eyes and steel myself. I'm going to talk to Mother and see if I can find some other job. I'm not cut out for this.

Another wave of dizziness. I grit my teeth and set off up the stairs.

One more flight to go.

I wonder what Aleesha would think if she saw me now. Picturing her expression of disgust makes me giggle, and the noise bounces off the walls down the stairwell.

She'd think you were a spoilt, drunken rich kid.

The thought sobers me and I straighten, forcing myself to walk normally up the rest of the stairs. I look out the window, down onto the street, and press my hands to my cheeks. My skin burns.

How much did those drinks cost? How much food could they have bought Outside?

I don't know. Would she be disappointed in me? Probably. Mind you, she'd probably laugh at me too.

The thought makes me smile and I push open the apartment door. It's quiet inside, the ticking of the oversized clock on the wall the only noise to break the silence.

"Mother? Ella?"

I walk into the living room and freeze. My mother is lying motionless on the sofa, her face pale. My eyes flit to the table where a pill bottle lies open. The effects of the alcohol vanish, as if someone's poured a bucket of ice over my head.

"Mother!" I drop to my knees beside her and shake her roughly.

I need to call a medic. Is she breathing?

"Trey?" She looks up at me through bleary eyes. "What's wrong?"

I rock back on my heels, my body trembling from the shot of adrenaline. "You're okay. Sorry, I just saw you lying there and thought …"

She follows my gaze to the pills on the table and sits up. "I was just having a lie down, that's all. I was tired."

She reaches for the pill bottle but I grab it and stand up, looking down at her. Her face is thinner than it used to be and her hair is dull and lifeless, the sheen of the rejuvenation treatments prematurely worn off.

I had put her altered appearance down to stress and grief, but maybe I was wrong. She looks sick, not tired.

The bottle has a prescription label on it. The name of the medicine means nothing to me, but I can read the dosage instructions. *Take 1-2 tablets a day as required. Do NOT exceed the maximum dose.*

When I'd asked Ella why Mother couldn't go to work, she had refused to meet my eye.

"What's this for?"

My mother reaches for the bottle, her eyes pleading. I hold it out of reach. "Not until you tell me what they're for."

I take a deep breath and close my eyes. That's a mistake. The dizziness hits me again. I sink into the chair opposite her.

"I know you're hiding something from me. You and Ella. Please, just tell me what it is. I'm not a little boy any more, you don't need to protect me. If I'm earning money for this family, I have a right to know what's going on."

She looks down at her hands, clasped tightly in front of her. "Please, Trey—"

"You're sick. I can see that. What's wrong? Why haven't you been to a medic?"

"I have been to a medic, Trey." Her voice is small, like a child's. "They can't fix it."

"What do you mean they can't—" I clamp my lips shut as her words break through the fog in my brain. "They can't fix it?" I whisper.

But the medics can fix anything.

My mother shakes her head. "No." She sniffs and wipes her eyes. "They think it's some kind of brain cancer. They tried the usual cancer treatments, and for a while I thought they might have worked. But then the symptoms came back, even worse than before. They think it may be some kind of genetic mutation."

The silence thickens the air, the ticking of the clock like a timer counting down the seconds, hours, days that remain.

“Are they looking at new treatments? You can’t be the only person affected by this? What caused it?”

I get to my feet and begin to pace the room, but it’s so crammed with furniture I barely get five steps.

My mother shrugs listlessly. “They don’t know. The labs are looking into it, but they’re busy with so much other work …”

“We’ll pay them.”

She looks up at me, her eyes filled with sorrow, though I’m not sure whether it’s for her or for me. “We *are* paying them, Trey. Where do you think all the money’s been going?”

I press my head against the doors leading out to the balcony. The Plexiglas cools my burning skin.

“Did Father know?”

“Yes. I kept it from him for as long as I could, but he noticed something was wrong when he started spending more time at home.”

No wonder he’d looked so gaunt and bowed over. He was carrying so many worries. All I did was add to them.

My breath mists the window pane. Life Outside seems almost simple now. I long for Abby’s kitchen. My fingers twitch to run over the strings of her guitar, to surround myself with soothing music.

Strange how you always want what you can’t have.

“But that’s enough about me. How was your first day?” My mother’s voice is artificially bright.

I turn from the window and sit down beside her, placing the bottle on the table. My fingers ache from clenching it.

“They’re for the pain.” She smiles weakly. “About all they can give me. Your first day, how did it go?”

“Fine. It was great.” I stare at the pill bottle. “Might take me a while to learn the job, but I’ll get there. I … I can see if they’ll give me my first paycheck early?"

"No, we'll be fine this month. We still have a few savings." She takes my hand and tears shimmer in her eyes. "I feel better just having you here, Trey. Thank you for coming home."

I give her hand a squeeze, but I still can't meet her eye. I feel like I'm riding in a pod that's suddenly swerved in an unexpected direction, the life I'd wanted fading into the distance behind me.

This is where I need to be. I know that now.

Then why do I feel like I'm betraying the people I care about?

* * *

"Good night out?" Emilie asks as I walk into the office.

I grunt and slump into my chair. A dull drumbeat pounds in my skull and my stomach churns. Eating breakfast had been a bad idea. I eye the giant pot plant at the side of my desk.

"Here. Swallow this." She places a pill and a large glass of water on my desk.

"What is it?"

She laughs and I wince as the sound rings in my ears. "Have you never had a hangover pill before? How do you think Louis and his mates turn up for work every day? Drink the water and the pill and in half an hour, you'll feel fine."

I do as she says. "They do that every night?" I mutter, leaning my head on my arms.

"Well, a couple of times a week. Burning through their paychecks." She refills the water glass for me. "Did you have fun?"

I glance up, wondering what I'm supposed to say. She seemed pally with Louis – is she his friend? But her smile is open and she's so nice that I can't help but like her.

"No," I say finally. "But I need to figure out some good excuse not to go again. I can't afford that kind of lifestyle even if I wanted it."

I bite my lip, suddenly conscious that I might have said too much. But Emilie just turns away and walks over to her desk.

Half an hour later, I feel miraculously better. The wonders of medical science. I'd always taken it for granted, assuming that the medics could heal any injury or sickness.

They'll find a cure for her cancer. They have to.

"Are you okay?"

I realize I'm hunched over my desk again, my fingernails digging into the artificial wood surface. "Yes. Just shaking off the hangover."

"You're due to meet Barnes for a tour of the factory in fifteen minutes. Would you like me to postpone it?"

"No, I'm fine, honestly." I get up and walk over to perch on the edge of Emilie's desk. "What do I need to know about Barnes?"

Emilie smiles. "Good question. Well, you saw the figures yesterday?" She plucks a film from a slim file on her desk and hands it to me. "Here they are again if you need a refresher. They're all down to her. Since she's been foreman, we've been top of the department for productivity."

I scan down the figures. They're impressive. "What's her background? Why's she so good?"

Emilie leans back in her chair. "She's just a genius when it comes to figuring out why something isn't working and fixing it. I don't know if it's her training or if she just has a knack for it."

"So why hasn't she been promoted? Why isn't she production manager?"

"She's an Outsider."

My fingers tighten on the film. That explained her accent then. She had been better spoken than most of the Outsiders I'd come across, but her articulation wasn't quite clipped enough for an Insider. "What's wrong with that? Aren't most of the workers Outsiders?"

Emilie gives me an odd look. "Sure, the factory workers are. But most of the foremen are Insiders."

I keep my head down so Emilie can't see my flushed cheeks. "Her and Louis seem to have a tense relationship," I say to change the subject.

"Yes."

There's a pause and I look up. "What is it?"

"Well ... Louis would kill me if he knew I'd told you."

"He won't hear anything from me."

She smiles, the twinkle back in her eye. "Well, you know how he likes the ladies, right? Well, he hit on Barnes. And she refused him. Not only that, but she put in an official complaint to Phillips. Louis can be, um, persistent. Some of the guys think they can do what they want with the Outsiders." The smile falls from her face.

The film slips from my hand. "He *raped* her?"

"No, of course not! Just pushed a bit too hard. And he definitely came out worse from the encounter. Apparently, Barnes threatened to quit unless Phillips got rid of Louis."

"So that's why he got promoted."

"Yup." She glances up at me. "Look, Louis can be a bit of an idiot and a cad, but he's not that bad. It's just how he's been brought up."

That's no excuse.

I stand and walk over to the window. Far below me, I spot

Barnes talking to two of the factory workers. "Did he try anything with you?"

"He's not my type." Her voice is flat.

My hands clench into fists. "If you ever hear of anyone trying to do that to any of my team, you tell me immediately."

"Sure." She sounds surprised at the intensity in my voice.

I straighten my jacket and grab the holo pad from my desk. "Right, I'm off to find out what we do. See you later."

Barnes is waiting for me as I exit the decontamination room. Her green eyes are bright but her face still wears a slight frown and I wonder if she ever smiles.

"Ready?"

I nod. "Let's go."

She turns sharply and the tip of her ponytail whips across my face. I grit my teeth. *That was deliberate.*

"We'll start over with the vats," she says over her shoulder. "That's where the meat is grown."

"Grown?"

She stops and turns. "Do you want the overview or the technical detail?"

"I'm a details person."

She smiles sardonically. "You asked for it."

A few hours later, I'm regretting that decision. My holo pad is full of notes, along with the recording I made of her explanations so I can listen back and actually try to understand everything she was saying.

We return to the elevator and Barnes folds her arms. "Any questions?"

"At the moment, no. But once I've had time to digest this, I might come back to you."

Her lip curls. "Well if that's all, I'll be getting back to work."

Her tone is insolent, and as she turns to leave I grab her arm. "Wait, please."

She stiffens and I let my hand drop.

"Barnes, I want to be clear about something. I've looked at the production figures for the past five years. We are consistently the highest performing production line in this factory, apart from a couple of blips—"

"They were out of my control. The machinery they provide us w—"

"I know," I interrupt her. "I wasn't blaming you. You are clearly very good at your job. Exceptionally so." Her eyes narrow as if she's waiting for a "but". I sigh. "Look, I'd be a fool to interfere when you've clearly got things running so well. That's not what I'm here to do. My job is to make sure you've got the resources you need and keep the senior managers off your back so we can keep our place at the top."

At least, I think that's my job.

A small smile tugs at the corner of her lips. I lean forward. "But to do that, I need two things from you. Number one: respect. *They* need to know you respect me, and your workers need to know you respect me. Got it?"

She doesn't reply.

"Number two: if anything goes wrong, anything at all, you come and tell me about it. I can't defend you or make decisions if I don't know what's going on. Do we have a deal?"

Barnes looks at me and there's a flicker of respect in her eyes. She smiles. "Sure, we have a deal. Perhaps you're not such a fool after all, Goldsmith."

She turns to walk away, her long ponytail swinging behind her.

"Wait!" I call after her. She pauses and turns to look at me.

"What's your first name?" I spread my hands. "Come on, I'm not going to call you by your surname like you're some ..."

"Servant? Outsider?" She smiles. "Thanks, but I like Barnes."

She turns and marches into one of the aisles behind one of the production lines. I sigh, wondering if Louis was pushed out of his job or if he got himself out. But he'd been right about one thing – keeping Barnes under control could well be the toughest part of my job.

As I walk toward the elevator, I wonder if she'd think differently of me if she knew where I'd come from, what I'd done. If she knew that, for a time, I was an Outsider too.

But even if I wanted to, it would be too dangerous to tell her. I get the feeling that Barnes is hiding something. And she's not someone whose trust is easily bought.

11

Aleesha

There's a bang on the door. "Aleesha?"

Rogue.

I freeze, the water from the cup over my head trickling down onto my wet hair. "What is it?" I eye the door handle warily and shiver, the water cold on my naked body.

"Update from the headquarters. And Samson's here."

"I'll be out in a minute."

I hear his footsteps move away from the door and finish washing quickly, emptying the dirty water down the drain in the centre of the room. A private room to wash in. Luxury.

As much as I hate to admit it, Bryn's idea had been genius. With a bit of persuasion, and, I suspect, a transfer of money, the monks at St George in the East agreed to take in the officers and members of the Snakes who didn't want to stay under Primo's rule. There are about thirty of us altogether.

The church is an ancient building of white stone. Its tower reaches into the sky, even higher than the eight-storey apartment blocks that surround it. Four miniature turrets poke up above the tall walls, making it feel from the outside as if someone is always watching you. Inside, most of the space is divided into smaller rooms, but at the centre is a large chapel that looks like it's seen better days.

Danny, who had been Jay's second, had stolen some chits from the headquarters before leaving and we eke them out as best we can to pay for our share of the food. The monks grow fruit and vegetables around the crumbling headstones in the graveyard, and even though the growing season is just starting, they have winter cabbages in the ground and squashes stored away. In many ways, we're eating better than we have before. The officers always look hungry – I guess this food is measly to what they ate inside the compound – but they don't complain.

The abbot laid down a few rules. No fighting, and we had to hand all our weapons in on arrival for them to lock away. We have to be respectful inside the church and attend their religious services twice a week. It's a small price to pay for safety. I'd never had much time for religion before, but I like the church. It feels peaceful, and the monks are kind. It's a sanctuary I never knew existed in the wilds of Area Four.

Technically, we're on the Bigland Boys' patch, but as they're under Samson's control, they didn't put up much of a fuss. Not for the first time, I wonder just how far across the city his influence stretches.

I dress quickly and hurry barefoot out of the room, picking up my boots on the way past. Most of the gang are already gathered in the larger of the two rooms the monks had given us. It smells stale from too many people breathing, sleeping and sweating. Samson lounges on a chair next to Rogue and a small boy stands in front of them, shuffling his feet nervously. They were clearly waiting for me to arrive.

I sit down and lift my legs to cross them in front of me. It feels good to have my boots off for a change. "What's the latest?" I ask the boy.

"Jax says it's gettin' worse. They've bin raidin' the shops for food. Too much food, he said." He looks nervously around.

Jax had agreed – reluctantly – to act as our spy in the Snakes' headquarters.

"What else?" I prompt.

"Jax said they're 'biding their time'," the kid enunciates, focusing on each word in turn. He screws up his face. "He's not sure what their plan is yet."

"What about the Snakes? How are they being treated?"

"I dunno. Don't really see 'em out an' about that much. Seen that Vihaan sumtimes. He looks like he's been given a golden chit or summit."

Anger flares inside me. *Traitor.*

I smile at the boy. "Anything else?"

He shakes his head. "Na. Can I go now?"

I nod and Samson hands him half a chit. The kid clutches the scrap of metal and runs from the room. There's a shout of annoyance from one of the monks as he legs it through the church.

"That matches up with what I've heard." Samson rubs his chin. "He's got the local people even more terrified than normal. At least with the gangs, they knew the rules. Primo doesn't know the rules, or if he does, he's not playing by them."

It's been a week since the fight. A week since Primo took control of the Snakes. A week since Trey went back Inside.

I take a deep breath. "So, what do we do? Any news from the President?"

Samson narrows his eyes and gives a slight shake of his head.

I raise an eyebrow. Curious eyes turn to us. "There are no screens in here. And the monks aren't that interested in politics."

Samson relaxes. “Nothing. Metz patrols have started in other areas, but they're still not venturing near this part of the city. I think they're waiting to see what happens to the officers they lost. They'll be tracking you obviously.” He glances around at the men and women sat along one side of the room. The remnants of the Snakes sit on the other side. Both groups are wary of each other.

“The captains who returned to the compound will have updated them on what happened.” Rogue looks down at his hands. “We can never go back now.”

His words hang in the air until the silence is broken by a sandy-haired officer. “I wouldn't want to, now that I know.”

The woman next to him nods her agreement. “I won't do that stuff again.” She shudders.

“Nevertheless, while they can track you, there are limits to what you can do out here. I doubt you'll be able to access rations or money through your chips – they'll have shut them down.” Samson frowns.

“We need to get the chips out then,” I say.

Rogue winces. “Is that really necessary?”

“Yes,” Samson and I reply simultaneously. He lets me continue. “There's no benefit to you having those chips – you can't do anything with them. But we don't know exactly what they do, which makes them dangerous. Plus, if the government and Metz can track you, they'll know where to find you.”

Rogue nods reluctantly. “But how … who's going to do it?” He looks warily at Danny, who's scraping dirt from under his nails with the tip of his knife.

“Amber,” I say, thinking of Abby's auburn-haired friend. “She's the healer in these parts. You've seen her out in the garden, she uses the herbs the monks grow.”

"Fine," Samson says, getting to his feet. "One other thing. I'm not sure Primo will be happy about some of you not being under his control. He may try and consolidate."

"Consoli-what?" Little Tommy screws up his face.

"Take us down," I supply for the benefit of the Snakes, most of whom look puzzled. *I must tell Samson to keep things simple.* "You think they'll come after us?"

"Perhaps not here. But you can't stay in here forever." He nods to Rogue. "You lot need to teach this lot how Metz officers fight." He grins at the Snakes. "And *you* need to show them how Outsiders fight."

"The abbot said no fi—"

But he's already gone, sweeping out of the room like he owns the place, leaving behind the scent of wood and needled trees.

I turn back to the room. "Any ideas?"

"There's that area at the back of the garden, behind the sheds," Danny volunteers. "Just a bit of wasteland. An' we'd be out of sight of their precious church." He runs his hand over his shaved head as if stroking the snake tattooed across it.

Tommy's face brightens. "Yeah, an' it's got high walls."

The corners of my mouth twitch but the smile drops from my face as I look at the remnants of the gang in front of me. Tommy's not the youngest and there are more kids than adults among them. *How can we hope to fight off Primo and his army? We'd be slaughtered.*

"Okay. Rogue, can you speak to the abbot? He seems to like you."

Rogue nods and leaves the room.

They respect him, but in that black suit, they fear him a little too. Whereas me, they dismiss without a second glance.

I sigh and curl my feet up on the chair. Muttered conversations start up. There's still so much distrust between the Snakes and the officers. They need to be brought together somehow, to learn to trust one another.

Rogue returns ten minutes later. "He's agreed, reluctantly, but he said we're to be civil about it and he won't give us the weapons back."

"Fair enough, it's a start." I yawn.

"What's that?" he asks, sitting down beside me.

I follow the direction of his gaze to the small amulet that hangs on a cord around my ankle. I tilt it toward him, the green glass at the centre sparkling in the light. Three pointed ovals overlap on top of it, made of some bronze-coloured metal, a circle weaving between them.

"It's something my father gave my mother. She gave it to me before she died."

Rogue's brow furrows in concentration. "You said that she was killed by the Metz?"

I look up at him. "Your memories are coming back?"

He nods and buries his head in his hands. "It's frustrating. There are flickers of them, at the back of my mind, but every time I try to focus, to remember more, they just slip away. I wish there was some way …"

"Of getting them back? Are you sure you want that – isn't what you have bad enough?"

He gives me a miserable look. "But what if I did something worse? What if I was involved in her … her death?"

I shake my head. "You couldn't have been. You're too young. She was killed twelve years ago."

His face relaxes. "Good. I mean, I'm glad I wasn't involved." He looks at me anxiously in the manner of a child seeking approval from a parent.

"It's okay." I reach down and pull on my socks and boots. This place is getting too close. I need space. Freedom.

"Where are you going?" Rogue asks as I stand.

I shrug. "Out. This isn't a prison, you know."

He stands and grips my arm, looming over me. "No, but it's a sanctuary," he says quietly. "And we need you here. Go out in the garden if you must but stay *here*."

Now I feel like the child, being ordered around. Irritation flares in my chest. His closeness isn't helping. Part of me wants to lean into him and feel his arms wrap around me.

I unpeel his fingers from my arm. "Don't tell me what to do," I say through gritted teeth.

When I storm from the room, he doesn't follow.

* * *

I don't go out the main gate – I reckon Samson at least is having it watched, and I wouldn't put it past Murdoch to have some spies looking out for us. But there's a gnarled old tree in the churchyard and it's easy enough to climb up it and over the high walls.

I pull the hood of my light jacket up over my head and skirt through the streets, slipping through the Wall just south of the concrete jungle. At least Inside, Primo and his gang won't be able to find me.

Once through the wall, I filch a bright scarf and wrap it around my head and across my chest. Hopefully, it looks like a style choice and not a desperate attempt to blend in. It's early evening and the streets are full of people making their way home from work, or taking kids to play in the park.

And I thought I could have all this, once, if I found my father.

Shame my father isn't the rich Insider I'd thought he was. Though I guess being leader of the Chain must have its perks.

But what has he done to earn those perks? How many has he killed?

I push the thought away, but it returns like an annoying niggle. I may have his genes, but I knowing nothing about this man apart from his name. Ricus Meyer. And, if I'm honest, even that could be fake.

Trey's family's apartment is in an area of older apartment blocks. I couldn't call it run down – compared to the housing Outside, it's luxurious – but it's not quite as pristine as other parts of the city. I lean on the wall of the block opposite, looking up at the balconies. There's only one that isn't crowded with plants or possessions.

I don't want to press the comm, so I hang around outside, hoping to catch him entering or leaving the building. Twenty minutes later, I hear quick footsteps approaching and look up to see him hurrying down the street toward me. He's wearing a bright blue suit the colour of his eyes, a tie that matches and gleaming black shoes.

He looks older. Handsome. Like an Insider.

"What are you doing here?" he mutters to me, pulling at my arm and glancing anxiously around. "Someone might see you."

He pulls me into a narrow passageway between two buildings and around a corner so we're out of sight of the street.

I yank my arm from his grasp. "I came to see you. Is that *allowed?*"

"Sorry." He pinches the bridge of his nose between forefinger and thumb. "It's ... it's good to see you."

"It doesn't sound like you want to see me." I swallow, realizing I sound like a petulant child.

"How did you find me?"

"Got Abby to tell me your address. She got it from Bryn." I hesitate. "They miss you, Trey. Why haven't you been to see them?"

He rubs his right forearm absentmindedly. "I can't go Outside."

"What, you're banned? Or are they tracking you? You could meet them somewhere else, you don't have to go to Abby's house."

"It's not that." He pauses and bites his lip. "I … I tried to go through the Wall the other day. Just to make sure I could still do it, you know? But as soon as I got close to it, I got this shooting pain up my arm, like an electric shock or something." He pales at the recollection. "I pulled back a few metres and the pain faded. I tried it again, but the same thing happened."

"But the Wall doesn't hurt people, it kills them."

"No, it wasn't the Wall. I didn't even touch it." He looks troubled. "It must be something to do with my chip."

"But Bryn said—"

"Bryn must be wrong," he snaps. "How else do you explain it?"

"I-I don't know."

His face softens. "Sorry, but it makes sense, right? You're not chipped and you can get through. I wasn't chipped and I *could* get through, but now I can't anymore."

"Trey, I'm not the only person out there who hasn't got a chip. And I've seen people die when they touch these barriers. Remember Sanders? He couldn't have had a chip, otherwise there's no way the Chain would have put him in the team to break into the government headquarters."

Trey sighs in frustration. "You're right. I … I just wish I knew how it worked."

"Don't we all." I change the subject. "So, you have a job out here?"

Trey looks down at the ground. "Yeah."

"What are you doing?"

"Oh, just a management thing." He waves his hand around. "You wouldn't be interested."

"I *am* interested." I frown. *What's he hiding?*

He doesn't answer.

I grab his arm. "Why won't you tell me?" Still, he stares at the ground. A cold feeling develops in the pit of my stomach. "You're not working for the government, are you? Or … the Metz?"

Trey shakes his head. He looks up but refuses to meet my eye. "Mother got me a job as a production manager at Coleman's. The food company."

My hand falls from his arm. Boxes of Coleman's food lines the top shelves of the stores. They make Chaz too, though that's the only product of theirs I've been able to afford, their prices are so high. That's why most Outsiders are forced to eat the government rations. The food containing tronk.

Tronk.

The word seeps into my mind. Saliva rushes to my mouth and my fingers claw at my pockets, tingling in anticipation.

No, you don't need it anymore.

"Aleesha?"

I open my eyes and Trey's anxious face swims in front of me. I swallow, trying to push the thought and temptation of the drug away.

"You're working for Coleman's?"

"I didn't have a choice. No one else would employ a boy who didn't even finish school. Not in a job that would pay enough anyway."

"So that's what it's all about? Money?" He reaches for me, but I push his hands away. "Don't touch me!"

He flinches and drops his arms to his side. "You don't understand. Please just listen to me!"

I take a deep breath. "Fine. Tell me."

"It's my mother." His face sags. "She's sick. Really sick. They … they don't know what it is." His fists clench at his side. "We need the money to pay the labs to find a cure. Before it's too late."

The anger inside me melts away. Of course there was a reason. *He wouldn't betray us for nothing.*

"I'm so sorry, Trey." I touch his arm lightly, then impulsively pull him into a hug.

He collapses onto me and I hold him tighter as his body wracks with sobs and his tears wet my shoulder. He smells of air, fresh water and green trees, of everything that is good, and tears of my own spring to my eyes, though I don't let them fall.

Tears for Trey. Tears for Jay.

We cling to each for what feels like hours and I remember the time when Trey had comforted me, after Lily's death, and I had cried on his shoulder.

We have been through so much together, in such a short time.

Finally, Trey pulls away, wiping his eyes with the sleeve of his posh suit. "I-I'm sorry," he hiccups.

I keep hold of his arm, not wanting to let go. "It's okay. That's what friends are for, right?"

He gives a weak smile. "Right."

His fingers trail across my cheek, my skin tingling under his touch. I lift my face to his, my arms snaking around his waist to draw him to me again.

But he pulls away. His hand falls from my face and he steps back, his cheeks pink. "I-I'm sorry."

Sorry for what?

"I have to go. Say hi to Bryn and Abby from me. Tell them … tell them I'm fine."

I stare open-mouthed as he turns and walks away, his shoulders slumped and his shiny black shoes catching on the uneven paving as he walks. If it wasn't for the colour of his suit and his blond hair, I'd have thought he looked like another man, bowed over in defeat.

Andrew Goldsmith.

Trey may be trying to convince himself that he's fine. But he's not.

12

Trey

Ella looks up as I walk into the living room. "What's up?"

"Nothing," I mumble, opening the sliding doors that lead out onto the balcony. I look down at the street, but there's no sign of Aleesha.

Her light footsteps sound behind me. "You've been crying." She places a gentle hand on my shoulder. "What is it, Trey?"

"I told you, nothing. Now can I just have a minute alone? There's no privacy in this place."

Ella pulls her hand back. "Fine. Sorry."

I lean on the rail of the balcony as she walks away. *I shouldn't have snapped.* I guess I could have gone to my room if I'd wanted to be alone. Ella moved into Mum's room, but the tiny room she left me is still full of her stuff. There's nowhere else for it to go, and it's not as if I have many possessions of my own. So it doesn't feel like my room.

Not like my bedroom at Abby's house.

I swallow back the tears that spring to my eyes. Aleesha was right. I should at least have sent them a message to let them know I'm okay, even if I don't dare to go see them. There's an ache in my chest when I think of Abby's bright, welcoming kitchen, and I have to push the thought away because it hurts too much.

Just like I pushed Aleesha away.

It's too soon. I still look at her and see the gun in her hand and my father's body toppling forward.

But that doesn't stop heat rushing through me when I breathe in her sweet vanilla scent. If I close my eyes, I can almost imagine the sparkle of electricity that races from her fingertips across my skin …

My eyes snap open. This isn't doing me any good. This is my new life. I need to make the best of it.

I straighten and walk back inside. "We need to get some plants for the balcony. It's looking bare." I force cheerfulness into my voice.

Ella emerges from the kitchen and makes a face. "I know, haven't got around to it yet. It's a bit shaded, but we could try and grow lettuce or something. What doesn't need much sun?"

I shrug. "I don't know. Do you want a hand with dinner?"

She gives me a look. "I'm just putting packets in the food heater. It's hardly cooking. But, you *could* come out with me tomorrow. Everyone wants to meet you." She leans in, resting her head on my shoulder. "There are some hot girls there too."

"Ella …" I shrug her off my shoulder. "I told you. I'm not interested – in girls or whatever it is you're playing at."

Ella looks hurt. "I thought you wanted to help Outsiders? Or have you changed your mind now you're a proper citizen again?"

"That's not it. But if you had forgotten, that kind of talk is illegal. And if I lose my job, there'll be no money to pay for Mother's medicine."

She looks crestfallen. "Well, it's up to you. I just … I know this job isn't what you wanted. But that doesn't mean you can't have a life in here. You shouldn't just be going to work then coming home in the evening. You need some kind of social life. It's just one night. If you don't like it, you don't have to come again."

"No."

A silence falls between us. Ella turns and walks back to the kitchen and starts ripping open packets and shoving them roughly into the food heater. She's angry, not in the way that Aleesha is angry, an explosive rage that threatens to tear her apart, but a quiet anger that shows in the tension of her shoulders and the tight line of her lips.

She doesn't understand. It's not just one night and it's not about me not wanting to help Outsiders. It's about protecting her. Protecting what I have left of my family.

"I'm sorry, Ella," I say finally. "You don't understand—"

"Don't I?" She whirls around to face me. "I've seen the holos, seen the news of what happens out there. I know what you've been through. I understand exactly how bad it is. Which is why we need to *do* something about it."

"But what can you do? It's not as if you've got guns or a trained army."

"No, but we can move around Inside. We have people who work in the government, the corporations, even in the government labs. Wars aren't just won by guns."

"Aren't they?"

She pauses to catch her breath, her eyes alight with an intensity that scares me. "We can help change the system from the inside, Trey. And if you don't want our help, we'll find someone who does. Tell me about the Chain and the Brotherhood. Who's in charge? What are they aiming to do?"

The food heater pings but she ignores it. “Ella …”

“If you don’t tell me, I’ll find out some other way. I’ll walk right out there into Area Four if I have to.” She folds her arms.

Bloody stubborn women.

But I wouldn’t put it past her to do just that. I sigh and collapse into a chair. “Fine, but you are *not* going after them. You won’t want to once you know what they’ve done.”

“Let me be the judge of that.” She plops down on the sofa next to me. “Go on.”

I pause to collect my thoughts, wondering where to start. “Well, you know about the Chain already. They’re the ones who murdered Father. They’re an international organization, led by this guy they call the Leader.” I decide not to mention he’s Aleesha’s father. “From what Murdoch said, they’ve been active in London for a while, but they’ve not had the people or resources to do much. They’ve mainly been gathering information, making contacts, that kind of thing. Katya came in a few weeks ago – she’s the woman who shot …” My voice breaks and I swallow back the tears that prick at my eyes. “She seems quite senior. And now the Leader himself is coming, Bryn says.”

“But what do they *want*?”

“To take down the government. Murdoch said they’ve done the same thing in Dublin – made it a better place. They … I think they want to open up our borders. Bryn says we’re too insular. That we could solve our population problems easily if we’d trade with other countries.”

“But I thought other countries didn’t want anything to do with us? Not since the Great Flood and the dark times. They bombed us, didn’t they?” Ella looks confused.

I shrug. “That’s what we were taught. But is it the truth? I don't know. We were also taught that the Great Flood killed so many people because Europe didn't warn us, but in the government papers I found, the truth was the other way around. *We* didn't warn *them*. No wonder they bombed us. But that was decades ago – would they still hold a grudge, even though everyone who was in charge then is long dead? Perhaps our government wants us to stay cut off from the world."

"We should ask Anabel," Ella says. "She's lived out there. She'd know. I ... I haven't really had a chance to talk to her properly since she got back. Not with everything going on."

We fall into silence. Ella pulls back a strand of hair into the loose bun on her head. A ray of sun cuts through the gloom in the room, causing red to sparkle in her brown hair.

"So what about the Brotherhood?"

"I don't know much about them. A guy called Samson's in charge." I shiver, remembering the huge man with the long thick dreadlocks and deep voice who'd towered over me after the Commander's pod had been brought down. "He's pretty scary. Aleesha said he'd managed to terrorize most of the gangs in her area into following him. Killed the gang leaders who refused to follow him." I hesitate. "But Aleesha seems to trust him more than the Chain. He's got – or had – some link with the President. So it's not really clear what side he's on. Anabel was right, Ella. You can't trust any of these people. They'll just use you."

"Not if we don't let them." She twists a curl of hair around her finger. "Besides, if they do take down the government, we may be safer being on their side."

"*If* they take down the government. They haven't done a very good job so far."

Ella stands and goes to look out the window. "The government is weaker than you think, Trey. It's like an eggshell – one hard tap and it'll break apart into a hundred pieces."

I stare at her. "What do you mean?"

"Father used to talk to me a bit about his work. Mother wasn't interested and most of his so-called friends abandoned him after he got demoted. Not everyone in the government is happy about the status quo. There are some quite senior people who want things to change. Really, it was stupid of the Chain to kill Father. He could have been very useful to them if they'd played their cards right."

This isn't the kind, laughing Ella I know. It's like a different person has taken over her body, drained the warmth from her voice.

"And you know these people?" I ask uncertainly.

"I could make an educated guess. I'm not as naive as you think, Trey. Quite the opposite." Her voice is calm and quiet. "I know it's a risk dealing with them, but I have to take it. Father would have wanted me to."

"No, he would have wanted you to stay safe and look after Mother." I stand and walk over to her, grabbing her arm and pulling her around to face me. "He didn't want any of us to be involved in this. He just wanted to protect us." My voice cracks but I harden it, trying to speak like him, to say what he'd want me to say. "Go back to your friends and your job and your parties, and stay out of this. Promise me you will? You'll only get yourself killed, and just think about what *that* would do to Mother."

I hate myself for saying it, but if it's the only thing that will make her see reason, I have no choice.

Ella pulls her arm away gently. "Since when did my little brother grow up so much?" Her words are light but there's a sadness in her eyes as she wraps her arms around me and kisses my cheek. "Don't worry, I'll be safe."

She lets me go and walks over to the food heater. "Time for dinner. It'll be cold at this rate."

I stay staring out the window. I'd always thought I'd known Ella the best of anyone in my family. But now, I'm not so sure.

* * *

Barnes had been right. After the initial overwhelm of learning what our production line did and what figures we were working to, my job was to let her do her job. Apart from writing the weekly and monthly board reports and checking that we were keeping up with our quota – which we never failed to do – I didn't seem to have any other responsibilities. Emilie dealt with all the administrative work, and a bit more besides, freeing me up to "make decisions". Except there weren't really any decisions to make.

By day two of my second week, I'm actively searching for something to keep me occupied. I stare out the window over the factory floor, wondering how I'm supposed to feel in charge of this when I don't actually control anything.

White-suited workers scurry along the lines, checking readings off the machines and robots. Barnes is barely visible, flitting between the vats where the meat is grown and the lines of robotic arms that chop and package it. If it wasn't for her red hair, it would be impossible to pick her out from the other workers.

My fingers stop their tapping on the desk. Now that's something I haven't looked into yet. My employees. I chide myself and turn back to the holo screen. *Call yourself a manager.*

The employee record system is locked down but ten minutes with one of the HR officers gives me access to the records for my workers. I quickly scan Emilie's information but there's nothing in there I don't already know. Barnes's record, on the other hand, is more interesting.

"Home time." Emilie waves a hand in front of my face when I don't look up. "You've been staring at those files for the past hour. I don't think you've even blinked. What are you looking at?"

I swipe my finger to close the records and rub my neck. "Nothing important. Just lost track of time." I glance up at her. "Thanks for interrupting me."

"Any time." The smile that seems to linger permanently on her face broadens. "Fancy going for a drink? If you need someone to drag you away from this place."

"Uh, no, I'm fine, thanks." I close down my holo screen and stand, just in time to see the smile drop from her face. Heat flushes my cheeks as I realize what she was actually asking.

"No worries, another time perhaps." Emilie turns and walks quickly over to the door.

"I'm sorry, I didn't mean …" I take a deep breath as she glances back over her shoulder and force a smile. "I mean, thanks for asking."

She smiles again but it doesn't reach her eyes. "No, it's fine. You're the boss, after all. No socializing outside the office." Her voice is artificially light.

I walk over and open the door for her. "I just meant, I'm not really very good at socializing." I give a wry smile. "You saw what happened when I went out with Louis."

Emilie laughs, her eyes searching mine. "Sure, no worries. But if you are … interested, let me know."

I nod and close the door behind her, pressing my back to it and closing my eyes. Her perfume still lingers in the air. I glance back at my desk, debating whether to delve back into the employee records, but decide Emilie's right. It is home time.

I take a pod back Inside but don't go straight home. Instead, I wander the streets until the Wall looms up in front of me. It's green this evening, the dark greens of the deep forests in Wales and the light yellow-green of apple tree leaves withered by the sun.

I halt a couple of metres away and stretch out a hand toward it, wondering if I'd imagined the pain I'd felt last time I tried this. Nothing happens and I take a step forward, relief flooding through me.

"Argh!"

A hot, burning pain flashes up my arm, sending me reeling backward. I trip over my own feet and fall to the ground. I stare down at my arm, half expecting to see scarred, mangled flesh, but the skin is smooth and unblemished. The pain fades to a dull throbbing and then disappears altogether.

I look back at the Wall. Was it just a few weeks ago that I'd been able to pass through it as I pleased? What's changed? Only the chip in my arm and the Coleman Corporation chip in my hand.

Bryn must have been mistaken. It has to be something to do with the chip.

A familiar dull thumping sounds in my head. My body responds instinctively, a surge of adrenaline dragging me to my feet and sending me stumbling away from the Wall.

Ahead of me, a pair of Metz officers round the corner, marching perfectly in time. In their black suits, they tower above me, their helmets disguising the people within.

Every fibre in me is screaming to turn and run from them, toward the Wall. But that would be admitting I've done something wrong. I force myself to stand still until they come to a halt in front of me.

"Hold out your arm," one of them rumbles.

I obey and it scans my forearm.

"Darwin Trey Goldsmith. It is not permitted to go near the Wall. That is the law."

Its voice is gravelly and robotic from the amplifiers in the helmets that make every officer's voice sound the same.

"You know the law?" the other one asks.

I nod. "Y-yes."

Was it a coincidence that they found me? Or was I being tracked?

"This is the second time you have tried to touch the Wall. It will kill you if you go any closer."

I nod again.

The second time. So they know I tried before.

"This time you get fined. A tenth of your monthly wage has now been removed from your bank account. Next time, you will be arrested. No more chances. Good evening."

Perfectly in time, the two officers pivot and walk away. I stumble over to a bench and collapse onto it, letting my head fall into my hands. Sweat beads on the back of my neck.

That was close. Too close.

They're tracking me. I can't try going through the Wall again, and even if I took a pod to Area Six and walked to see Abby or Bryn, all I'd be doing is leading the government right to my friends.

My heart feels heavy as I make my way slowly back to the apartment. To my home, I remind myself.

Voices filter along the narrow corridor from the living room.

I recognize my mother's high-pitched laugh but it takes me a moment to place the other voice.

"Is that you, Trey? Come in here."

I shuck off my shoes and pad down the short hallway.

"Hello, Trey."

Milicent turns to look at me, her iron-grey hair pulled into a knot on her head. She's perched on the edge of Father's favourite wing-backed chair, holding a cup and saucer. Mother's best tea set.

"What are you doing here?"

Mother shoots me a warning look. "Milicent was kind enough to drop in to see how we're doing."

"How's your new job going?" Milicent asks, her gaze boring into me.

"Fine," I mutter, earning me another glare from my mother.

"Sit down and have some tea."

Reluctantly, I obey and take the delicate cup and saucer she hands me. The china is so thin it feels as if I could snap it like a twig. Not like Abby's handmade mugs – rough and uneven, but beautiful and solid. A mug you could wrap your hands around.

Mother places her cup down on the table. "Now, I just need to nip out and pick up some bread for dinner. Will you be staying, Milicent?"

Milicent smiles up at her. "No thank you, Miriam."

My mother hurries from the room and I stare after her, then look back to Milicent. The older woman waits until the front door clicks shut, then puts her empty cup on the table and walks over to the balcony doors.

"How are you finding going back to your old life?"

"It's different. Not really my old life, more a new one."

She glances back at me. "I'll be honest with you, Trey. We've been interested in recruiting someone in the food production companies for a while. There are the Outsider workers, of course, but they have no access to the computer systems."

My pulse quickens as her words spark a dwindling hope inside me.

They killed him, remember. The Chain killed him.

As if she can read my mind, Milicent continues. "I know you don't trust us, and I can understand why. I advised strongly against what they did to your father, but Katya refused to listen. Things *are* changing. We are getting more resources, recruiting more people, but Outsiders are still being held to ransom by the government and food companies." She turns to me and spreads her hands in a gesture of defeat. "Everyone needs food. But if we could infiltrate the corporations, find some way of taking control of the food supply, it could tip the balance …"

I stare down at the patterned carpet. "Did Katya ask you to come to me?"

"No, I suggested it."

"If people could afford proper food – the food produced by Coleman's and Hendricks, they wouldn't have to eat the government rations. They wouldn't have to eat *tronk*." I spit the word out.

"Yes."

"You know they're following me? Tracking me? I can't go Outside anymore. Even going to the Chain's headquarters in Six would be a risk."

"That is why you'll report to me."

I hesitate. "But won't it blow your cover?"

She turns toward me, a faint smile on her smooth, unlined face. "What? Taking an interest in the son of an old friend after his death?"

"I didn't think you were that close," I mutter darkly.

She waves a hand dismissively. "It's not a problem. As long as you don't act suspiciously it will be fine. We can set up a regular weekly time for you to come for dinner ... Say, the day after tomorrow. You can let me know whatever you've managed to find out then."

"What sort of thing do you want to know?"

"Food production and distribution rates, where food supplies are held, if there are any stockpiles, that kind of thing. Plus any weaknesses in security and how they go about distributing food out to the areas."

"I'm not sure I can get access to that kind of information. Although ..." A thought strikes me.

"Although what?" Milicent looks at me sharply.

"Louis – the man whose job I've taken over – now looks after distribution."

"You don't mean Louis Coleman, do you?"

I nod. "He's the son of the CEO. Guess he's being trained up to take over the company."

Her lips curl into a smile. "Perfect. Get to know Louis better then. Take him out for drinks or something – that's what young men like to do, isn't it?" She doesn't wait for me to reply. "And see what you can find out about the Coleman family. Your mother may know something – she's friends with Brad Coleman." She walks over to the door.

"Wait!"

Milicent turns to me expectantly. I stand, not quite sure what I want to say. "I ... When I came in here, I thought I had made a choice. To be an Insider again and help my family. You're now telling me I can do both? Look after my family and help Outsiders?"

"Yes." Milicent's voice softens. "But it's your choice, Trey. You can continue to help us make this city a more equal place, but I would be lying if I said there was no risk. You mustn't get caught. And working with us is not a safe path. It has cost you already, and it may cost you again." She pauses. "I understand if you don't feel able to help us."

It has cost you already ...

My father kneeling on the stone step of the monument. The baying crowd. The shot.

It has cost me.

But I have felt more guilt in this past week than I have ever felt in my life. I can't just go back to how things were and forget everything I've learned about the injustice in this city. What kind of person would that make me?

"I'll help you."

Milicent gives a small smile. "Thank you, Trey. I will see you on Thursday at seven."

I show her out, then return to the living room, my mind racing.

Perhaps my job won't be quite as boring as I'd thought.

13

Aleesha

The sky seems darker Outside. A final ray of red and gold peeks through the clouds before they close together, blanketing the city in shades of grey. In the distance, there's a rumble of thunder.

I trip on a loose flagstone and stumble, just catching myself before I fall to the ground.

I miss him.

My hands ball into fists. Why couldn't I tell him that? Why did I have to berate him instead, for doing what he needs to do?

A hobie shouts my name but I ignore him and keep walking. It only hits me a minute later – how did he know my name?

It's then I realize that I'm in the wrong part of town. I've been walking on autopilot, letting my feet carry me through familiar streets.

I mutter a curse and turn back on myself. I'm in the centre of Snakes territory, just around the corner from headquarters. *You idiot.* I quicken my pace, heading south and east in the direction of the church. But there are footsteps behind me, footsteps that also quicken.

I walk faster, then break into a run, ducking into a side

street to get away from the main roads. Fifty paces ahead, the street spills out into another main road. People walk along it, heads bowed, clutching food or bottles of water to their chests. There's a break in the wall to my left: an alleyway running behind the rows of tall apartment blocks. As I approach it, a figure steps out.

Vihaan.

For a second, I think I can push past him, but another figure steps out to stand behind him, towering over him by a head. Three more follow, completely blocking my path.

I skid to a halt and turn to face my pursuer. The woman stares at me, her expression indifferent. She's still dressed in the black skin-tight suit the Metz officers wear and is poised on the balls of her toes, barely out of breath. In her hand is a thick, black baton.

I turn, slowly. Vihaan is the only Outsider. All the rest are former Metz officers.

"Do you really need five guards to look after you, Vihaan?" I taunt, my eyes searching the alleyway for some means of escape. A set of low outbuildings juts out from the apartment block to my left. Low enough for me to reach the lip of the roof if I jump.

"Primo wants to see you."

"Does he now." I take a step back, hoping to force the woman behind me to step back too and give me a bit of room to play with. She doesn't move.

Vihaan sneers. "It'll be easier for you if you come willingly … Though not quite so fun." He twirls the knife in his hand lazily.

Anger mingles with fear in my veins. But that's what he wants. He's trying to goad me into attacking him so he has an excuse to use that knife of his. He wants revenge.

I should never have fought him. Never have beaten him.

But then you'd have let him get away with being a bully.

I leap forward. Vihaan raises his knife, thinking I'm going to attack. But I jump up, my fingers curling over the edge of the roof. My feet scrabble on the wall and my shoulders scream in protest as I try and pull myself up.

Someone's hands close on my ankles. I kick out, but their grip is like iron. They yank my legs and I tumble from the roof like a rag doll. The face of the woman blurs in front of me before I slam into the ground.

The impact knocks the breath from my lungs and sends pain shooting up my side. Then Vihaan is on me, his foul breath choking me as he pins me to the ground.

I cough, fighting for breath. His blade nicks my neck and warm blood trickles down my throat. His dark eyes are bright as his hand cups my cheek, forcing me to meet his gaze.

"You thought you'd beaten me," he whispers.

"I … did beat … you." I close my eyes as a wave of dizziness washes over me.

Get off my chest, damn you!

I squirm under him, but this just makes him chuckle. "Now, now. There'll be plenty of time for *that* later." He strokes my cheek with the back of his knife.

I manage to get one of my arms free and punch up into his stomach. He grunts.

It earns me a slap around the face, so hard I taste blood. But I smile anyway.

His lip curls. "You won't be smiling for long."

I feel his weight lift from my chest just as a black bag comes down over my head. Something is pushed against my mouth, and for a moment I think they're going to suffocate me. I snatch a breath and a medicinal smell fills my nostrils. Then my head spins and it feels like I am falling, falling, into blackness.

* * *

"How much did you give her?"

"Not much. She should be coming around any minute."

"W-what was it?"

I recognize the third voice, though I struggle to place it. My head still spins and my brain's foggy. I also feel as if I'm about to puke, so I keep my eyes closed and focus on trying to breathe through my nose.

"Just a sedative." The first voice again. Male, cold, hard. "We use it to transport criminals. Stops them fighting and hurting themselves." I recognize that voice now. Primo.

"But she'll be okay?" The third voice again. Female. A trace of fear.

"Of course." Primo sounds amused. "I didn't think you cared about her anyway?"

"I don't." The voice softens to a purr. "But I can think of much better things to do with our time ..."

Primo gives a low laugh. "Jealous, my sweet?"

My sweet?

"Not at all. But why have her here ... like this?" I recognize the voice now. Megan. She's lost no time making her play then.

"She needs to be taught a lesson."

Keeping my eyes closed, I try and figure out where I am. There's a hard surface underneath me, smooth but not cold like concrete. A table perhaps. My arms are stretched out from my body, my legs splayed. I flex my wrists and ankles. They're bound tightly.

Cool air trickles over my toes, making them curl in protest.

My eyes snap open.

"Where are my boots?"

The room is small and bare, lit by a single dim bulb suspended above my feet. Primo stands at the foot of the table, his pale face made more ghostly in the white light. Megan stands in his shadow, clutching his arm possessively. She refuses to meet my eye. I sense a third person in the room, out of sight behind me.

"Your boots?" Primo sounds amused.

This must be one of the smaller rooms in the Snakes' headquarters. There are plenty of them, particularly on the upper levels, where no one really goes. I try to lift my head and peer into the shadows, but my arms are bound too tightly for me to do more than strain my neck.

They've taken my jacket too, though that's less of a problem. Without my boots, I can't run. I wouldn't get ten paces along the street without something sharp and dirty cutting into my foot.

That's presuming I can make it out of this room, of course. I eye Megan again. Her gaze flicks between Primo and me and she shifts nervously. Her hand grips his arm a little too tightly.

Stay calm. Think this through.

"Why remove my boots?"

My voice is steady. *Show no fear.*

"Why?" Primo holds up a thin short knife and my heart sinks. He tosses it onto the table, six inches from my right wrist. "We found your little weapons arsenal." A second knife lands between my legs.

He pulls away from Megan and walks around the end of the table. His fingers linger on the bare skin of my ankle, then trace up my leg, coming to rest over one of the knife pockets built into the seam of my trousers. "We found this one too. It's amazing where you can hide things. Any others you'd like to tell us about?"

His fingers continue their journey up my thigh, my body flinching under his touch. My pulse quickens.

"No!"

The fingers pause, inches from my hip.

I swallow, every part of me desperate to escape his touch. Revulsion dries my mouth, making it hard to form words. "No other weapons," I manage.

"Good."

The sickness returns and it's not just from the sedative. My stomach lurches and I just have time to turn my head to the side before my whole body heaves and I vomit. The bindings dig into my skin as my body contorts, out of my control, and I retch again and again until there's nothing left to bring up.

My eyes burn, my throat raw. Acid coats my mouth, a sour taste that reminds me of burning fevers, cold nights and the feeling of losing control of my body.

Primo looks disgusted. He waves a hand. "Clean up that mess. You gave her too much sedative."

A sheet of water hits me full in the face, sluicing over the table beside me. I gasp, coughing, and my body cramps again in protest. When I finally catch my breath, I lie back panting and close my eyes.

"Now get out of here."

Heavy footsteps. A door closing.

When I open my eyes, I am alone with Primo. His eyes bore into me, grey and hard like stone.

Thoughts flash through my mind like images on a holo screen. *What does he want? Is he going to kill me? Torture me? Does he know we're hiding out in the church?*

"I've been wanting to get you alone ever since I arrived here. But you're a tricky woman to pin down." Primo cocks his head to one side and I notice the snake tattoo – freshly inked – that winds around his neck. "Or at least, you were."

"What do you want?"

"What do I want?" He laughs. "I want a lot of things. Decent food, clean water, pretty girls." He waves his arm expansively. "My life back."

I don't know what to say.

Primo's face hardens. "But first, I want to know what you were doing in the Metz compound that evening. You and the blond boy."

"Why don't you ask—"

"ML486? The officer who was with you?" His hand brushes my arm, sending an icy chill shooting up through my shoulder. "I did. But he couldn't tell us much, even under interrogation."

I close my eyes and hope that's one of Rogue's memories that hasn't returned.

"Who are you working for?"

"No one."

His hand returns to my arm, resting lightly on my skin. "I thought you were smart, Aleesha. That's what your *friends* say."

"I don't have any friends," I reply through gritted teeth.

"If you're as smart as everyone says, then you'll realize that telling us everything you know is in your best interest." Primo's voice is soft, but somehow that makes it even more threatening.

His finger runs up to my shoulder and across my collarbone, tracing the neckline of my thin vest. I try and force myself not to recoil, but my body betrays me, trembling under his touch. The hairs on my arms and legs rise and my teeth begin to chatter.

It's not the cold of the water or this room that makes me shake, but the thought of what he might do to me.

Dark thoughts tug at me as a black pit cracks open in my mind.

I clamp my jaw, looking around for a distraction. There's a blue mark on the wall – a crudely drawn snake painted by an inexpert hand. An overly long forked tongue curls in a spiral and a single black eye gazes blankly out at the room. Perhaps this room was home for one of the gang members, a place of solitude, an escape from the chaos of gang life. A room …

Primo tilts my head, forcing me to meet his gaze. My eyelids flicker, desperate to close, but I can't let them. The pit widens, my grip on the present crumbling into its depths, and I know if I close my eyes it will pull me down into that deep dark place in my mind. The place where I can shut out what's happening around me in order to preserve a tiny bit of sanity.

The place I thought I'd left behind once and for all.

Primo's face melts in front of me, reassembling itself into the face of an older man with thin cheeks shadowed with stubble. His eyes bulge out at me from sunken sockets, hungry for the body of a girl turning into a woman.

A choked sob escapes my lips, and I try and turn my head away from this monster, but I can't. Then his face dissolves and another appears, a young boy with blond hair and a face that had seemed friendly, at first …

A hand slaps my cheek, jerking my head to the side. The taste of copper fills my mouth and I spit, spotting the table with blood. When I look back, Primo's chiselled jaw and flint-grey eyes are back.

"Who are you really working for, Aleesha?"

My eyes dart around the room as I suck air into my lungs.

"No one."

His hand returns to me, sliding under the thin strap of my vest. A shudder wracks my body and a twisted black thread rises from the pit, curling around my mind and pulling me down. And maybe it wouldn't be such a bad thing to let it draw me in.

Whatever he does, you can survive it. You can hide the memory away, with the others. Forget all about it.

But I know I'm lying to myself. You can never forget the bad memories. They just lurk at the corners of your mind like cobwebs you can't quite reach. Better not to make them in the first place.

I focus on my breathing, drawing air slowly into my body, then releasing it.

You are strong. You are strong.

The black thread retreats and my mind clears. I tug at the cords around my wrists. My hands are small. If I could loosen them just a little …

Primo's eyes flicker with amusement. "They're quite tight, I assure you." He walks around so he's behind me, his fingers never leaving my body. They travel up my neck to wind in my hair. I shake my head but he clenches his hand, yanking my head back. "Are you going to tell me? Or do we have to do this the hard way?"

He lowers his head so his eyes are inches from my own. His pupils are pinpricks despite the dim light.

"It doesn't *have* to be hard, you know. Many women appreciate my … attentions."

My anger flares at his arrogance and I strain my neck to break free of his grasp. "You think I would *choose* to sleep with you?"

"Per—" His voice breaks off, his head jerking up at the sound of a muffled explosion.

My heart leaps.

Primo mutters a curse and pulls back. I bite back a whimper as he yanks his hand away, ripping hairs from my scalp. He strides over to the door and opens it.

There's another explosion, louder this time, followed by screams and another bang. The table under me shudders. Primo glances back at me and smiles coldly. "Consider this a brief interlude in our conversation."

Then he's gone. The door hangs open behind him.

My breath comes in gasps, my heart pounding. Inside, the pit begins to close as my mind sharpens. Craning my neck, I inspect the cords binding my wrists. They're thin and the skin underneath is already rubbed raw from my earlier attempts to free myself. The cord on my right wrist is double knotted, the knot tightening every time I pull at it. But on my left wrist, there's a quick release loop.

If I can grasp the frayed inch of cord and pull out the loop, perhaps I can loosen the knot underneath enough to wiggle free.

I'm so focused on trying to draw my fingers down to my wrist that, at first, I don't hear the footsteps approaching. It's not until the hairs on my neck prickle that I look up.

Vihaan stands in the shadowed doorway, staring at me.

I redouble my efforts to try and reach the cord on my wrist. The end lies tantalizingly out of reach.

Come on.

My heart begins to race as Vihaan crosses the room toward me. He steps into the ring of light cast by the weak bulb and my lip curls at the barely disguised lust in his eyes. My vest and trousers suddenly feel a thin and inadequate barrier to his gaze.

I strain to close my legs, but the cord around my ankles bites into my flesh and a small cry escapes my lips.

His eyes flick to my face and the expression in them turns the blood in my veins to ice.

There is desire there but also hate. I'm not sure if one fuels the other – if it's me he hates or his own body for reacting to me in this way – but it doesn't matter. I've only seen that combination on one man's face before and the memory of him sends tremors coursing through my body.

The pit yawns open again, but I will not let myself be pulled down into it. I will not let him abuse me.

You are strong.

Vihaan's touch makes my skin crawl, like a thousand spiders skittering up my arm.

"Get your hands off me."

My voice is hoarse, my mouth dry with fear. I strain, trying to fold my hand unnaturally over on itself to reach the end of the looped cord.

"Just you and me now, Aleesha," Vihaan murmurs. He licks his lips and leans over me, his stale breath choking my nostrils.

My fingertip brushes the frayed end of the cord.

He tugs at the strap of my top, pulling it off my shoulder.

"Primo promised me I c—"

There's another explosion followed by a burst of gunfire. It sounds close at hand.

The door flies open. Dark figures storm in.

Someone grasps Vihaan's shoulder, throwing him back against the wall.

I feel cold metal on my wrists and look up into Bryn's blue eyes. He cuts loose my wrists, then my ankles. "Get up, quick as you can. We don't have long."

My hands shake as I find my boots, tossed in a corner of the room, and pull them on. Murdoch has Vihaan pressed up against the wall and is screaming at him, his pale face flushed with anger. Vihaan's eyes bulge and he trembles in terror at the knife pressed against his throat.

"Did you hurt her?"

Vihaan tries to shake his head but thinks better of it. "N-no ..." His eyes screw up tight. "Don't kill me!" An acrid smell fills the room as a trickle of urine drips from his boot to the floor.

"I should bloody well kill you," Murdoch growls.

Why is he so mad? I didn't think he cared about me that much.

I walk over to them and touch Murdoch's shoulder, wrinkling my nose at the stench coming from Vihaan. "Leave him, Murdoch. He's not worth it. You got here in time to stop him."

Murdoch doesn't appear to hear me.

"Murdoch!" Bryn shouts from the door. "Leave him. We've got to go."

Reluctantly, Murdoch pulls the knife from Vihaan's throat and shoves him to the floor, where Vihaan holds his arms above his head to ward off an expected blow. Then Bryn's pulling me through the door and out into a corridor. Smoke fills the air and the sound of fighting and cries of wounded people ring in my ears. My legs are sluggish, but I force myself to stumble after Bryn, keeping my head down. Down some stairs, fighting all around us, then out into the open air. I want to stop to catch my breath, but Bryn pulls me on.

We don't stop running until we're well into Area Five. I look around, recognizing a couple of other members of the Chain. Blood trickles from a cut on Murdoch's cheek but the rest mostly seem to have got away unscathed. Bryn lifts his wrist to his mouth and mutters something into his comm.

He nods to Murdoch. "Samson's pulled back. Light casualties."

"Did they get *him*?" Murdoch asks.

Bryn shakes his head. "Samson couldn't get close, and Primo was fighting off any opposition. Samson lost two of his people trying. Couldn't risk any more. That wasn't the purpose."

Murdoch's lips tighten into a thin line but he nods. "He's got the message anyway." He looks around. "We'll get back to HQ."

Bryn nods and glances at me. "I'll be along in a bit."

"Thanks, Murdoch!" I call after him.

He pauses and nods awkwardly. "Sorry I got a bit carried away. Reminded me of what they did to my sister." His face darkens. "Thought they might have done the same to you."

I remember what Trey had told me about how Murdoch had come to London. His sister had died after suffering terrible abuse at the hands of one of the gangs. I shake my head and give him a small smile. "You were just in time."

He nods and turns to follow the others.

Bryn takes my arm gently. "You alright?"

I fold my arms across my chest and shiver. "Yes, thanks to you."

"Thank Samson. It was his runner who spotted you getting caught. And Jax managed to get us inside. Murdoch and his team just happened to be in the area, so we joined forces." He scowls. "What the hell were you doing outside the church?"

I bite my lip and look down. A shiver runs through me and I lean against a wall as the adrenaline rushes from my body, leaving me feeling weak … and ashamed. "W-what were you doing there? Why did you come and get me?"

"I was looking for you. Went to the church and Rogue told me you'd done a runner. Figured you might be spying on the headquarters so I hung around, then I ran into Samson." His face darkens. "I didn't think it was like you to get caught."

"But why didn't you leave me?" This is what I don't understand. Why would they risk so much for me?

Bryn flashes me a look that I can't read. Then he sighs and his lips curl into a smile. "Well, I didn't want to be the one to tell your father that he'd arrived just in time for his daughter's death."

My heart stops.

He laughs at my face, frozen in shock.

"H-he's here?"

"Arrived this morning."

I take a deep breath. A thousand birds flutter in my belly. "And he … he doesn't know about me?"

Bryn shakes his head. "Figured you could tell him yourself when you meet him."

When you meet him.

Twelve years I have waited for this moment. And now it's here, I don't know what to say, what to think. I feel Bryn's hand on my back, guiding me forward. "First we go to Abby's. I don't believe you're quite as well as you're making out."

14

Trey

"Where's Barnes?"

The woman looks frightened. I smile reassuringly. "There's nothing wrong, I just want to chat to her."

"She's fixing the line." She points up the silent row. "About halfway up."

I walk up between the rows of robotic arms. One set moves faster than would be humanly possible to chop up and package the meat products, the other is silent, the robotic limbs frozen in mid-air. A technician crouches in front of the silent production line, an open toolbox in front of him. A pair of legs pokes out from underneath the machinery.

"Damn screws have wobbled their way out again." Barnes's voice comes from underneath the production line. "They need to sort out these vibration issues. Pass me a pair of number tens."

The technician scrambles to get the screws out of the toolbox. I hold out my hand and wave him away, pressing my finger to my lips. He looks frightened but scurries off up the line.

A hand emerges. "Come on, I haven't got all day."

"Here you go." I place the screws in her hand and sit with my back against the metal plating.

The hand freezes, then closes around the screws. A moment later, Barnes twists herself out from under the line. Her hair is mussed up and a streak of oil runs across one cheek.

"What are you doing here?"

"I came to talk to you."

She waves to the production line. "I'm a little busy right now. Can it wait?"

"I've been looking at your background."

"You've been investigating me?"

I shrug. "I like to know about my employees. You worked in the government factory for ten years before coming here. Why did you leave?"

"Look around." Barnes gestures with one hand. "Where do you think the money is, here or in some crumbling government factory?"

"You came here because they paid you more?"

"What's wrong with that?"

I stare into her eyes. "Nothing, except that I don't believe you."

Her eyes dart away for the briefest of moments. "Believe what you want. That's the truth."

"I don't think it is," I say quietly. "You found out the truth, didn't you? About what was in the government rations."

Still, she doesn't meet my gaze. "I don't know what you're talking about."

"Who was it, Barnes? Your mother? Father? Sister? Husband? Who was the tronk addict?"

Her face tightens and anger flashes in her eyes. "It's none of your goddamn business. Now get off my factory floor."

"*My* factory floor," I remind her.

She leans in, close enough for me to smell the oil on her clothing. "If you want to keep your job, then I suggest you let *me* get back to work and quit sticking your nose into my business."

"I'm not who you think I am." I force my voice to stay low and controlled.

"Oh, I know exactly who you are. Think I don't watch the news? Found life Outside a bit tough, did you? That why you came home to Mummy? A few weeks spent fighting the good fight and you think you know everything there is to know about Outsiders. Do you even know what happens off this factory floor?" She pulls back and shakes her head. "Thought not. Because you're one of *them*. Do your job and keep your mouth shut. That way we carry on being the golden boys and girls of the factory and *you* get to keep your job."

She stands, forcing me to stand too. I look her straight in the eye. "You finish here at six. I want to see you in my office then." Barnes opens her mouth to protest. "That is an order, foreman."

I turn and walk away, not looking back.

Back in the office, I collapse into the comfortable swivel chair behind my desk and turn to stare through the window to the factory floor. "Why is she so difficult?"

Emilie looks up from her holo screen. "What's she done now?"

I sigh. "Nothing, really." I glance at the clock. It's nearly lunchtime. At least the food in the restaurant is good and cheap. Perk of the job. Except …

I frown as something occurs to me. "I've never seen any of the factory floor workers up in the café. Don't they have a lunch break?"

"Sure they do. Thirty minutes. But they have a separate

canteen."

Things begin to click into place.

"They don't arrive by pod either, do they?" I say slowly. "No wonder I've never noticed anyone in the corridors."

"Their changing facilities are at the other end of the building." Emilie leans back in her chair and frowns. "Is there something wrong?"

I push myself up. "Where's their canteen?"

"Let me check." Her fingers fly across her screen, bringing up a plan of the building. "Level 10 East. But you can't go there."

I'm already heading for the door. "Why not?"

"Because it's for them, not us. You're not supposed to …"

I glance back to see a look of consternation on her face.

"Not supposed to what?"

She comes over to me and leans in. Her perfume wafts over me, jasmine and lemon trees. "You're not supposed to interfere with the Outsiders," she whispers. "You only deal with Barnes. The workers come under a different department."

Her brown eyes beseech me not to leave.

"They're my workers, aren't they? I just want to check on their welfare." I smile down reassuringly. "Surely I can't get in trouble for that."

Her hand closes on my arm, a surprisingly strong grip for such delicate fingers. "You have no idea."

I gently prise her fingers open. "Okay, well I'll head up to the café as normal then. I hear they're testing some new cake mix today." I flash her a smile. "Don't worry."

I feel her eyes following me as I walk down the corridor to the elevator. Once inside, I type in the code for Level 10. The panel flashes red. "Access denied," the robotic voice intones.

Denied?

Level 11, then. Also denied. I try more codes but it seems I'm unable to access any levels below sixteen. Still, they must have a staircase for emergencies.

The lift shoots downward, depositing me in a corridor similar to the one I've just left, except without the bank of windows. I wander around, looking for a stairwell. I don't find it, but I do spot a floor plan on the wall showing the emergency exit routes. There's a tunnel marked further up the corridor. It's open-ended with an arrow pointing along it and a label.

To the East Wing and lower levels.

Bingo.

I head back to the main corridor and fall into step behind a pair of workers in blue overalls. They glance around nervously as if they're not supposed to be here. One of them presses their hand to a panel beside a pair of large glass doors. The doors open and I slip through behind them just before they swish shut.

It's only then that they notice me. The woman starts and opens her mouth to say something, but her companion nudges her and nods at my suit. They exchange a look.

We're in a glass tunnel that extends as far as I can see. Outside is the void. I jump as something drops past, then look down to see a huge carrier pod hovering in front of a line of hanger doors set into the building below us. One of the doors opens and the pod shoots forward into the hanger.

"Sir?"

I snap my gaze back to the tunnel. In front of me is a pod, suspended in a trench. The door's open and the woman looks at me expectantly. I hurry inside.

There are no seats, just a bar at head height that extends around the inside of the pod. I hold onto it, but it's not necessary.

The pod shoots along the tunnel, the walls outside blurring, but inside, it doesn't feel as if we've moved at all.

The workers wait for me to leave the pod, but as soon as we're inside the main part of the building they hurry away, leaving me standing in an empty corridor, a mirror of the one I've just left. Except here, there's no colour on the walls or floors and not even a carpet underfoot. Everything is rough grey concrete. A battered sign on the wall proclaims it to be Level 16 East.

I find a staircase and bang on the door until someone opens it. People are flowing down the stairs, talking among themselves. Some are dressed in blue or green overalls, but others wear t-shirts, jackets and trousers in shades of black and grey. Their conversations trail off as they catch sight of me and they glance at me curiously, as if I'm not supposed to be here.

Perhaps Emilie was right. I shouldn't be here.

But something draws me forward, pulling me down the stairs and through the doors onto Level 10, following the flow of people toward a pair of open doors. A pair of security guards stand either side of the opening, scanning each person in.

One of the guards frowns when he sees me. "Sir? I don't think you're supposed to be here."

"I'm here to do an inspection of the canteen facilities." I smile at him. "Haven't you been informed?"

"No, sir."

I frown. "My assistant assured me this had been taken care of. I will have words with her." I glance into the room, thinking fast. "My name's Louis Coleman. I assume you know who I am?"

Recognition flashes in the guard's eyes, followed by fear. He knows who Louis is, and he also can't have met him otherwise he'd know that I'm not Louis.

"Of course, Mr Coleman, I'm so sorry. We weren't told to expect you." The guard nearly falls over himself to push back the flow of people trying to get into the canteen to usher me in. He shoots a worried glance at his companion.

I slap him on the shoulder, Louis-style. "Don't worry about it. These things happen." I make a show of checking the band on my wrist. "Now, I'll only be here ten minutes or so. Just keep things moving as normal. Don't want to hold up the lunch queue." I give him a wink.

I step into the room, past two more guards, and move to one side so my back's against the wall. The cavernous space is packed with tables and benches, but there aren't enough for all the workers, and people lounge with their backs against the wall or sit on the tables themselves. A bank of food dispenser slots is built into the wall on my left. Above that is a huge clock.

The smell of sweat and dirt mingles with the greasy odour of food. The room is stifling and I tug at my collar, feeling sweat build underneath despite the cooling effect of the shirt.

A grey-haired man passes me, his face lined and his shoulders bowed, like so many of his fellow workers. My eyes linger on him as he presses a button on the food dispenser slot, takes his food and slots himself into a space at one of the tables that's just been vacated.

He gobbles his food down, so fast I wonder if he's had time to chew it at all. But he keeps a portion of the burger back, curling it in his hand and glancing around surreptitiously to check no one's noticed. The people around him move and he gets up with them. They head toward the exit on the far side of the room.

I walk around the outside of the room, feeling the eyes of the workers on me. Some of them notice the direction of my gaze and murmur to themselves. I'm about ten metres from the double doors when the grey-haired man reaches them. The guard waves a wand in front of him. There's a beeping and the man shrinks back in fear even before the guard's heavy hand lands on his shoulder.

The guard yanks his arm up and, finger by finger, forces the man's hand open. I'm close enough to hear the snap as one finger gets bent back too far. The man screams and drops the mangled piece of burger.

"That's it for you." The guard slams him into the wall and reaches for a pair of cuffs at his waist. "Third offence – you're out."

The man begins to shake. He mumbles an apology, a reason. His wife is sick. They have no money for food. The guard pulls his wrists behind his back and cuffs them together.

I've closed the distance between us almost before I've had time to think. "Excuse me …" My eyes flick to the guard's tag. "Bates."

The guard whirls around at my voice. His eyes widen and his Adam's apple bobs up and down. "S-sir?"

His eyes flick to the entrance door to the canteen. "Did your colleagues not tell you? I'm inspecting the facility." I give him a cold smile. "Louis Coleman. I'm the new—"

"Oh, I know who you are, sir." The man gabbles. "I'm sorry, we weren't infor—"

"About the inspection? It's alright, I know." I pat his arm companionably. "Issue at my end, I think. Now this man …"

The guard clears his throat. "Caught taking food out again. Third time, sir. We'll get him out of here, along with the rest of them, as soon as our shift ends." He nods to two women and a man who are lined up against the wall. Their faces are drawn and their hands are cuffed to the wall.

"Good work, Bates, you've passed the test." I force myself to smile at him. "We asked these workers to try and smuggle part of their lunch ration out so we could test that our security procedures were working properly. I'm afraid you'll have to let them go this time, but I think they've had all the warning they need."

The workers on the tables nearest to us fall silent. It ripples through the room, like the shockwave from a pebble dropped in water.

"Sir?"

The guard is confused. No one's told him to release people before.

I lean in closer and lower my voice. "Release them. This was just a test."

I don't know if he believes me, but he's scared enough by my suit to do as I order. The grey-haired man gives me a confused look as he hurries through the exit, clutching his hand to his chest.

I look back across the room to find hundreds of faces turned to me. My fake bravado begins to slip away and a gnawing sensation develops in the pit of my stomach.

All these people will remember who I am. They see me as an Insider.

"Keep up the good work." I turn to the guards. "I've seen everything I need to make my report."

I glance back one final time as I leave the canteen, and a flash of copper in the sea of grey catches my eye.

Barnes.

Her ponytail swings as she snaps her head back to the table. But she was close enough to hear every word I said. And she knows I'm not Louis Coleman.

The question is – what will she do about it?

* * *

Barnes comes to see me at six, as ordered. Emilie has already left for the day. She barely spoke to me this afternoon. Even the cup of coffee and cake I'd fetched her from the café wasn't enough to placate her. Apparently, she'd gone to find me in the restaurant, and not being able to find me, had guessed where I'd really been.

She'd given me a lecture about risking my job and hers, before seeming to remember that I was her boss and cutting herself off mid-sentence. We'd spent the rest of the day working in an awkward silence.

Barnes walks over to join me at the windows that look down onto the factory floor and crosses her arms. "So you've been to see how the other half live?"

"I know how the other half lives." I glance around the room then lean in to whisper in her ear. "Will people be listening in?"

She stiffens and for a moment I wonder if I've made a mistake. If she is the one I need to be worried about turning me in.

"Assume so."

I pull back.

She raises her voice. "I need to show you an issue we've got with the production line."

We make our way down to the noisy factory floor. It runs all day and all night. The night supervisor gives us an odd look but I give him a nod and he doesn't ask questions. According to Emilie, he's lazy and leaves any problems for Barnes to fix.

We head for the section of line Barnes had been working on this morning. It's one of the noisier parts of the factory.

A white-suited technician walks toward us. "I thought this had been fixed already." I raise my voice as he walks past, then drop it to a whisper that only Barnes will hear.

"I may be young but I am not a baby. I was there in the Battle of Rose Square. I have seen my friends killed in front of my eyes, watched my own father's blood spill on the ground. I know what life Outside is really like. So stop playing games with me."

She runs a finger along a join in the metal, not meeting my eye. "Why come back Inside then?"

"That's my business."

She gives a thin smile. "Touché." After a pause, she speaks again. "What were you doing down in the canteen today?"

"Finding out what really goes on in this factory."

Her finger rubs a bolt head, almost fondly. "He'll find out, you know. Coleman has spies everywhere, even among the workers. People can be easily bought with extra rations or access to a nicer apartment. You shouldn't have gone there." She turns to look at me. "And pretending to be Louis was downright stupid."

Heat rises to my cheeks. "It'll be fine. I'll deal with it."

She studies me, her head cocked slightly to one side. "Don't underestimate him, Mr Goldsmith."

"Underestimate him or you?" I narrow my eyes. "Have you been bought already?"

She flinches and anger flashes in her green eyes. "I am not a slave to be bought." She spits the words and I smile, feeling a stab of satisfaction at having provoked a response from her. Barnes sucks in a breath, turns away and walks down the line of machinery, forcing me to follow her.

"You don't have to worry about me turning you in to Coleman." She stops and turns toward me. "But you *should* stop snooping around. You'll only get yourself into trouble and you won't help anything or anyone."

There's a sadness in her words that halts the reply forming on my lips.

"Look, Trey. I don't know why you came back to work Inside. Whether you wanted your old life back or fancied acting as a spy. But you need to figure that out, because otherwise you're just going to put yourself and others in danger." Her voice is soft and her green eyes are kind. "This isn't a game for rich boys to play at. I believe you mean well, but what you did today in the canteen? That was stupid. Any more stunts like that and you'll be hauled off by the Metz." Her lip curls into a smile. "And I for one was quite enjoying having a boss around who actually cares about his workers. Not to mention one who leaves me alone."

She turns and walks away, leaving me frozen on the spot, a hundred thoughts rushing through my head. But one lingers.

She called me Trey. I've never introduced myself as Trey ... Why would she call me that?

Unless she knows more about me than she's letting on.

15

Aleesha

I walk in a daze until there's a click of a gate opening, then a door and a familiar voice. Familiar smells of peppermint and herbs. I look up into Abby's concerned brown eyes.

"Aleesha, are you okay?"

I nod but I'm still trembling. She wraps an arm around my shoulder and I lean into her. Tears prick at my eyes, but I won't cry. Not because of *him*.

Vihaan, I can understand. He's just like half the guys in the gang, half the men in Area Four. They think they can take what they want because that's what life is like out here. But Primo ... he knows both sides. He has power and he could use that for good, to help us.

He and Rogue have been through the same. How can one be so caring and the other a monster?

I shiver again and Abby wraps a blanket around my shoulders. It's warm in the kitchen, but I still feel cold inside.

"Sit." She pushes me down gently into a chair. A moment later, a steaming bowl appears in front of me. It smells hot and delicious. I wrap my hands around it.

There's a sharp intake of breath. "What happened?"

I glance up then follow Abby's gaze to my wrists. They're ringed with red lines where the rope bit into my skin.

"And what were you doing away from the church?" Bryn sits down opposite me. His voice is gentle but firm.

"I-I went to see Trey."

Abby sits down next to me. "How is he?"

I dip my spoon in the bowl, rescuing a floating chunk of rehydrated protein. The saltiness eases the bitter taste in my mouth. "He says to tell you he's fine. He ... he's working for one of the food companies." I wonder whether to tell them about his mother. Had he told me in confidence or not? But Trey tells Abby most things, and I don't want them thinking he's sold out for no reason. "His mother's sick."

"How sick?" Bryn's eyebrows knit together and I remember, belatedly, about his relationship with Trey's mother.

"Very, I think. He said they don't know what it is." I take another sip of the soup and place the bowl back on the table. "He doesn't want to work at that place, I know he doesn't. But he feels he has to, because of her. Because they need the money." The heat of the bowl burns my hands.'

Bryn and Abby exchange a glance. "I didn't know," Bryn says finally. "I just thought it was Miriam wanting him back."

"Is there anything you can do?" Abby's expression is unreadable.

"About the money? I don't know. Perhaps." Bryn looks at me. "But it's up to Trey whether he stays Inside. We can't force him to come back."

"I know." I slacken my grip on the bowl.

Abby reaches out and rests a hand on my arm. "So what happened on your way back?"

Haltingly, I tell them about the ambush and how Primo had

recognized me from our trip into the Metz compound.

"But you didn't tell him about us?" Bryn asks.

I shake my head. "No."

"Good girl."

Abby scowls at him. "She shouldn't have been put in a position where she was being threatened!"

"She got herself captured." The smile drops from Bryn's face under Abby's look. "We went to rescue her!"

"Thank you," I say quietly. "You're right. I was dumb to let them catch me." My hands tighten around the bowl again. "But being shut up in that church all day, unable to *do* anything, it's just so ... so frustrating!"

"I know." Bryn sighs. "But at least you're all safe there. We just need to figure out what Primo's weakness is."

"Surely the government won't be too happy about him setting up his own empire out here?" Abby asks. "Perhaps they'll deal with the problem."

"And lose more Metz officers?" Bryn shakes his head. "They still think we've got that device, remember? You *do* still have the device, Aleesha?"

I shrug. "It's in safe hands."

Bryn doesn't look convinced.

Abby yawns. "Well, the President needs to do something to stop all this fighting. The city's falling apart."

"I doubt he cares," Bryn mutters into his tea.

I stare down at the lumps floating in my soup. The President's words ring in my head. *He tricked your mother into loving him ... Make no mistake, she died because of him.*

The President blamed my father for my mother's death. And my father blames the President. Which of them is right?

"Are you going to see him tonight?" Abby asks.

Bryn shakes his head. "It's getting late. We'll go first thing tomorrow."

"Good, well, you finish that soup, Aleesha. I'll go and make up the bed for you."

I drink the rest of the soup and rinse the bowl. It feels nice to be back here again. I wonder what they're having for dinner at the church. I turn to Bryn. "Can you get a message to the others? I … they'll be worried about me."

"Samson's already dealt with it."

"You know, perhaps you should join forces with him? You'd be strong enough to take on the government then."

"It's one thing to use him to rescue you but quite another to trust him to work with us." He stretches. "You need anything to help you sleep?"

I shake my head. "I'll be fine."

But as I curl up in the narrow bed in what I always think of as Trey's room, I begin to wish I'd taken him up on his offer. As hard as I try, I can't push away the image of Primo standing over me. The memory of his hand on my skin makes my stomach churn.

The sheets smell fresh and clean, but I wish that Abby hadn't washed them, that I could close my eyes and smell Trey, and imagine his arms around me, chasing away the bad dreams.

And finally, that thought pushes all the others away and sleep takes me.

* * *

When I awake, I stare up at the thin crack in the ceiling. Today is the day I finally get to meet my father. The man my mother had loved so much that she's died to protect him.

Today, my life could change.

The sun streams in through the small window, already warm despite the early hour. We're still some way off the real summer heat, but the air in the streets is already thick and muggy, and the rains are less frequent. I'm never sure which is worse, the constant rains and flooding of winter or the intense heat and drought in summer. But at least in winter, the water tanks are kept full.

I push back the sheet and dress, pulling my hair back into my usual tight braid. Then I go to the bathroom, wash my face and stare at myself in the cracked mirror.

I've always known I looked like my mother. I have the same long dark hair, straight as an iron rod. The same brown eyes and cool, light brown skin, burned darker by the summer sun. But the shape of my face is not hers. My jaw is more square, whereas her face was like a heart. My nose is slightly larger and longer.

Will he recognize me? Will he see her in me?

My heart beats a little faster. A thousand images flow through my mind. Him crossing the room in two strides to pull me into his arms. Me comforting him as he cries for my mother. Talking with him for hours about life in London – the good parts anyway.

That won't take long.

I swallow and look down at my dirty trousers, wearing through at the knees. Perhaps I should ask Abby if I can borrow some of her clothes. Try and look a bit nicer, so he doesn't think his daughter is some street hobie.

In the kitchen, Bryn's finishing a bowl of porridge and Abby's sat with a mug of tea. She rises when I walk in. "Porridge?"

I shake my head. My stomach is a ball of knots, there's no

room for food. "I'm not hungry."

She smiles at me sympathetically.

Bryn licks his spoon and places his bowl in the sink. "Ready to go?"

"I-I think so." I pluck at my jacket. Underneath, my top is coming apart at the seams.

Abby comes to stand in front of me and places her hands on my arms. "You look fine," she says quietly. "Don't worry. Any father would be proud to have you as his daughter."

Even after everything I've done? Everything I've become?

"Show him the person you are, not the person you were."

It's as if she can read my mind.

Abby smiles and gives me a gentle push toward the door. "I hope it goes well."

"See you later," Bryn calls as he shuts the door behind us.

We walk in silence up to the Chain's headquarters in Area Six. A man and a woman lounge against the pillars that flank the stone steps up to the front door. I pause before we reach them. "Who knows he's my father?"

Bryn purses his lips. "Me, Katya, probably Milicent. I haven't told her, but I'm sure she's figured it out."

"And they won't have told him?"

"No."

My fingers tap nervously against my legs.

Bryn looks at me. "Do you want me to speak to him first?"

I take a deep breath and shake my head. "No. It's fine."

At the entrance to the building, Bryn stops with his hand on the door. "I forgot to say. We don't know him as Ricus Meyer – the name you saw on the file. He calls himself Richard Masterton now."

Richard Masterton. Right.

Muffled voices filter down the staircase as we step inside the entrance hall. Katya emerges from a room on the right. "Aleesha." She smiles and hurries over. "How are you feeling?"

Her tone is warm and friendly, but I take a step back, away from her outstretched arm. If she's looking for my forgiveness for Andrew Goldsmith's death, she's not getting it any time soon. "Fine."

"Good." She turns to Bryn. "He's upstairs. Murdoch's updating him on our assets. He's … not in the best of moods."

Bryn nods.

"Well, I'll be down here if you need me." She saunters off.

"Not in the best of moods?"

"I'm sure it'll be fine," Bryn replies, though he doesn't sound at all certain.

I walk slowly up the stairs, running my hand along the ancient wooden bannister. As we reach the top, a door off the landing opens and Murdoch storms out, slamming the door behind him. His face is dark, his eyebrows furrowed together and he pushes past us without a word.

My fingers tremble on the polished wood. Bryn walks forward and opens the door.

A man stands in front of the holo table in the centre of the room. His fingers fly across the display, pulling up lists of names and numbers and moving them onto an outline map.

He's not a tall man, not by Insider standards, or particularly stocky. He wears a light blue shirt, open at the neck, and his rolled-up sleeves are tight on his muscular forearms. Stubble traces his jaw and his dark hair is streaked with grey.

He looks up as we enter and starts, frowning at me. He may be older than the man I'd seen in the Metz files but his blue eyes are just as piercing.

My breath catches in my throat and, for a moment, I'm frozen in place. His eyes move on to Bryn and I shake myself, released from some invisible bond.

"What is it, Bryn?" His voice carries a trace of irritation.

Bryn glances to me and raises an eyebrow.

I search his face for some flash of recognition, an understanding that he knows who I am. But all I see is annoyance.

"I-I'm Aleesha." My voice sounds small in the big room.

Show him the person you are.

I take a deep breath and step forward. "I'm your daughter."

For a split-second, his eyes widen in disbelief. Then he throws back his head and gives a harsh laugh. "Not another one. Bryn, get her out of here." He flicks his hand impatiently and turns back to the holo display. "I don't have time for this nonsense."

Bryn clears his throat. "It's not nonsense. She's Maria Ramos's daughter."

The man's shoulders tense at the mention of my mother's name. "I told you I didn't want to talk about her."

"Why? Did you forget about her that easily?" My fists clench at my sides.

His eyes tighten as he zooms in the display. "What are you doing here?"

"I thought you might want to know that she had a daughter," I say through gritted teeth.

Richard Masterton shrugs. "Maybe she did, but that doesn't make me your father."

Anger explodes inside me.

"You bas—"

"Aleesha!" Bryn's hands close on my arms, pulling me back. "Calm down," he hisses in my ear. I respond by stamping down on his foot. His grip slackens and I pull free, closing the distance to the holo table in five strides.

"My mother loved you!" I grab the man's arm and pull him to face me. "She *died* because of you. You left me to survive on the streets alone. I have ..." Tears spring to my eyes and thicken my throat, but I swallow them back and fight to keep my voice under control. "You do not know what I have had to do to survive. All these years, I dreamed of finding my father. You. And now you stand here and call her a whore?"

The slap of my palm on his cheek echoes in the room. I freeze, my hand still in mid-air.

Silence hangs heavy in the air between us. Finally, he looks at me, but if I was expecting to see compassion or love in his eyes, I was wrong.

"You do look a bit like her ... But it's been so long ..." His voice hardens. "Besides, do you know how many kids I've had coming up to me, claiming that I'm their father? Wanting my money, my protection? Hundreds. And they all have a sob story to tell."

A fire rages inside me. Is that all she was to him? One woman of many?

I hate him. Hate myself, for being such a fool to believe ...

"And why is that? Because you have a woman in every city?" I jab my finger in his chest. "Did she know that she was just your London woman? The President was right – you tricked her into loving you. You *used* her."

"No!"

He yanks my wrist away, twisting it painfully. The fire in his eyes reflects what I feel inside, but I don't know if it's directed at me or her or someone else. "Maria was everything to me. Everything! You don't know what you're talking about." He pushes me away. "Now get out!"

I stumble backward.

He doesn't believe me. Why doesn't he believe me?

I've spent so many hours imagining meeting my father for the first time but never did I think it would be like this.

I scrub my fist across my eyes to brush away the tears that threaten to spill down my cheeks but my arm freezes as a thought hits me. "Wait. I can prove it to you." I lean over and claw at my boot. "I have the amulet."

"The amulet?"

He remembers. I can see it in his eyes. I pull my boot off, hopping awkwardly on one leg and reach for the amulet tied around my ankle.

But it's not there.

My heart skips a beat. Time slows while my mind tries to make sense of what I'm seeing.

I always wear it. Except...

Except Primo had taken off my boots. And in the rush to leave the headquarters, I hadn't realized the amulet was no longer around my ankle.

I feel suddenly sick. I've kept it safe for twelve years. The only thing I had left of my mother. The only thing I had of my father. And now *he* has it.

"Aleesha?" Bryn's voice breaks through the bubble surrounding me.

"He took it. Primo must have taken it when he had me tied up. It's still at the Snakes' HQ." I turn back to my father. "My mother gave me an amulet before she died. Green with a—"

"Shut up!"

His words cut through me. "Stop wasting my time. Get out of here."

Never have I seen eyes that seemed so cold. Power and anger

radiate from him, and I take a step back, suddenly afraid. Bryn tugs at my arm. "Come on, Aleesha, let's go."

I want to speak, want to say something more, but I can't. I let Bryn pull me from the room and lead me down the corridor into a smaller room. There's a sofa against one wall and a small table with a withered pot plant.

Bryn walks over to the window and looks out. Then he gives an exclamation of frustration and bangs his fist against the wall. "I'm sorry, Aleesha."

"About what?" My words are dull and lifeless.

He didn't believe me.

"I should have talked to him first. Prepared him to see you."

"Would it have made a difference?" I stare at the wood panelling on the wall. So much wood in this building. Enough to keep a dozen hobie fires burning.

"Perhaps." He leans against the window frame. "He doesn't want to believe. Doesn't want to accept responsibility, perhaps." A smile twists the corner of his mouth.

"Like you."

"Yes, like me." There's a pause. "He did love your mother. I know him well enough to know that. But he's burying the hurt and pain inside." He glances over at me. "Like you."

"So what happens now?"

"We prove it to him. I'd hoped it wouldn't come to this but he can't deny the results of a DNA test. Swab the inside of your mouth with this." He pulls a tube from his pocket and hands me what looks like a toothpick with a soft, round head. "Just in here." He pulls his mouth open and points.

I do as he asks and hand it back. "Are you going to ask him to do the same? I can't see him taking part in some stupid test."

"Leave that to me." Bryn puts the toothpick into a plastic tube and screws a cap on the end. He shoves it back in his pocket. "Don't go after the amulet. Whatever it is, it's not worth risking your life for. We're not going to come and rescue you a second time."

I glance toward the door.

He smiles. "I know you're thinking it. I'd be thinking the same thing. I'll do what I can to help you get it back. But Primo isn't someone you can manipulate like an Outsider. He's clever and cunning. You know that. Don't do anything stupid."

I nod and turn to leave.

"Aleesha?" I pause with my hand on the door handle. "If … if you see Trey, can you tell him …" He looks awkwardly down at the floor. "Tell him I support him in whatever he decides."

I yank open the door, irritation flaring.

What am I, his messenger?

"Tell him yourself. I thought you were taking *responsibility*."

The door slams behind me, and I run down the stairs and out into the street. As I walk away, I get the strange feeling someone's watching. I whirl around and look up, just in time to catch sight of a face pulling back from a window.

I force myself to turn away and march resolutely down the street. Tears burn at my eyes and I'm so focused on not letting them fall that I walk in a daze, back through the streets of Area Six and down into Five.

As I cross the boundary into Four, a large figure steps out in front of me. I open my mouth to greet him, then close it as I see the anger that fills his deep blue eyes. His fists clench at his sides as he steps toward me.

I lick my lips and find my voice. "Rogue?"

He doesn't answer, just takes another step closer. His hand closes around my arm in a vice-like grip as he begins to drag me through the streets.

16

Trey

I glance up as the office door bangs open, my finger frozen over the holo screen in front of me. Instinctively I snap down the window displaying the files I'd been trying – and failing – to access.

The man who stands in the doorway exudes power. Like an overpowering scent, it wafts toward me and I find myself frozen in his stare. His eyes are dark and piercing and a mane of black hair, with a single thick streak of silver, surrounds a sculpted face that looks vaguely familiar. He's heavyset, carrying some extra weight around his stomach, unusual for an Insider.

"M-Mr Coleman, sir ..." Emilie stammers, shooting to her feet. Her eyes are wide and her fingers twitch nervously as she clasps her hands together. She gives me an anxious look. From her reaction, I can only assume that this is *the* Coleman: CEO of the Coleman Corporation.

I try to speak but no words come out.

The man surveys my office dispassionately. He gives Emilie a nod. "Please leave us, young lady. I would like a private word with Mr Goldsmith."

Emilie almost bolts from the room, only pausing at the door

to cast a panicked look in my direction. I swallow and press my hands into the table so he can't see them shaking.

Or perhaps I should offer to shake his hand. Is that what I'm supposed to do?

Coleman walks over to the window that looks down onto the factory floor. "Darwin, isn't it? I don't think we've met. You were always ... away when I visited your parents."

"Yes, sir," I mumble.

"I'm sorry about your father. He was a good man. Not good enough for your mother, of course, but she had such hopes for him. She believed he was destined for the top. But it wasn't to be." He sighs and turns toward me. "And you, Darwin, what do you want to do with your life?"

I don't know what to say. I feel like a mouse caught in the gaze of an adder, like the time Peters had called me up in front of the class and asked me to explain why I had let my schoolmates down.

"I-I'm not sure, sir." My answer is honest, at least.

Coleman frowns, a crease wrinkling his smooth brow. He pulls something from his pocket and makes a flicking motion with his hand, then walks closer. I try to refrain from pulling back. His suit is perfectly tailored and made from real wool. It probably costs more than I make in two months.

"I gave you this job as a favour to your mother, boy. But you have to earn your place here. Your mother promised me that you'd turned over a new leaf – left all that ridiculous rebellious nonsense behind." His voice is low but intense. "Have you, Goldsmith?"

"Yes, sir. I-I want to do a good job." I try and make my voice confident but the blood in my veins turns to ice as I look up into his eyes.

He knows.

"Good. Because I would hate to have to go back to your mother and tell her that you had betrayed my faith in you by snooping around and impersonating my son."

I try to swallow but my mouth is too dry. I'm sure he can read the terror on my face. Aleesha always said I was terrible at lying.

"I-I wanted to know more about the layout of the factory, more about my workers so I could manage them more effectively. I appreciate your generosity in giving me this job and want to do the best I can. I-I apologize if I've broken any rules."

He surveys me for a minute, then takes a step back. I try and look as open and honest as possible. "To be perfectly honest, sir, Barnes and Emilie do such a good job that there isn't really enough to keep me occupied here. If there's any other work that I could help you out with, to help repay you for giving me this job ..." I let my words hang in the air between us.

Coleman purses his lips. "Well, you're keen at least. And Phillips says your reports have been good. What did you excel in at school?"

I wrack my brain. I'd come bottom in most of the traditional subjects we'd studied at school. History, politics, economics. "I'm pretty good with computer programming and technical solutions," I say, more confidently than I feel. "I've made some minor improvements to the model we use for predicting efficiency in this department already."

"Show me."

Shakily, I bring up a new window on my holo display and talk him through the changes I'd made to the model. His expression doesn't change but when I finish talking he nods. "Very well, there may be some other work you can assist with. But please keep your activities only to those you have been assigned. You know what they say about curiosity."

He strides over to the door and opens it.

"W-what do they say?" I ask, confused.

He turns and flashes me a smile and I'm reminded of a lion, baring its teeth before its prey.

"It killed the cat." And with that, he turns and leaves, slamming the door shut behind him.

* * *

Milicent lives in a six-storey townhouse in the east part of the city, a short distance from the Wall. Stone lions sit atop pillars, guarding the path through the flowerbeds to the steps leading up to the polished black front door. I've only ever seen it from the inside – when Bryn brought me in through the secret underground passage that connects the house to a shop Outside – and even then I was amazed that one person had so much space.

Even if she's wealthy enough to afford it, is it right for one person to have so much?

The scent of orange trees lingers on the warm breeze and I'm grateful for the new shirts my mother bought me. Another thing I'd taken for granted – clothes that keep you cool. I can't remember ever spending a summer in London – I spent the school holidays at my family's home in the Welsh countryside, being kept away from society – but I suspect it's unbearably hot.

I walk up the narrow path. As I approach, the door swings open and a butler dressed in an old-fashioned black uniform ushers me in. He shows me through into a dining room that looks out over the back garden. A long mahogany table is set for dinner. Milicent is already seated. The smell wafting from the covered dishes makes my stomach gurgle.

"Come and sit down, Trey. I thought you might be hungry." Milicent smiles and waves to the chair next to her. I slide into it. The butler lifts the domed lids off the platters, revealing dishes of meat, vegetables and potatoes. "Please, help yourself."

I haven't seen this much food since … I can't remember when. If I ate like this every day I'd quickly put back on the weight I'd lost living Outside.

"It's the one luxury I allow myself," Milicent says, helping herself to a modest portion. "The cook has been with me since he was a boy. I don't ask where he finds half the stuff he does. Eat what you want – it's not often I have company."

I try each of the dishes in turn: beef with spicy peppers and a sauce that explodes in my mouth, fresh green beans and garlic, roast potatoes that are crisp on the outside and soft and fluffy inside. There's duck too, in a plum sauce, and a vegetable I don't recognize but which tastes delicious.

I've barely finished half the food on my plate when my stomach starts to protest that it can't handle any more. And then the guilt hits, twisting my stomach tighter and threatening to purge the contents of it back up my throat.

This could have fed a family of four for two days. Three, if they were careful.

"It won't go to waste," Milicent says. "The staff will eat the leftovers for dinner and lunch tomorrow. I suspect the food is the one reason most of them stay working for me." She smiles wryly.

I push my plate away, wondering if she actually is a mind reader or if I'm always that much of an open book.

Milicent pushes back her chair and stands. "Let's go into the drawing room and talk."

I follow her into a large sitting room. Heavy brocade curtains shut out the last of the evening light and an assortment of lamps cast a soft glow around the room. Away from the smell of food, my nausea fades, though my stomach feels tight and uncomfortable. Milicent waves at me to sit on a low sofa and seats herself in a tall, wing-backed chair opposite.

The door opens and the butler comes in, carrying a tray with a teapot and a pair of cups. He sets it on a low table, nods to Milicent and leaves.

"Mint tea," Milicent says as she pours steaming liquid from the teapot into the two cups. "It'll help settle your stomach. I imagine it's been a while since you had rich food."

The sharp scent of the mint reminds me so strongly of Abby's kitchen that a thickness develops in my throat. I take a sip of the hot liquid, letting it scald my mouth, the pain pulling me away from the memory.

I never thought I would miss being Outside.

To distract myself, I look around the room. It's decorated in an old-fashioned style with pastel wallpaper and a polished wood floor. Real wood, I suspect, though it must have cost a fortune. Unless it dates from the time before the Great Flood, when there was a seemingly never-ending supply of the stuff. Large oil paintings in gilt frames hang from a rail, mostly landscapes, except for a portrait of a young man. He looks a few years older than me, with dark hair and a square jaw shaded with stubble. The portrait is so life-like that I almost feel his eyes on me.

Milicent follows the direction of my gaze. "My son." She adds a small spoon of sweetener to her tea and stirs it, the silver spoon chinking against the china.

I look back at her in surprise. "I didn't know you had a son."

"He died," she says shortly. "A long time ago."

"I'm sorry." I take a sip of my tea and look back at the portrait. Now I know, I can see the resemblance. They both have the same long straight nose and blue eyes. But while Milicent always has a trace of coldness in her gaze, her son's eyes smile down on me.

The tinkling of the spoon on china stops. "You don't know about the Rose Rebellion, do you?"

I shake my head, then pause as I think back a few weeks. "You mentioned that once before, didn't you?"

She nods. "I thought you would have been taught about it in school. Though, on reflection, perhaps not. They only teach you about the successes of governments, not the failures."

"That's not true," I object. "We learned about the Great Flood, and the two World Wars the century before, and lots of other events."

"Yes, but they were all *before*. You didn't learn much about what came after the Great Flood, did you? The dark times. The bombing and the starvation and the fighting. They didn't tell you that more died from that than in the flood itself." She glances up at me. "I thought not. Just like they didn't teach you about the Rose Rebellion. Our young people have to be taught to respect the society we're in and not question it. How else can the government rule?"

Her voice carries a trace of irony.

"Did … did your son die in the Rebellion?"

"He *was* the Rebellion. And yes, he died. They all did."

I try to remember what she'd said about the Rose Rebellion. It had been before Aleesha and I had broken into the Metz compound. We'd been at the Chain's headquarters. Aleesha had been talking about her mother's death and Milicent had butted in, saying something about death without trial. I'd meant to ask Bryn about it later, but so much had happened it had slipped from my mind.

Milicent sips at her tea. "I was a child during the dark times, you know. Yes, I am that old." She gives me an ironic smile and I blush, realizing my shock must show on my face.

That must make her a hundred at least? But she looks barely eighty.

Then again, there aren't many old people to compare her to. Most give up their lives so new babies in their families can be born. It's one of the foundations of our society – a consistent, steady population means we can provide for everyone.

Except we don't provide for everyone. We provide for Insiders.

"The dark times lived up to the name. Even the little I remember still gives me nightmares sometimes, and I know I was one of the lucky ones. Those of us who were around at that time understood why the government put in new laws around population control, why the Metz were created, even why we cut ourselves off from the rest of the world. Our belief in that was why we only decided to have one child – to do our bit for population control."

She takes another sip of her tea, a faraway look in her eyes. "William was the kindest, most delightful boy. And very clever – top of his class. He could have had any career he wanted, but all he wanted to do was help others. He trained as a doctor – this was when the automated medics were first being developed, so most medical care was carried out by highly trained doctors and nurses. And William, being William, wasn't interested in helping Insiders, with their moans and minor complaints. He wanted to treat Outsiders.

"Back then, the laws were stricter about contact between Insiders and Outsiders. My generation remembered why the Wall had been put up and there was still a fear of Outsiders. Outside was the Wild West." She gives a small smile. "But William thought the best of everyone. Which was fine, until he met and fell in love with Rose. And that is when everything went wrong."

There's a knock on the door and Milicent starts. The butler enters and walks over to her in quick, short strides to whisper something in her ear. Milicent nods and smiles up at him before looking back at me. "I'm sorry, Trey, I was getting carried away there. Lost in the past – that's what happens when you get to my age. So tell me, what have you managed to find out so far at Coleman's?"

I recount my exploration to the workers' canteen and what I'd managed to find out about how Outsiders are treated in the factory. Then I tell her about Brad Coleman's visit.

"Hmm, stands to reason they'd be keeping an eye on you."

"And I've got two chips now – my citizen chip and the one in my hand that controls my access and authorization inside the factory. I can't go anywhere without them knowing."

"It is a problem, but not insurmountable, I don't think. Let's see what projects he gives you to work on. Have you been out with Louis recently?"

I shake my head. "Not yet. It's only been a few days." I wonder if she sees through my excuse. The longer I can put off going drinking with Louis again, the better.

"Fine, well, plenty of time." Milicent stands. "I'm afraid I have to go and deal with another matter. Was there anything else of interest?"

I hesitate, wondering whether to tell her about Barnes. But I don't really *know* anything about her yet, or whose side she's on. If she's even on anyone's side. "No, that's all for now."

"Well, same time next week then. Unless anything urgent comes up, in which case you can comm me." She nods to the new comm band on my wrist and holds out her own. We press them together to connect. "Don't say anything on the message – the government monitors all comms – but if you need to speak to me urgently, say it's about ..." She pauses to think. "About your mother. And if I need to speak to you, I'll say it's about a book I've got for you."

I nod.

"Thomas will see you out."

As if on cue, the door opens and the butler walks in. He holds the door open for Milicent, then gestures for me to follow her out. As I leave the room, I glance up again at the portrait of the young man. His eyes seem to follow me.

"Were you the reason Milicent joined the Chain?" I murmur under my breath.

"Sir?" The butler looks at me, a placid expression on his face.

"Oh, nothing." I smile awkwardly at him and hurry from the room.

I walk home quickly, driven by curiosity to find out more about the Rose Rebellion and the young man with the smiling eyes.

17

Aleesha

"Let go of me!"

Rogue ignores me, as he's ignored my first two requests to let go of my arm. Furtive eyes follow us from under hooded cloaks but no one makes any move to help me. He cranes his neck over the heads of the crowd, apparently following someone. I hope he knows where he's going.

The last thing I need is to end up back in Primo's hands.

My heart skips a beat. I trip and stumble, falling to the ground. My arm wrenches in its socket and a yelp of pain escapes my lips but Rogue doesn't slow.

I fumble at the pocket in my trousers, trying to grab hold of my knife. Just as I pull it out, Rogue turns sharply into a narrow alleyway, dragging me with him. He lets go and I stumble back, tripping over something on the ground. I brace myself for a hard landing.

Instead, the ground gives beneath me and I land softly on my back with a faint *whoomph* as brightly coloured wrappers fly up around me.

A rubbish pile. Great.

I sit up, rolling my shoulder. It makes a crunching sound but still works. Even better, I'm still clutching my knife.

Rogue is staring down at me. His hands are balled into fists at his sides and his face is twisted in anger but he doesn't say a word as I push myself to my feet and stand in front of him. My left ankle is twisted and aches when I weight it.

"What the hell was that all about?" I jab the knife toward him and he sucks his stomach in.

Not that there's much to suck in. He's one hundred percent muscle.

My eyes dart around the alleyway. There's a movement at the entrance but I can't see past Rogue's bulk. I draw a second knife from my belt. "Why have you brought me here?"

Rogue raises his hands, the anger on his face turning to confusion. "Hey, put those away. I'm not going to hurt you."

"You've already hurt me." I glare at him, trying to ignore the pain radiating from my ankle.

He looks abashed. "Sorry, I just wanted to get you somewhere safe. I forgot ..."

"That I'm a person? Or that you're no longer a Metz officer?"

That hits home. He winces and drops his hands. There's another flash of movement behind him.

"Who's that?"

Rogue steps aside.

"Tommy?"

The kid sidles into the alleyway, followed by a younger girl.

"And Helen ... Gollin, isn't it?"

I sigh and pocket my knives. I look carefully at the dark-haired girl, but there's no sign of recognition or fear on her face. But then there's no reason for her to associate Rogue with the faceless Metz officer who'd threatened her and her brothers with their lives at Rose Square. "What are you doing here?"

"Just givin' Rogue a hand. Showin' him around, like." Tommy's voice rings with pride. "Been findin' out some in-form-ation from Helen 'ere." He enunciates the longer word carefully and jabs a thumb in the girl's direction.

I pull a scrap of chocco wrapper from my hair and sniff my top, eying the rubbish pile suspiciously.

"Sorry," Rogue says sheepishly.

"You never know what's underneath a rubbish pile out here." I scowl at him. "Could have been nails or blades or anything. Anyway what were you doing out here?" I turn to Tommy. "And you. You should be safe in the church."

"I came looking for *you*." Rogue's voice is tight. "Half the group think you got taken by Primo and his lot and the other half believe you ran off and left us. You've been gone a full day. What the hell did you think you were doing?"

I look at him in surprise. It's the first time I've heard him speak like that – obviously being around the Snakes is rubbing off on him. "Bryn said Samson had sent a message …"

I guess it didn't arrive.

He glares at me. "I'm serious, Aleesha. People look to you. They think you're the leader of the group. You can't just go running off like that."

I feel a surge of irritation and push past him, limping toward Tommy and Helen. "I didn't ask to be the leader of anything."

"You think you have a choice?"

"Of course I have a choice!" I snarl, turning on him. Pain shoots up my leg and I stagger back into the wall. Concern flashes in Rogue's eyes but it quickly disappears. I take a deep breath and carefully weight my ankle. It holds. "We need to go. If we're around the corner from the HQ building then Primo's people will be all over the place. And I bet he's pretty pissed right now."

Tommy's eyes are like saucers. Helen tugs at his arm and whispers something to him. He nods at her. "We'll go ahead an' look out fer you," he announces. "They won't notice us."

I nod and wince again. *Stop moving, you idiot.*

I'm not sure about Helen, but Tommy's smart for a kid and he's been in the gang long enough to know a few things. And I'm glad I don't have to worry about keeping us all safe. My head's throbbing and all I want to do is lie down in a quiet room with my leg up.

Tommy leads us through Area Four, keeping to the smaller alleyways and passages between the backs of apartment blocks. As we get nearer to the church, Helen says something to him, then falls back. Tommy pauses and scowls at her but Helen just shakes her head.

"What's up?" I hobble over to her.

Her pale face stares up at me, pinched tight. "I need t'go back. Me da'll be wakin' soon."

I smile down at her. "Thank you Helen. How is— How are you all now?"

The girl gives a shrug. "Da cries a lot, when he doesn't think I can hear. The boys just ask for Ma. They don't understand she's not comin' back, but they will."

My breath catches in my throat. "Your da still has his job, right?"

She nods and wipes her nose on a filthy sleeve. "Nights at the food factory. He used to be able to smuggle us some bits out, but not anymore. An' that new man keeps takin' all the food from the shops so there's nothin' for us to buy."

"New man? Do you mean Primo?"

Helen shrugs, but Tommy nods and answers for her. "'Ee's been raidin' everythin'. All the food an' water an' everythin'."

He cuts his hand through the air emphatically. “Gone.”

My heart sinks and I glance to Rogue, who looks away. I turn back to Helen. “Will you be okay getting home?”

She nods. “I know the way.” She smiles shyly at Tommy. “See you again, mebbe.” Then she turns and runs back up the street.

“She doesn’t ’ave many friends,” Tommy announces, as if he’s known her for years. Perhaps he has. I never paid much attention to the kids who wander the streets.

We walk the rest of the distance to the white church in silence. Tommy runs ahead, then forgets I’m limping behind and stops to wait. I lean into Rogue for support. My head barely reaches the top of his chest he’s so tall, and his arm wrapped lightly around my back feels strong and comforting.

A pair of monks sit by the main gate, nodding at the people walking past and inviting them into the church. Most people ignore them. Religion isn’t a big thing out here, however hard they try. One frowns as he sees us approach, but he silently opens the gate and lets us in. I smile at him. It was kind of them to take us in, even if Bryn is paying them.

I hobble up the steps into the coolness of the church, leaning on Rogue’s arm for support. Tommy’s already running ahead of us.

“Tommy!” I call after him. He shuffles back to us, his head down, clearly wondering if he’s in trouble. I smile at him. “Don’t tell anyone where you’ve been, okay?” He nods reluctantly. “And don’t run around the church. You know the monks hate it.”

“Aww, but Aleesha—”

“No buts.” I squeeze his shoulder and lower my voice. “You’ve seen what Primo is doing. And I don’t think he’s treating the Snakes who are with him much better. If it wasn’t for the monks, he’d be after us too.”

Tommy mutters something I don't catch and trudges off, dragging his feet.

"What's up with him? Why isn't he happy to be safe?" Rogue sounds puzzled.

"He is. But we're not used to following rules – sometimes people rebel against them even though they're designed to keep them safe."

"But that doesn't make sense. It isn't logical."

"People *aren't* logical, Rogue."

"This is another feelings thing, isn't it." He sounds miserable.

I sigh inwardly, wondering what it must be like to feel nothing and then everything. It must be overwhelming. I pause and look up into his deep blue eyes, feeling a sudden urge to run my hand over his stubbled cheek.

He could do with a shave.

The thought makes me smile.

"What makes you happy?"

I shake my head and look away. "Nothing."

His finger brushes my cheek, then turns my chin back toward him. Electricity dances on my skin. His eyes capture mine.

"I'm sorry I shouted," he says quietly. "I was worried about you."

I try and nod but I can't move. "I know. I'm … sorry too. Just don't go throwing me on any trash piles again." The joke sounds lame.

Rogue frowns. "I won't. I promise," he says in all seriousness. He releases my chin and brushes his hand over my hair. "I think—"

"Aleesha?"

Rogue breaks off as a voice echoes down the corridor. Relief floods through me and I pull away from Rogue's hand and turn to see who it is. The former Metz officer with the sandy hair and freckled face is standing ahead of us.

"Samson wants to see you." He gives an apologetic shrug.

I try and remember his name. Anders, that was it.

"Thanks …" I hesitate. Samson isn't one to be kept waiting but I really want to clean the smell of the rubbish from my hair and clothes.

"I'll tell him you'll be ten minutes cleaning up," Anders says. "Do you want to speak to him outside, in the graveyard?"

I nod. Anders flashes me a smile and ambles back off down the corridor.

"Do you know him?" I ask Rogue.

"Anders? Not really. I must have seen him around the compound, but I don't remember him from before that. He … he has coped with the transition better than most. I think he remembers a lot."

And unlike most of the Metz officers, he's good at reading people too. Interesting.

I make a mental note to get to know Anders a bit better.

Rogue's body is warm against mine. I pull away from him and grit my teeth as I hobble down the corridor, doing my best to walk normally. "I'm going to the washroom," I say over my shoulder. "I'll come and see everyone after I've spoken to Samson."

I sense Rogue coming up behind me, probably to offer his arm again, or maybe continue the conversation we were having before Anders interrupted us, and I quicken my pace. If I can put *that* off for a few days, so much the better.

There are two buckets of clean, cold water in the wash room. I twist the handle at the end of a pipe that leads down from a small tank on the roof and warm water, heated by the sun, gushes into the bowl underneath. I strip and dunk my clothes in an empty bucket, sloshing cold water over them and adding a bit of soap.

I wash with the cold water first to get the worst of the sweat and dirt off. Warm water is a luxury, even here, and the monks' system wasn't designed to wash thirty extra bodies. Perhaps I'll see if some of the officers can figure out a way to expand the tanks.

Must stop thinking of them as officers. They've given that up now.

But who are we? The Snakes? Primo has taken the name for his gang now, and he's got the tattoo to go with it. We're just the outcasts – the remnants of a broken gang and a handful of confused lost souls who are still coming to terms with what they had been forced to do. They need something to bind them together. They need hope.

I need hope. Hope that we can be something more …

My body is stiff and sore, bruises already darkening my skin. Soap stings my eyes.

There's a knock on the door. "Aleesha?"

A woman's voice and not one I recognize. "Yes?" I ask cautiously.

"It's Amber. I'm a healer in Area Four. Rogue mentioned you might be in need of some salve. Can I come in?"

I wring the water from my hair and grab a towel from the pile in the corner, wrapping it under my arms. "Sure, come in."

The door opens and a curvy woman with long, curly auburn hair walks in. She smiles and holds up a small pile of black clothes. "I think these are yours." She shrugs out of her long dark overcoat and hangs it on the back of the door.

"Rogue said he dragged you along the ground a bit. Seems a bit of an extreme way to get your attention." Laughter dances in her eyes. "What hurts the most?"

"My shoulder and ankle. And my side."

I turn over one of the buckets and sit on it while Amber feels around my foot. I clench my jaw to stop a whimper escaping my lips.

"Hmm, I think it's just a bit of a sprain. Try and stay off it for a day or two." She opens a pot of cream and rubs it in. "This should help with the pain and reduce the swelling."

She does the same with my shoulder and smears a bit down my left side, then hands me the pot. "Keep it. It's fairly potent so only use it on the bruises and no more than twice a day." She pulls a small packet of herbs from a different pocket. "Make a tea from these with hot water before you go to bed – it'll help you sleep."

"Thank you." I stand awkwardly, the towel held up in front of me. "How much—"

Amber waves a hand. "Anders gave me some chits to remove their chips ..." Her voice trails off and she looks at me curiously. "They're Metz officers, aren't they? What have you done to them?"

"It's a long story," I mumble under my breath.

She surveys me and I get the feeling she sees a lot more than she lets on. *Perhaps she's like Abby – an Insider who chose to live Outside.* Her accent is posh for Area Four, for all she tries to sound like she's from around here.

"Some of them have mental trauma." She lifts the overcoat from the back of the door and sticks her arms through the over-large sleeves. "Which isn't surprising if they remember what they've done. They may need to talk about it ... or not. Different people have different ways of coping." She opens the door and smiles back at me. "The monks know where to find me if you need me again."

The door clicks shut behind her. I dress as quickly as I can and re-braid my hair. Whatever the cream was she put on my shoulder, it's already taking the edge off the pain. I rinse out my dirty clothes, empty the buckets and carry them outside to refill.

I'm hanging my clothes up to dry when I sense someone behind me.

"Need a hand?"

Samson. Of course.

"You could fill the water buckets for me," I say, not turning around.

Now I'm listening, I catch his faint footfall as he walks over to the empty buckets.

How does he move that quietly?

Water rushes down the pipe from the tanks on the roof of the church and quickly fills the buckets. I finish pegging the clothes out and turn to face him. "They need to go back into the washroom."

Samson raises an eyebrow but obliges, picking up the heavy buckets as if they weighed no more than a bag of flour. I show him where to put them, then he follows me back outside. I try to walk normally, but even with Amber's cream, it's hard not to limp.

"You were stupid to get caught," he says quietly as we approach a secluded corner of the graveyard.

Does he think I don't know that?

"Is that all you came to tell me?"

"No, but I thought you might need reminding."

A trace of a smile flickers over his face. I was going to thank him for rescuing me, but I'm not going to give him the satisfaction now.

"He's terrorizing Area Four, you know. And it won't be long before he spreads – takes over the other gangs." I stop walking and turn to face him, folding my arms. "He's a threat to you."

Samson nods thoughtfully. "Perhaps."

Anger flares in my chest. "So what are you going to do about it? You were too late to stop him from killing Jay." I narrow my eyes. "Or was that part of your plan? Were you watching the fight all along?"

Samson's face remains placid. "Even I don't interfere in the leadership challenges. No one does."

"But afterwards – you could have challenged Primo then, when he was already tired!" I glance around and drop my voice. "You're the only one who's strong enough to beat him. You *have* to stop him."

"Do I?"

"Yes!"

I bite my lip and turn away. *Why is he being so damn difficult?*

"Unless you're scared, of course." I glance at him out the corner of my eye and catch a flicker of anger in his eyes. But he composes himself immediately.

"It's not that."

"Then what?"

There's a pause before Samson speaks again. "I am not the right person to lead the Snakes. It would … complicate relationships with the other gangs if I were to take over."

"It would complicate things if Primo makes a move on the other gangs. Everyone's afraid of him."

Samson nods again. There's another silence. "The President has asked to speak with me," he says finally.

I turn to look at him in surprise. "I thought you'd decided you weren't going to work with him anymore?"

Samson shrugs. "It depends what he's offering. I suspect the government aren't happy that a number of their best Metz officers have gone rogue, even less so that one of them appears to be setting himself up as some kind of new leader out here."

"Would they take him down?" I try and work through the implications of this. If the government got rid of Primo, that would save anyone having to challenge him. But I can't see Primo negotiating and he won't go down without a fight. More deaths.

"I don't know." He turns to look at me. "But it's got to be worth a try, right?"

"So you're going to see him?"

"Yes. A lot has happened since we last spoke. He may be more willing to compromise on some aspects of what we discussed previously."

I snort. "I doubt that. He sent an army of Metz officers to slaughter us. Twice! And you want to give him another chance? You'd be better off cutting a deal with the Chain and joining forces against him. Maybe then you can take him down."

Anger flashes in Samson's eyes. "Have you not learned your lesson about them? I warned you that they didn't have the Outsiders' best interests in mind. That they were only after revenge. And I was right, wasn't I?"

His eyes bore into me and I look down at the floor, unable to meet his gaze. He had been right. He'd warned me, and if I'd listened maybe Andrew Goldsmith would never have died.

Guilt sours my mouth.

"Once I've spoken to the President, I'll know one way or the other whether he will help get rid of Primo. If he won't, we can think of something else then. The device you used to deactivate the officers' chips … There's definitely no way you can reverse the effects?"

"No."

"You still have it though?"

I avoid his gaze. "It's safe."

"Well, keep it that way. I'll see you in a day or two. In the meantime, don't do anything stupid." He gives me a withering look and turns and strides away toward the church.

"Wait!"

He pauses and waits for me to catch up.

"How do I find you? Where's your headquarters?"

His lips curl in a smile. "My headquarters is my business. I'll come back once I've spoken to the President and let you know what happened. Until then, stay out of trouble and focus on making your bunch of ragtags a force to be reckoned with. That should keep you busy."

"They're not *my* bunch of ragtags," I say, but he has already gone.

18

Trey

"So, what did Coleman want with you yesterday?" Emilie shuts down her holo and comes to stand over me.

I glance at my wrist. "It's two minutes to leaving time and you're asking me now?"

Particularly as you've barely said a word to me all day.

"Well, you looked pretty busy. I didn't want to interrupt." She folds her arms, then unfolds them, glances up at the corners of the room and lowers her voice. "Did you get into trouble? I told you not to go poking around the East Wing."

"Everything's fine."

Emilie gives me a look and I spread my hands. "Honest! I actually asked him to give me some more work to do so I don't spend all day making you coffee." I pause. "Look, I'm sorry I went off. I didn't realize you might get into trouble too."

Her shoulders relax slightly. "It's okay. I know you want to know everything, but sometimes it's safer not to. And I really can't lose this job. Not if I'm to help Leona get through university."

"Leona's your sister?"

"Yes. She's fourteen. I worked out if I can save a third of

my wages every month, by the time she's eighteen she'll have enough to pay her fees."

I lean back in my chair, stretching my arms above my head. "I hope she appreciates what a generous sister she has."

Her lips part in a smile that lights up her eyes. "Obviously, I've told her that once she's the top researcher at the government labs, she'll be buying us a nice new apartment." There's a slight undercurrent to her words, for all their lightness. Insiders might have access to better food, education and healthcare but it still comes at a price. "What have you been working on so intently today then?"

"I'm just trying to find out more about what goes on in the factory. Did you know that the premium steaks are held in the vats for six months to mature? No wonder they're so expensive." I close down my computer. "Wish I'd paid more attention in chemistry class, though – I don't know what half the compounds that go into the food actually are and can't find anything on the system about them."

"I don't think I *want* to know what they are." Emilie wrinkles her nose. "Not when we're eating the stuff."

I pull on my suit jacket and we head out the office and up to the pod station, joining the queue of people waiting for a ride home.

"I'm meeting a friend in Six for dinner. There's a cute restaurant with a live band – real musicians, not bots. Fancy joining us?"

"Live band?"

"Yes. Probably the only place in the city you'll hear one. They're not as good as synth music, of course, but it's a fun novelty." Emilie steals a glance at me from under her long lashes. Her corkscrew hair is tied back with a bright green band of fabric that matches the tunic she's wearing.

I hesitate, wondering if she really is meeting a friend or if this is her way of asking me out again.

Do you think everyone lies to you now?

But the music is tempting, and besides, I feel like I owe her something as an apology.

"Your friend won't mind?"

"Na, it's an open invitation." Emilie flashes me a smile. "Chances are he'll bring along a friend or two as well."

See? Not everyone's trying to trick you.

I shake my head, marvelling at the person I've become.

"Well, maybe next time."

I look across at her, just in time to catch the disappointment on her face and curse inwardly. "No, I mean, I'd love to come. If you don't mind."

Emilie looks at me, confused. "Are you sure?"

I nod. "Sorry, I was just thinking of something else. I love live music."

Her face lights up. "Great!"

Emilie chatters away as we cram into the pod for the short trip to the Area Six pod point. She doesn't seem to mind my limited responses and I find myself relaxing in her company. She's so … uncomplicated. Open, honest, easy to talk to. And pretty, too.

There's another queue to get the elevator down to street level at the other end. We'd have been quicker walking from the factory if there had been a pedestrian exit.

The restaurant's in the northern part of Area Six. I wonder where we are in relation to the Chain's headquarters and the thought crosses my mind that maybe I could try to find it on the way back and see if Bryn is there. Then I remember the

Metz and the tracking chip in my arm.

As we approach the restaurant, the comm band on my wrist vibrates. I bring the message up. It's my mother, asking when I'll be home for dinner. I reply quickly, saying I'm out with a friend tonight, and hit send, shrugging an apology to Emilie, who's paused to wait for me.

The comm band bleeps again. "Come home now. I need you." My mother's voice is insistent. My heart begins to beat a little faster. What's happened now?

I look up at Emilie. "I-I'm sorry. I have to go home. My mother needs me. She's sick and she wouldn't call unless it was something important ..."

Emilie's face radiates disappointment.

"I'm sorry, I really would like to hear the band. Perhaps we can go another time? Next week, maybe?"

She gives a small smile and shrugs. "Sure. I'll see you tomorrow then."

"See you tomorrow," I echo.

I hurry back through the streets to the pod point, tapping my fingers impatiently at the wait for the elevator. Fifteen minutes later, I burst into the apartment, panting from having run up the four flights of stairs.

My mother looks up at me in surprise as I rush in. "Trey? Whatever's wrong?"

"What do you mean, what's wrong? You called me back." I glance around. Ella's messing with something in the kitchen, but everything else appears normal.

"Yes. Anabel's coming over. I thought we could have a nice family dinner for a change."

I stare at her in disbelief. "I've just run all the way back from Six for that? I had a nice evening planned with a ... a friend. I thought something was seriously wrong!"

Mother looks crestfallen. "Oh, I'm sorry, Trey. It's just that it's not often Anabel takes an evening off – you know how busy she is. I thought it might be nice for you to get to know each other a bit better."

Oh, right. Because her job is obviously more important than our lives.

"Who's your friend?" Ella's face appears around the corner, smiling impishly.

"Just someone from work." But I feel the heat rise to my cheeks.

"A female someone?" Ella wheedles, sauntering out the kitchen. I glare at her but am saved from replying by a buzzing from the door.

"That'll be Anabel. Go and let her in, would you, Trey?" Mother smiles up at me. "You can tell us about your friend later."

Glad for the reprieve, I walk over to the door access system. Anabel's face looks up at the camera, four floors below. I push my thumb to the pad and the door to the apartment block clicks open.

Ella goes to greet her at the apartment door. Anabel's still dressed in the dark grey uniform of the palace guard. I wonder if she ever takes it off. She kisses Mother on the cheek, then unclips the belt laden with weaponry from around her waist and drops onto the sofa.

"You look tired, love." Mother gives her a fond look.

Ella disappears back into the kitchen. "Dinner in five minutes!"

"Good, I'm starving." Anabel props herself up on her elbows. "Didn't have time for lunch. They've taken a third of our best guards to join the Metz, so I'm horribly understaffed."

"Why are the Metz taking your guards?"

"Didn't you hear?" Anabel gives a short laugh. "Guess they're covering it up. They lost a bunch of Metz officers in the last riot Outside. They've gone missing."

She shoots me a meaningful look.

"But surely guarding the government headquarters is just as important?"

"You'd think so, right? But I guess they're more worried about further riots Outside." She shrugs. "Our men and women are already trained fighters, so it's easier to use them in the Metz than taking a bunch of new recruits and starting from scratch."

"Do you even know what they'll do to them? What the Metz are?" The words burst from me.

"Well, they'll get better armour and weapons than we have. I'll bet they won't want to come back to the boring palace guard." Anabel's expression turns curious as she catches the look on my face. "That wasn't what you meant?"

How can they not know?

My hands clench into fists and I can feel the anger building inside me. There's a warning hand on my arm.

"Let's not talk about this now."

I turn to face my mother and she flinches under my gaze. "Why, is this another thing you don't want to know about?"

She stiffens. "I would just like us to have a nice family meal *in peace.*"

"Fine." I take a deep breath and school my face into a neutral expression.

"Dinner!" Ella calls from the kitchen. We move to the large dining table that's crammed up against the wall behind the sofa. There's barely room to pull the chairs out.

Mother goes to help Ella dish up. "Are you happy to be back in London?" I ask Anabel, wanting to forestall any more questions about what happened to the missing Metz officers.

The frown on her face relaxes as slides herself into the chair at the end of the table. "It's nice to be able to see Mother and Ella again, and catch up with some old friends." She smiles and it softens her face, taking the edge off her strong jaw. With her hair loosened from its tight knot, her severe face would be transformed into a beautiful one. "You know, for years I hated you for being the reason I was sent away. But now … now I'm glad I did leave. I used to think this city was everything, but really, it's nothing."

"What do you mean?"

"You're so cut off from the world here. And so *backward*. You know we're the laughing stock of the world. Like the provincial cousins at the farm at the end of the road, refusing to adopt modern technology."

Ella sets down a steaming bowl of chicken noodles. I wonder which vat the meat was grown in and sigh inwardly. Perhaps Emilie was right; it's better not to know what we're eating. Anabel ladles noodles onto her plate and digs in, without waiting for the others to join us. "Delicious," she mumbles through a mouthful.

"I see the rest of the world hasn't taught you manners, then?" Mother sits down next to me and looks pointedly at Anabel, who shrugs, unrepentant.

"What's it like out there?" I ask curiously.

"Well, I'm not really supposed to tell you. Part of the deal for letting me back into the country. They don't want people to get jealous of what they're missing. You'd have thought someone would have found a way of bypassing the communications lockdown by now, but apparently not." Anabel sighs. "Or perhaps everyone here is just happy to live in their own little bubble. People thought I was mad to come back. Mind you, I'd hoped they would at least have let me keep *some* of my toys, but no. Any technology that doesn't already exist here can't be imported."

I help myself to a spoonful of noodles. "What did you want to bring in?"

"Booster boots, my bubble shield, a stun gun that's actually effective." She smiles wickedly. "And my whip blade."

Mother shivers. "I wish you'd chosen a career in politics or business, as your father wanted, rather than fighting."

"And that's exactly why I didn't choose a career in politics or business." Anabel rocks her chair back. "Besides, security is more interesting than you might think. You may be glad I chose it one day."

Mother gives a *harrumph* of disgust and reaches over me to ladle more food onto Anabel's plate. Her own portion lies untouched.

"Come on, Mum, eat up." Ella gives her a nudge. "It's good for you."

"Oh, I'm not really hungry." Mother smiles weakly and Ella gives her a mock glare.

"You can't expect to fight this … disease if you don't eat."

Mother sighs and lifts up her fork. "And I thought I was the parent around here."

I spear a piece of chicken and lift it to my mouth. "Do they have real meat outside Britannia?"

"Yeah, but it's expensive like here."

Mother stabs at the noodles on her plate. "That's enough talk about the rest of the world. Let's just enjoy our meal, shall we?"

We have coffee after dinner, then Anabel yawns and says she needs to get back. The evening is warm and there's a slight buzz as the ancient cooling system in the apartment kicks in. Suddenly, the air feels thick, the room too cramped and close. I need space to breathe, to think.

"I'll come and see you out."

Anabel looks surprised, but nods. She says her goodbyes to Mother and Ella and leads the way down the stairs and out into the street. Immediately, a sense of relief washes over me and I stumble forward.

"You okay?"

I nod. "Just gets a bit cramped in there. Wanted some air."

She chuckles softly. "Missing being Outside?"

"Not exactly. If you think it's bad in here, you should see out there."

There's a pause. "You know, there are poorer areas in other cities," Anabel says finally. "It's not all perfect. I wouldn't want you to think that." She glances across at me and there's something in her expression that I can't quite read. Then she reaches out and presses her comm band to mine so we're connected. "Let me know if you need anything. And make Mother eat – she's wasting away."

I lean against the wall as she jogs off down the street. Dusk is falling and low-level lights burst into life along the street. I close my eyes and draw in the fresh air, feeling it fill my lungs. The days seem to go past so fast now.

I'm about to turn and go back inside when I hear quick, light footsteps further up the street. A dark shape flits in and out of the shadows cast by the street lights. I back away, my hand fumbling behind me for the access pad to the apartment.

"Trey? Is that you?" Aleesha's voice comes out of the darkness.

I relax and step out from the doorway. As Aleesha comes closer, I see she's moving awkwardly, as if she's trying to disguise a limp. Seeing her sends a bunch of conflicting emotions surging through me. My cheeks flush as I think back to the last time we'd spoken. I'd spent the whole time crying on her shoulder, never even asked her how she was.

"Hey," she says.

"Hey."

I reach out for her arm, but she flinches from my touch, breath hissing through her teeth, and I pull back as sharply as if I'd been stung.

"Sorry. Hurt my shoulder." She looks down at the ground.

"What happened? And what's been going on Outside?"

"Stuff." She wraps her arms across her chest and scuffs her toe across the ground. "Lots of stuff. How's your mother?"

"Not too bad." Concern wells up in my chest. "What's wrong? Is it Abby? Bryn?"

"No, they're okay, I think." She shrugs. "I haven't seen them for a few days."

I glance around at the empty street and take a step closer to her. "What are you doing here then?"

"I don't know. Rogue would be so mad if he knew I was here. And Samson," she adds, almost as an afterthought. "Guess I just wanted to say hello. See how you were doing. If you're busy, I'll go."

She turns and a streetlight flickers across her face, reflecting off eyes bright with tears.

"No, don't go." I grasp her uninjured arm. She stiffens but doesn't pull away. "Come on, let's go somewhere we won't be seen."

I lead her around the corner to a small, secluded park where tall trees hide the benches underneath from sight. An old air mattress lies punctured in one corner, left behind by the refugees from Six who'd been camped out here until a few days ago. I perch on a small bench next to a trickling fountain.

"So, what's happened since I left?"

Aleesha lowers herself onto the bench, wincing. She stares up at the leaves forming on the tall maple tree. "Jay's dead," she says flatly. "One of the Metz captains I deactivated challenged him to the leadership of the Snakes and won the fight. The gang is split – half of them stayed with Primo, along with most of the officers. The rest of us are hiding in a church Bryn found for us."

I stare at her. "Jay's dead?"

She nods.

We fall silent. I hadn't liked Jay the first time I'd seen him, but he'd defended Aleesha in the Battle of Rose Square, and he'd meant something to her, however much she denies it.

"This Primo ... what does he want? And surely he can't take over a gang if he's not an Outsider?"

"He challenged and won in a fair fight. That's the rules. No one's happy about it, but no one's brave enough to challenge him. Not even Samson."

I think about the giant of a man pushing Metz officers aside and tossing bags of rocks as if they were stones. If he's afraid to challenge, what does that make Primo?

"Anyway, you've met him. Remember when we broke into the Metz compound? He was Rogue's captain before all this." She waves her hand around.

"And did he hurt you? Primo?" I ask quietly.

"No, at least, partly." She looks down and picks at the frayed hem of her top. "I walked into a trap and he caught me. He ..."

Her voice breaks. "Anyway, the Chain and Samson's people got me out. Rogue came to find me afterwards and that's how I twisted my ankle."

I stare at her. "He hurt you?"

"Oh, he didn't mean to." She looks up in surprise at the anger in my voice. Her hand closes over mine and I realize my fist is clenched. "I'll heal in a few days, honest. It's not that bad."

"Yeah, well, it's good to know you have a protector." My voice is bitter and Aleesha pulls her hand away. I wish she'd put it back. I miss her touch.

"What do you mean by that?"

I close my eyes and take a deep breath, forcing a smile onto my face, though it's so dark I don't know if she can see it. "It's good you have someone to watch your back. He's a good fighter, I'll bet."

"Trey, I—"

"What about the Chain?" I don't want to talk about Rogue anymore. "Can't they help get rid of Primo?"

Aleesha shifts uneasily beside me. "The Leader ... my father has arrived. He ..." Her breath catches and she looks down, turning her face away from me. "He doesn't believe I'm his daughter."

"What? But you look like your mother, from what I saw. And what about your amulet? I thought you said he gave it to your mother?"

"He did. But Primo took it from me." The words come out reluctantly, as if I'm dragging them from her. She looks up at me and her eyes are wide and fearful, her voice a whisper. "I don't know what to do, Trey. Primo's a monster. There's no one who can beat him."

"There must be some way. You just have to find it." I reach

out for her hand, as much for my comfort as hers, and run my thumb across her palm. "It's not like you to give up. Go to your father again. If he's got the power and resources Bryn seems to think, he's got to be able to help."

"Perhaps." She doesn't sound convinced.

Silence stretches between us. The shadows under the trees deepen. I should be getting home, but I don't want to leave.

"How's your job going?" Aleesha asks eventually.

"Well, it's more interesting than I'd thought." I drop my voice and tell her in a whisper about Milicent coming to me for help and about my conversation with Coleman.

"Be careful." Aleesha frowns. "If he knows you're up to something …"

"It's fine. Now I know, I can cover my tracks better. I just wish I could do something to help you. I feel so useless in here."

"At least in here you're safe. I don't have to worry about getting you out of any scrapes." Her teeth flash white in the dark.

I give her a mock punch, forgetting her bruises. "Crap, sorry." I touch her shoulder gently as she winces, my hand naturally moving across her back to wrap around her other shoulder.

"Trey …"

She turns her face toward me and I have to fight the urge to pull her to me and press my lips to hers. Just the thought of it sends a shiver down my spine.

"Yes?"

"Do you think you'll ever be able to forgive me for what I did?" she asks in a small voice.

I pull back slightly. "You mean, with … with Father's death?"

"Yes." She stares at the collapsed mattress. "I'm sorry, I really am. If I could just go back to that day, I'd never have taken him out there."

"It's okay."

"I don't know what I was thinking, really. I was just so upset about what happened to my mother and—"

"Aleesha, it's okay." I turn her face to mine. "I mean, it's not okay ... he shouldn't have died. But I don't blame you."

"Really?"

"Really."

And it's true. For every night I've lain awake with my father's death playing through my mind, there's been another where I've spent hours trying to push the memories of mine and Aleesha's one kiss from my mind, trying to convince myself that I don't need her, that she was responsible for his death. But every time I fail. Because in my heart I've already forgiven her part in what happened, knowing that she was used as much as I. And I don't think I can push her away any longer.

Her breath is warm on my lips, our faces inches apart. Butterflies dance in my stomach as I lean closer, my body aching to touch her.

"What was that?" Aleesha pulls back with a start. Her eyes dart around the shadows.

"What?"

"I heard something." She seems oddly agitated. "We've been here too long. I have to go. You need to get home – you'll be safe there."

She stands, pulling me up with her. We walk out of the park together and down the street to the corner of my road where she stops and turns to me. "Please stay safe, Trey." Her eyes search mine, then she stands on tiptoe and kisses me lightly on the mouth. Before I can react, she's pulled back, disappearing into the shadows like she is a shadow herself.

19

Aleesha

The road is dark as I walk quickly away from Trey, unable to shake the sense that someone was watching us.

I round the corner and duck into a narrow passageway, pressing my back to the wall. I strain my ears, listening to the dull silence that hangs over this street. And then I hear it. Footsteps. They're light, and if I'd carried on walking I wouldn't have noticed them, but they're definitely footsteps.

Someone's following me.

My fingers find the handle of the one knife I carry. I hope it'll be enough. The footsteps come close, pausing as their owner reaches the turn in the road, then becoming louder as my pursuer pads toward me.

A slim, shadowy figure darkens the entrance to the passageway. Silently, I slip out behind them. The figure pauses, perhaps sensing my presence, but it's too late – I've already sprung. I wrap my arm around their neck, pulling their head back. The tip of my blade nestles in the slight hollow of their neck where their heartbeat pulses.

Soft hair tickles my face. I can smell her scent, mingled with fear.

"Aleesha?"

I start slightly, my knife scraping her skin. She lets out a whimper.

"Why are you following me?"

"I saw you meeting with Trey. I … I wanted to talk to you."

"What do you want with Trey?" Cold panic seeps through my veins.

The woman swallows. She has her fear under control though; her voice is steady and she doesn't tremble despite the blade at her throat. "He's my brother."

Her brother?

"Please, I only want to talk to you … to offer help. Just let me go … please?" There's a pleading note in her voice now. She's afraid, but trying not to show it.

I remove my knife from her throat and push her forward so she stumbles into the glow of a street light. She's a little taller than me, slim, her features fine and delicate like a bird's. Wisps of dark hair hang loosely from the rough bun on the back of her head. She wears a loose t-shirt made from some soft, patterned material.

I try and remember what Trey had said about his sister. Or sisters … he has two. Which one is she?

I hazard a guess. "Ella?"

The woman nods and straightens, eying the knife in my hand warily. I keep it out. Just because she's Trey's sister, doesn't mean she's not a threat.

"You wanted to talk? Talk."

She starts, her eyes wide. "Yes, of course … I …" She gives a nervous laugh and runs a hand over her hair. "Sorry, I should have known it was a bad idea sneaking up on you. I just didn't want Trey to see me. I …" She falters and takes a deep breath. "I'm part of a group of Insiders who feel that our society, our system of government, isn't fair. We want to do something about it. I know you and Trey have been working for a couple of gangs and I wondered if you'd know of someone who might be interested in our assistance."

"And what assistance is that?" She's telling the truth, I can tell that much. But why would a group of Insiders want to help us?

"We have people who work in the big corporations, and in government. We can find out information that may be helpful."

"And what would you want in return?"

Ella looks surprised. "Nothing. I mean, we just want to help." She laughs nervously. "We know things need to change, but we don't want Insiders getting hurt. At least," she amends hurriedly, "not innocent Insiders." She tucks a stray piece of hair behind her ear. "You know, most people are terrified of change. And the Metz operate Inside too – it can be dangerous to not fall in line with what society expects."

A flash of irritation surges through me. *What can these people know about danger?* But I keep my face schooled into a blank expression.

"Why didn't you ask Trey about this?"

"I did. He … he didn't want to help us." She lets out a sigh. "He thinks he can protect me, like I'm a child or something. He can be a little naive sometimes." She takes a step toward me, still eying the blade in my hand, and lowers her voice. "Look, if you want to take down the government and build something better, you're going to need people who work in here. Any Outsiders who are allowed in here are closely monitored, and very few have jobs where they'd have access to any information that might be useful to you."

I consider this. She's got a point. I don't know what connections the Chain and Brotherhood already have Inside, but they both seemed keen enough to use me and Trey as their runners. Either way, I'm pretty sure she's not a danger to me. I pocket the knife. Ella looks relieved.

"So who do you want to speak to?"

"Trey told me about two organizations – the Chain and the Brotherhood. The Chain killed Father." She swallows. "So perhaps the Brotherhood? He didn't know much about them …"

"No one knows much about them." I shrug. "Whoever you want to approach, it's a risk – you know that, right? They may not want your help, and even if they do, they'll probably just use you."

Like they used us.

Ella nods and gives a small smile. "Don't worry, I'm not quite as naive as my brother." She takes a deep breath. "I know they have their own agenda and we have ours. But I do think we can help each other."

I wonder what Trey would think of Ella working with Samson. But the fact that Ella's going behind his back tells me that. And Trey is so fiercely protective of his family, especially now …

And now you're going to betray him again. Put his sister in danger too.

I almost turn and run then. Because Trey's right – this will put Ella in danger, however smart she is. But I can also sense the determination in her and know that if I don't help her, she'll look for someone who will. And that could end up being even more dangerous.

Besides, Samson may not want their help, and if he says no perhaps Ella will give up on the idea.

And it's her life. Her choice – not Trey's, whatever he thinks. "Okay, I'll try and speak to Samson. If you're sure?"

I hold my breath, the question hanging in the air between us.

Say no, say no.

Ella nods. "Yes, I'm sure."

My heart sinks. "Fine. But he may not want your help."

Ella's face relaxes into a smile. "Thank you. And I appreciate that, but at least we can offer." She reaches into a pocket and hands me a small piece of film. "This is my office address. Don't come in, but I leave work about five and go out for lunch most days."

I nod. "Might be a few days before I can speak to him."

"That's fine." She reaches out hesitantly and touches my arm. "Please, don't tell Trey we've spoken. He's worried enough about Mother and his job. It's best that he doesn't know about this."

I turn and walk away, back toward the Wall, feeling as though a weight has been hung around my neck.

So Ella doesn't know Trey's working for Milicent and he doesn't know she wants to work for Samson. I guess even families have secrets.

* * *

Low murmured voices come from the other side of the door. I strain my ears, words flickering at the edge of my hearing, but I can't hear anything clearly enough to piece together a full sentence.

Frustrated, I pull back and pace across the landing. Five steps forward, five steps back. My stomach keeps flipping. I wipe my palms over my trousers and clench and unclench my hands, wishing I had something to occupy them. Six days it's been since I was last here.

I'm drawn back to the door. The voices are raised now – one in anger, one trying to soothe. I squeeze my eyes shut and press my head to the wooden doorframe.

I told Bryn it wouldn't work.

"You can't deny the DNA test, Richard." Bryn's voice, suddenly louder, filters through the crack where the door meets the wall. "She's your daughter. I know this must be difficult for you. But you have to accept it."

My father mutters something too low for me to catch.

"She's not a baby. She's a grown woman, and a smart one at that." Bryn sighs. "I've been here too, remember. Twice, actually. I ... I never treated Daniel right. And then I lost him. Now I've been given another chance and I'm damn well not going to screw it up again. Trust me – if you walk away from her now, you will always regret it."

There's another mutter. I only catch one word – Katya.

"Well, that's for you to sort out." Bryn lowers his voice and I miss his next words. Then I jerk back as footsteps come toward the door.

I lean against the far wall, trying to make it look as if I've been casually waiting here all along. The door opens and Bryn waves me in. He gives a slight nod, which I think is supposed to be reassuring, and leaves, closing the door behind him.

I stand awkwardly just inside the room, wondering what to do, what to say.

The silence lengthens.

"I loved her, you know," he says finally, still staring out the window. "Loved her so goddamn much. She was so full of life and love – the light to my darkness. When she died, it felt like that light was ripped from me."

He falls silent. I don't know what to say, so I just stand there, hands twisting awkwardly in front of me.

"And now you are here. With her hair, her eyes." He turns to face me and his hand twitches as if he wants to reach out for me. "She never told me she was pregnant."

I find my voice. "It must have been a shock."

A ghost of a smile flickers across his face. "That's rather an understatement. I never even considered it a possibility. Maria always wanted children. We used to talk about it. But we were kids then." His lips curl into a wry smile. "We had years ahead of us. Thought ourselves invincible."

Did she get pregnant deliberately? To keep him in London?

There is so much I don't know about this man. So much I don't know about my own mother.

"How old are you?"

"Eighteen, I think."

He raises an eyebrow. "You think?"

I shrug and lift my arm. "Not chipped. I scratched notches into a wall to try and keep count, but I may have missed a few months."

Something flickers in his eyes and he turns away again. "Maria was eighteen when we first met. You look like her, you know. Very much like her." There is pain in his voice and I wonder if that's why he doesn't seem to want to look at me. If it brings back memories he'd locked away, like I have, over the years.

I swallow. "She was beautiful."

He nods and turns further away from me. "You don't sound like her though. Your accent is ... different."

"Yes, well, that's how people talk out here. Down in Four." I take a deep breath and force my fingers to relax. "She was an Insider, wasn't she?"

"Yes."

"And you?"

"I guess I was an Insider too, for a time."

"Your records said you came here from South Africa after your parents died."

His head jerks around. "You've seen my records?"

I flinch back, though he is five paces away. There's something about him that makes me want to cower and beg for forgiveness like a slave who's angered his master. It's the same feeling I get when I'm around Samson and when I was face to face with the President. But in Ricus Meyer – or Richard Masterton, as I'm supposed to call him – it seems magnified.

Power.

He reeks of it.

I glance down at the floor and swallow, collecting my thoughts. "I saw it when we broke into the Metz compound. That's how I knew who you were."

"Ah yes," he says softly. "Bryn briefed me on that. It seems as if you have inherited your mother's looks and my traits. You must have been, what, six when she died?"

I nod.

"And what happened to you after that?"

Where to start?

But I start at the beginning, standing there in the middle of the room like a school kid reporting to a teacher. I tell him about the children's home taking me in, only to hand me over to the Metz when they realized I wasn't chipped. I tell him how I escaped and tried to survive on the streets. I tell him *everything*, even the really bad stuff – the stuff I had refused to face for so many years – and feel a strange sense of satisfaction from the pained look on his face and the horror in his eyes when I describe exactly how I was used.

This is what you could have prevented.

When I finish he just stares out the window. All that, and still he can't look at me.

"I'm sorry," he says finally. "If I'd known …"

"You'd have done what?" I cross my arms, irritation sparking in me again. "Rescued me?"

"I—"

There's a knock on the door. His brows furrow. "Yes?"

The door opens a fraction and Katya sticks her head around. "Sorry to interrupt. Can I come in, Richard? It's important."

My father nods reluctantly. Katya pushes open the door and walks across to him, flashing me a smile on the way past. But I can read her better now, since Rose Square.

She's not sorry at all.

I see her take his arm and lean in to whisper something in his ear, and there's something about their body language, the close, comfortable intimacy between them that makes my breath catch.

It can't be. Her … and him?

"Aleesha?"

I force my eyes up to meet his and get the confirmation I need. Katya gives a small, satisfied smile, her hand resting on his arm almost possessively.

I feel as if I've been punched in the gut, and it takes all my self-control to keep my face calm and to turn and walk slowly from the room, down the staircase and out of the building.

It's only once I've ducked into the small alleyway leading to the main street and I'm out of sight of the headquarters that I break into a run.

* * *

I take the long way back to the church, partly to give me time to think and partly so I don't risk coming across Primo's gang.

Primo's gang.

The words ring in my head. I wonder what Samson has said to the President and if the President sees Primo as a threat. I think about what I would do if I were him. Not send more Metz officers out here, that's for sure. Not when they know we have a way of deactivating them. But the President is clever and he has the resources of a country at his fingertips. Perhaps he'll think of some other way of bringing Primo down.

I keep my hood up and my head down as I skirt through the Dragons' territory and down into Area Three. I don't know the gangs here so well – they keep out of our way, we keep out of theirs – but it's never good to draw attention to yourself.

As I get closer to the church, I slow my pace. Something feels wrong. There's a gnawing sensation in my stomach that I've learned to trust.

I move to the side of the road and duck down beside a street hobie. He jerks his head up and shies away from me, clutching something to his chest. "S'okay," I mutter. "I just want some information."

I glance at him out the corner of my eye. Paper-thin skin stretched over bone and hollow eyes with that dulled glaze that speaks of tronk. He can't be more than a few years older than me, but he doesn't look like he has long left in this world. You never grow old on tronk.

I find my eyes straying to his chest. Is that what he's protecting so fiercely? A packet of white powder? Perhaps not even that much – a twist, more likely. My tongue tingles, saliva filling my mouth.

I could take it from him. He's weak. It'll be street tronk, cut with something bad, but a taste of it, just a taste ...

I tear my eyes away and swallow hard. My hand's trembling. Ridiculous.

You're better than this. Stronger than this.

I thought I had beaten it. I haven't had a craving for days, weeks perhaps.

"What were yer wantin'?" The man's voice is thin and dry. He sounds suspicious. Has good reason to be.

I take a deep breath, reminding myself why I'm here. "There's something going on. Down that way." I point in the direction of the church. "You heard anything?"

He shrugs, bony shoulders hunched. "Heard there's some people hidin' out in the church."

"More recent than that. Today."

The man shrugs again. "Don't know nothin'." He eyes me speculatively. "You got some?"

"No." I don't need to ask what he means. I stand, fighting the urge to close my fingers around his wrist and see what he's clutching.

I strain my ears against the background hum of the city. Then, just as the tower of the church comes into sight, I hear it. A muffled explosion.

Around me, people look up. But when there's no sign of an immediate threat, they carry on with their business. Explosions aren't that unusual out here. Sometimes the gangs get their hands on explosives. Or a homebrew experiment goes wrong. But not this time, I don't think.

I take to the rooftops. If there's danger ahead, it's usually at street level. Not many people think to come up here. I run along the long apartment block that butts up against the church walls. From the end, I'll have a view down onto the front of the church.

Another explosion, closer this time. I duck down and crouch behind the parapet, then lift my head to peer over. My eyes take in the carnage below quicker than my brain can process it.

My instincts have saved me again. If I'd carried on walking down the street I would have walked straight into Primo's arms. But this time, I don't think it's just me he's after. It's all of us.

20

Trey

When I was Outside, there was nothing to distinguish one day from the next, but now I'm living Inside, I have to get used to weekends again. It makes me feel guilty, having all this free time and not being able to do anything with it. Nothing productive anyway.

As much as I try to distract myself, my thoughts always stray back to Aleesha. I wonder what she's doing, if she's got enough to eat, if she's with Rogue. Just thinking of the two of them together in the same room is enough to sour my thoughts.

I run my finger around the comm band on my wrist. How much easier things would be if I could contact her through this. At least I'd know she was safe. But the government monitor all communications. So the people I want to talk to most – Aleesha, Bryn, Abby – are out of reach.

The nightmares still wake me most nights. Sometimes, I'm back at the Battle of Rose Square, stumbling over bodies, trying to reach Abby before the Metz officer blows a hole in her head. However many bodies I trip and climb over, she never seems to get any closer. But most of the time it's my father I see, and Katya behind him holding the gun to his head. Sometimes it's

Aleesha holding the gun and firing the shot that kills him, and when I wake I have to tell myself over and over again that it was not real, that she did not kill him – would not have killed him.

I don't blame her, not now. But I still can't forget what happened.

My mother doesn't mention the screams in the night, other than to comment occasionally on how tired I look. But perhaps she doesn't hear me – she takes a sleeping draught before bed to help her sleep through the pain. She's getting frailer every day and taking more painkillers than she should be.

Ella tried to broach the subject of my nightmares, but I just told her I didn't want to talk about it. Since then, she hasn't asked again, though occasionally I find a packet of sleeping pills beside my bed, letting me know she hasn't forgotten.

I'd logged into my holo screen on Monday morning to find a series of messages with random tasks to complete. A day later and I've just about finished the first of them. Seems Coleman took me at my word when I said I didn't have enough to do. My screen bleeps twice and a holo of Phillips, my boss, appears.

"Goldsmith, we've got a problem," he barks without preamble. "Quality control have picked up an issue with your line. They're on their way down to the factory floor now."

My breath catches. "What issue?"

He shrugs and tugs at the tie that's cinched around his thick neck. "Some ingredient that's been missed out. I'm not sure. Get down there now and report back to me ASAP, understand?"

"Yes, of course." I nod, but Phillips has already cut the connection.

I push back my chair and head for the door. As I open it, I nearly run into Emilie, who's carrying coffee and pastries. She looks surprised. "What's up?"

"Got to go down to the factory floor. I'll be back in a bit." I grab one of the coffees and take a gulp before handing it back and rushing toward the lift.

Barnes is taking reports from the technicians, ticking off checks on her data pad. She looks up as I hurry over, her expression of annoyance turning to wary concern when she sees my face. She dismisses the technicians and walks toward me.

"Quality control are on their way. What's this about?"

"How should I know?" She looks down at her data pad and shrugs. "All systems are normal."

The lift pings and the red light above the decontamination chamber turns green. "Well, we're about to find out."

A tall woman emerges, dressed in a white lab coat. I walk over and extend my hand. "I'm Darwin Goldsmith. Nice to meet you."

The woman doesn't take my hand. Nor does she introduce herself. "We've been testing samples from your production line, Mr Goldsmith. It appears that some of the meat products are missing an essential ingredient."

I force a smile onto my face. "I'm sure that's not possible. There must be some kind of mistake." I glance at Barnes, but her face is expressionless.

"Are you saying I am lying, Mr Goldsmith?" The woman's voice is ice.

"N-no." I take a deep breath. "But all our systems are working normally, isn't that right, Barnes?"

The woman shoots Barnes a disparaging look and refers to her data pad. Her face is set in what appears to be a permanent frown of displeasure, the expression emphasized by her slicked-back hair.

"You're missing an ingredient in the lower-grade product lines. Androcibus nanite."

Barnes stiffens beside me. I turn to her. "Is this something you're aware of?"

Barnes ducks her head, her fingers flying over the data pad, though I get the impression she has all the relevant information in her head. "The deliveries didn't come in," she says finally. "I raised a query and was told there was a delay in getting the ingredient from the labs." She glances at me. "This was just before you started. I reported it up but didn't get any instructions to stop running. It's a new ingredient anyway – only been added in the past month or so. I figured it wasn't essential."

"Wasn't essential?" The woman looks about to have a fit. "And who are you to decide what is essential, *foreman*? I don't recall you possessing a biochemistry degree. You should have stopped the production process immediately as soon as you realized you had run out."

Barnes bristles. "I may not have a biochemistry degree, but I do know how this product line works. You can't just turn it off and on as if it were a child's toy. It takes *days* to restart the line once it's been stopped. We have to go through hundreds of checks and there would have been wastage across all product lines." She glares at the woman. "That kind of decision is above my pay grade."

Tension crackles in the air. I step between the two women and smile.

"I apologize for the oversight. I've only been in this position a few weeks and my predecessor had moved on to his new role before I arrived. The message must have been lost in the confusion. We'll take steps to get this sorted as quickly as possible. H—"

"I don't care for your excuses. Stop this production line now!"

I swallow down my rising anger. I'll be damned if she's going to bully me into submission.

"It's not that simple. Barnes is correct when she says that stopping and restarting the production line is a major undertaking. It usually only happens once a year for a deep clean. Now, what is this ingredient for and when are we going to get fresh supplies of it?"

Her face turns beetroot red. If looks could kill, I'd be as dead as a dodo. "It doesn't matter what it's for. What matters is that it isn't in the meat products in those vats." She jabs her finger in the direction of the huge tanks. "As for the supplies, you will have to take that up with that department. My concern is with the meat that has been processed and gone to distribution."

"Well, we should be able to track that easily enough." I glance at Barnes, who nods. "We'll process the records and get a list of all product codes to you by the end of the day."

"And you will stop the production line until the new supplies arrive?"

"I will speak with my manager," I say, hedging my bets. I still don't know who this woman is and whether she outranks me. "But a better solution may be to keep the system running and just isolate the products that don't contain this androcibus nanite. That way they won't accidentally get sold. If the ingredient doesn't affect the safety of the food, perhaps the items could be given away instead."

"Given away? What do you think we are, a charity?" The woman sneers. "We will not risk our reputation by letting any substandard food out of this factory." She touches her data pad, then lowers it to her side. "I have a full record of this conversation. My recommendation will be to shut down this production line immediately, pending delivery of the nanite. Thank you for your time."

She turns and strides across the factory floor toward the lift.

"Well, that went well," Barnes comments. "Nice work, boss."

"No thanks to you. Why the hell didn't you tell me about this before? And why have you been running the line at full capacity with an ingredient missing?"

Barnes looks abashed – possibly the first time I've seen anything approaching consternation on her face – and stares down at her data pad. "I did report it to Louis …"

"And you knew very well that he'd be busy with his new job." I narrow my eyes. "What is this ingredient anyway?"

"How should I know? I don't have a biochemistry degree, do I?"

"Barnes …" I let a warning note enter my voice.

"Look, it's something that's only been added in the past few weeks – it can't be that important or anything to do with product safety as we've been running the same recipe for years. It's not my fault the supplies didn't come in. I queried it with the department but they refused to respond as I'm only a foreman." Her voice is laced with sarcasm. "So I included it in my report to Louis. That's all I could do. There's no bloody way I'm stopping the production line on a whim – it could cost me my job!"

Her face is set into hard lines, but still she refuses to meet my eye.

I sigh. "I'll speak to Phillips, see if we can get the affected products marked as not for sale, and I'll chase up this ingredient, whatever it is. I need you to collate and send me all product codes affected and whether any are likely to have been shipped out yet."

"Of course."

"I'll come back down once I've spoken to Phillips and let you know what he says. Now, is there anything else you've forgotten to tell me about? We had a deal, remember?"

Barnes has the courtesy to look chagrined. "No."

"Fine, well, let's get this mess sorted out."

Barnes nods and turns to leave.

"Wait!" I hesitate. "The other day … you called me Trey. Why?"

Something flickers in her eyes, too quick for me to catch. "Did I?" She shrugs. "Sorry. Slip of the tongue. Is that all?"

I nod reluctantly and watch her walk away. It bothers me that she lied, and there's something else about her that I can't quite put my finger on. But I have more important things to worry about now. I shake myself and head back up to my office.

* * *

"Is it okay if I head off a bit early today? I was in at eight this morning," Emilie says.

I tear my eyes away from the holo screen and run my hand through my hair. "Sure. Thanks for your help this afternoon."

"No problem." Emilie stands and begins to pack away her things. "I'm sorry I didn't pick up the androcibus nanite issue at the time, but Barnes included it in a private report for Louis that I couldn't access." She shrugs. "Still, not too much harm done by the sound of it?"

"Other than pissing off quality control, no. At least Phillips agreed with me about keeping the production line going."

My manager had been curt about the whole thing. "Bloody quality control, sticking their noses in," he'd said with a grunt.

"Just make sure we keep the products separate from the others. I'll speak to supply about getting the ingredients in – I'm not having this messing the whole system up."

"Well, don't stay too late," Emilie says, heading for the door. "I'll see you tomorrow."

I finish double-checking the figures Barnes had sent me and send them through to the quality control officer, having looked her up on the system. Ann Davies, senior quality control manager. So she does technically outrank me. I'm glad I hadn't known that before speaking to her.

With that done, I run a search on the system for androcibus nanite. There's no record of what it is, but it appears in the ingredients list for most of the lower-grade product lines. I also try and find the message that Barnes had sent to Louis, but draw a blank. It must have gone to his personal account.

I try and comm him, but he doesn't answer. I hesitate, then look him up on the internal staff system. When I click on his office number, a three-dimensional map of the factory appears above my desk, flashing dots indicating my location in relation to his.

I log off the system and try Louis again on the comm. Still no answer. Perhaps he's in a meeting. Or in the bathroom.

Outside the office, I pause. Coleman warned me about wandering around the factory. But I have a genuine reason for wanting to speak to Louis – I need to find out whether he knew about the missing ingredient and if he knows what it is. Surely that's got to be acceptable?

I don't pass many people as I navigate through the maze of corridors and lifts. It feels like there's a lot of space for not very many people on this side of the factory, whereas on the other side, where the Outsiders are, there is little space for many people. From what I've gathered, around seventy percent of the factory staff are Outsiders, but they all seem to work on the factory floors; I don't see them anywhere else in the building.

The door to the distribution department looks to be secured, but it slides open as I approach and a tall woman with curly blonde hair steps out. She looks at me enquiringly.

"I'm looking for Louis. Is he still around?"

Her face flushes slightly at the mention of his name. "He's just in a meeting. What were you wanting to see him about?"

I introduce myself and explain that I need to check something with him relating to his previous job.

She glances over her shoulder at the corridor behind her, then back at me, apparently torn. Finally, she reaches a decision. "I'll let you into his office. You can wait for him there. He shouldn't be long – the meeting was due to finish at five, but they do sometimes run on."

I follow her back up the corridor. She pauses and presses her hand to a door on the left and motions me into the room

"Thank you ..."

"Elaine," she supplies. "I'm Louis's personal assistant," she adds, somewhat unnecessarily, though the tinge of pink on her cheeks and the way she avoids my eye makes me wonder exactly how personally she takes her duties. I remember what Emilie had said about Louis being a ladies' man.

"Thank you, Elaine." I smile at her and step inside the room. The door closes behind me.

Louis's new office is larger and more richly decorated than his previous one. What looks like an antique leather sofa sits regally in one corner opposite a pair of high-backed chairs. There's a large desk that faces the door, and most of one wall is taken up with a huge screen designed to mimic a window. In the far corner is a discreet transparent door that presumably leads to Elaine's workspace.

I cross to the desk, wondering if there are cameras on me, recording my every move. Or perhaps that's just in my office. Surely if anyone is exempt from surveillance, it would be Coleman's son?

There's little in the way of personal possessions on the desk, just a digital photo frame with a rolling series of photos. I pick it up and study them. A couple of Louis with a pretty smiling girl who bears a strong resemblance to him. His sister, I guess. One of Louis with his father. Coleman's eyes seem to pierce through me and a shiver runs down my spine. There's a couple of Louis's parents and one of Louis and his father with two older men.

As I place it back on the table, the holo screen jumps into life. I step back, a spike of adrenaline shooting through me. Then I shake my head.

You idiot, Louis must have left it on.

A map fills the air above the desk. I study it for a moment, trying to figure out what it represents. Different coloured lines span out from a cube in the centre to different points. Hesitantly, I reach out and pinch my fingers to zoom out. Then it becomes clear. It's a map of London. The central cube is the factory and the other points must be distribution centres. I click on an information symbol and an explanatory box pops up. The different colours represent different grades of food.

My heart begins to race. This is the sort of information the Chain is after. I press my finger to one of the distribution centres. Another information box appears, this time detailing delivery times, live supply levels and access codes.

I try to memorize the information, focusing first on the

distribution centres in the east of the city, Outside the Wall. It would be much easier to stream the image direct to Milicent, but they'll be monitoring my comm band. I can't risk it.

I'm moving around to the northern distribution centres when a hissing sound from the door gives me a split-second warning that someone is about to enter.

I snap my fingers and the display disappears just as Louis steps into the room.

21

Aleesha

The church gates are open and the two monks whose job it is to welcome people are sprawled face down in the dirt. Black figures swarm around the graveyard; Primo's officers are wearing their protective Metz armour again. No helmets though – just the suits.

They have the church surrounded, but they haven't managed to break in. The heavy wooden doors stand closed, and there's no sign of life from inside the building.

I breathe a sigh of relief. They are safe enough for now, at least.

I spot Primo and Vihaan near the main gates. They seem to be arguing about something and Vihaan cowers back into the wall as Primo raises a gloved fist over him. But the blow never falls. Primo turns and walks away. Even from up here, I can see the disgusted look on his face.

I slump down with my back to the parapet, wondering what's going on inside the church. I should never have left them. Rogue was right – my place is with them. Last time I went to see Trey, I ended up in trouble. This time, they're the ones being attacked and I'm not there to help.

But they're trapped, and you're not.

Primo's people are focused on the church. Too focused. I glance over the parapet again, counting eight men and women in Metz uniforms, plus Vihaan. Presuming they have a similar number on the other side of the church, and a few lurking in the large graveyard to the rear, there's probably about twenty of them. Not many, but they're armed with Metz guns, grenades and batons.

Still, they won't be expecting an attack from behind.

I crawl away from the parapet, get to my feet and run back along the rooftop and down to the street. I need reinforcements.

The Chain? Not if I can help it. Bryn said they wouldn't help me again.

Samson on the other hand … He may not have wanted to challenge Primo directly, but here, he won't have to. I still don't know how big the Brotherhood is, but he's got the gangs at his beck and call too. And if we can take Primo down at the same time, then no one will have to fight him one-on-one.

There's only one problem. I have no idea where to find him.

But he seems to have eyes and ears everywhere. Perhaps he'll find me.

I walk through the streets with my hood up, stopping people at random and asking if they know Samson. Most of the time they just shake their head, but a few start when they hear the name, and though they deny knowing him I can tell they're lying.

I ask them about Primo's mob too – some of them say there were twenty of them, some two dozen.

"Thought they was Metz officers at first," a young prostitute confides in me. "But they 'ad no helmets on. Then I guessed they were that new group as what taken over the Snakes." She gives me a hopeful look. "Are you goin' to get rid of 'em? They took in a few girls last week. One of their bodies was in the river yesterday."

It seems he left the members of the gang behind, with the exception of Vihaan. I'm not sure if that's because he doesn't trust them or because he believes they wouldn't be any use in a fight.

Half an hour later, I'm wondering if I'm going to have to go to the Chain after all. I duck into an alleyway and lean against the wall, closing my eyes.

No. I'll damn well deal with this myself. I don't need my father to fix my problems.

"Looking for someone?"

A man leans against the opposite wall, studiously cleaning his nails with a four-inch blade. His hair is part-shaved, the rest gathered in a tight thin braid that hangs down over his shoulder to his waist.

"You know Samson?"

He looks up and his thin face triggers a memory.

"You were with him at Jay's leadership fight."

"You've been asking for him?"

"I need to speak to him. Now."

"You can't."

He holds his hand out, inspecting his fingers, then switches the blade to his other hand.

I push myself off the wall and make a grab for it, but I'm a fraction too slow.

"Now, now. Back off." He waves the blade in front of him like a sword. "You can't speak to him because he's not here."

"I know that. I want you to take me to him."

"You don't understand." He returns to picking his nails, but his hand trembles slightly and the tip of the blade catches on the skin under his nail. "Dammit!" He sucks at his finger.

"Don't understand what?" I'm starting to lose patience.

He says some unintelligible, then removes the finger from his mouth and looks at it dolefully. "He's not here. Or *there*. He's missing."

"What?"

The man shoves his knife back into his belt. "Samson's missing. He was supposed to be back at the main base two days ago, but there's been no sight nor sound of him."

I shake my head. "Impossible."

Samson missing? He'd been going to see the President, to ask for his help with getting rid of Primo. But what if the President still hasn't forgiven him for his role in bringing down the Metz Commander and capturing the officers? Does he even know Samson was involved?

He must have been detained by the President. It's the only explanation. I curse and start forward.

The man jerks his head up, alerted by my sudden movement. "You know something?" He grabs my arm.

"No." I twist myself free from his grasp. "But if Samson can't help me, I need to find someone who can."

The thought of going back to the Chain's headquarters and asking Katya for help makes my stomach clench. The smug expression on her face haunts me. Has she been playing us both off against each other?

As for my father ... *I can't face him again. Not yet.*

But if I don't go to the Chain, there's only one option left.

The Bigland Boys.

You knew you'd have to face them at some point. How long do you think they'd let you camp out in their territory? They're biding their time, waiting until your group falls apart so they can sweep you all up into their gang.

And by going to them now, I'm playing right into their hands. But without their help, there may not be anyone left alive for them to take. And the clock is ticking. I don't know how long they can last in the church. Don't know how long it will be before the anger and fear escalates and someone decides to make a break for it. At least with Outsiders I know how to cut a deal, and the leader of the Bigland Boys isn't known for his brain power.

I stride out into the street, weaving between people, ambling along with my head down.

A figure looms in front of me. I lift my arms instinctively and bounce back as if I've hit a stone wall. I look up, my hood falling back from my face.

"Aleesha?" The round face looking down on me breaks into a smile.

"Anders?"

I've never been so relieved to see a Metz officer in my life.

Former Metz officer.

"Did you escape from the church? Have they gone?"

"No. At least, I don't think so. You know then?"

Danny steps out from behind Anders, his eyes constantly scanning the crowd around us. "Let's get off the street."

Danny leads us down a side alley and onto another street. He pauses in front of a tattoo parlour and glances around before opening the door and ushering us in. The owner – a thin man completely covered in tattoos – looks up from the woman he's inking, but when he sees Danny he just nods to an unobtrusive door at the back of the shop. We step through into a single room that obviously acts as the man's living quarters. It smells stuffy, of fried food and sweat.

"We were training at the back of the graveyard when they attacked," Anders says. "Danny heard them first and we managed to get over the back wall before they saw us. There's twenty-two of them, all ex-officers, apart from that greasy-haired kid you beat in the fight."

"Vihaan. I saw."

Danny gives Anders a look. Anders shrugs. "What? She needs to know."

Danny folds his arms and gives me an aggressive look. "What I want to know, is where you were while all of this was going on. Seems pretty convenient that you just happened to be out and about when they attacked."

I meet his gaze levelly. "I went to see if I could get some help."

"Oh yeah? What kind of help?"

I take a deep breath and try and swallow down the anger I can feel building inside me. Danny is right to question me. To him and the others, it must seem like I've been doing nothing.

And what have you been doing? Going to see Trey and your father. Nothing to help them.

"Jay had an arrangement with Samson. And Samson has a hold on most of the gangs in this part of the city. It's not in any of their interests to let Primo take over."

"And what did Samson say?"

"I haven't been able to speak to him." I shrug. "He's on some other mission at the moment."

"So what's your next plan?"

"Well, the three of us can't take them on, not when they have armour and guns." I pause, reluctant to tell Danny my plan. I can guess what his reaction will be. "We need to ask one of the other gangs for help. The Bigland Boys, as this is their patch."

As I expected, Danny explodes. "Over my dead body. What

d'ya think you'll get from them? They've had their eye on us for ages. Probably just waitin' until Primo finishes us off an' then they'll move in and take over our patch too. Even if you do talk 'em into helping us, they'll stab us in the back as soon as the fightin's over."

I wait until he's finished ranting. Anders just stands there, looking thoughtful.

"That's the point, Danny," I say when he's finished. "They'll help us because Primo is a threat to them too. Their leader was on the jury when Primo won, right? They must be aware of what Primo's doing in Four. None of them can beat him in a leadership contest, and the Snakes' headquarters is impenetrable. Well, almost impenetrable," I add, remembering how the Chain and Samson had broken in to rescue me. "But out here, with a handful of them focusing on breaking into the church, they're vulnerable. They're not going to get another opportunity like it."

"But yer handin' us over to them—"

"Listen!" I reach out and grab Danny's t-shirt, yanking him toward me. He's so shocked by the action that he gapes at me, mouth open like a fish. "I am *not* going to let them take us over. But if we can use them to get rid of Primo, then we can bring the whole gang back together. With the officers included, we'll be by far the biggest and strongest gang in Area Four."

I push him away from me, trying not to wince as pain shoots through my shoulder. Danny's face is twisted in concentration as he tries to work this through. Anders, though, is nodding.

"I don't like it," Danny says finally, though he sounds less confident than before.

I let out the breath I'd been holding. Ten minutes and he'll be resigned to it. Give him an hour and he may even think it was his own idea.

"There may be another way," Anders says into the silence.

He looks at me as if waiting for approval to continue. I nod.

"They're not wearing helmets, which means the armour isn't complete. It'll provide some protection from direct blows but it won't be as effective, and they're not charged."

He sees our blank looks and explains. "The suits are charged between uses to activate the circuitry that powers the exoskeleton and regulates the user's body temperature."

"The what?" Danny looks at him blankly.

"With the exoskeleton activated, the suit stiffens to provide a hard, weight-bearing shield that's responsive to the nerve impulses of the person inside. So it feels both weightless and part of you. Like an extra layer of clothing that keeps you cool and enhances your ability to fight." His face drops for a moment but he quickly recovers. "There may be some charge still left in the suits, but it's irrelevant anyway, as the exoskeleton is activated only when the helmet is fastened into the body of the suit."

He pauses and looks at us, his smooth brow furrowed. "Does that make sense?"

"So, if the exoskeleton isn't activated, it'll just feel as if they're in a heavy suit?" I say slowly, still trying to figure out where Anders is going with this.

Anders nods enthusiastically. "Exactly. We're built to carry the weight, of course, but it will definitely slow them down a bit, not to mention being hot in this weather." He tugs at the tight black suit all the officers wear and smiles ruefully. "This is bad enough. It's designed for the air-conditioned climate of the compound, not the weather out here."

I nod absentmindedly. *So they may not be as strong as I thought.*

"What about the guns? I guess they might have spent most of the bullets in the fight at Rose Square?"

Anders' smile broadens. "That's the really neat thing. They won't work. For safety, they can only be activated by the current running through the exoskeleton. They're just carrying them for show – as a deterrent."

"So that's why we couldn't get 'em to work? Because we don't have an exo … skeletal thing?"

"That's right, Danny. That's one reason for the design. We can't risk civilians turning our own weapons on us."

Danny's brow furrows. "So why don't they just put the helmets back on?"

Anders shrugs. "Would you? Knowing that's what controls you? Presumably, you still have that device you used to control us?" He cocks his head and looks at me.

I ignore the question. "So they're giving a big show of strength to scare people. But there are still twenty-two of them and three of us."

"*They* don't need to know that."

Slowly, it begins to dawn on me what Anders is proposing. "They're all inside the church walls, spread out through the graveyard," I say, thinking aloud. "If we can find some way of taking them down one at a time from outside the walls, they won't know who is attacking them from where."

Anders nods and waits for me to continue. I glance at him and realize he had already worked this all out, but he was letting me say it so Danny would think it was my idea.

Interesting. He's clever. Manipulative. But he seems happy for me to take the lead.

"If we can stay hidden and move around, they may think we're a bigger force than we are. It'll distract them from the church –

allow the others to come out. Then, we'll have the advantage in terms of numbers."

"And we don't have to go to the Bigland Boys?" Danny says.

"No, we don't. But we do need something we can throw … some kind of explosive perhaps? Even a flaming bottle would do it." I glance at Danny. "Any ideas?"

"Rich made those explosives we used to blow up the depot wall that time, back when Dane was in charge." He looks slightly mournful. "Before all this shit happened."

"Can you get your hands on some?"

He looks thoughtful. "Reckon so. If not, there's plenty of bottles an' rags to be had."

"Can I come with you? Or will I get in your way?" Anders looks at him enquiringly.

"Na, I reckon you'll be okay." Danny grins. "'Sides, no one will mess with me if you're there."

An odd sort of companionship seems to have struck up between the two men. Of Anders' doing, no doubt, and yet it doesn't feel as if he's using Danny in any way. More like he's trying to bridge a gaping divide, one stone at a time.

Definitely not someone to underestimate.

I turn to Danny. "Are we okay to meet back here?"

He nods. "Sure. Jake's a mate of mine. Did this beauty for me." He runs his hand over the snake tattoo that covers his head and coils down to his neck. It's delicate work. "You lot should get 'em done too if you're going to be part of the gang like."

Anders pales slightly and I hold back a smile. "I'll scout around the church and see where our best attack positions are likely to be. Meet back here in an hour."

* * *

Danny and Anders make it back to the tattoo parlour first. When I walk in, Danny's stuffing rags into a set of glass bottles filled with a clear liquid. Three backpacks are set out in front of him. Anders hovers suspiciously near the door. He gives me an awkward smile as I walk in and shifts uncomfortably.

I eye the backpacks and bottles. "All sorted?"

Danny nods. "Got some similar to the ones Rich made. Used 'em in Rose Square, so we know they work." He reaches into one of the backpacks and pulls out a metal can. "Gotta treat 'em gentle like. Otherwise, they might go off before we want 'em too. Snap these caps onto the end just before you throw 'em." He pulls out a piece of cloth and wraps it delicately around the can before placing it carefully back into the bag. He waves at the glass bottles. "These are just normal firebombs. Lighting sticks in the backpack. Hope it'll be enough. We'll 'ave to aim straight."

I walk over and look in the backpacks. "Do you think we're taking down an army?"

Danny grins and shrugs.

There's a pile of films on a table in the corner of the room, most of which are covered in sketches and tattoo designs. I find a blank film and a pen and draw a rough outline of the church boundary and the surrounding buildings and streets.

"You take this side, Anders, and Danny you take this side." I point out a couple of low buildings. "Once you've thrown a couple, scarper and move along here. Work your way back along the building. I'll take the front and pick up any that try and escape through the main gates. I'll throw first."

"It might just work," Anders says slowly.

"Three take on twenty and win! Now there's a story to tell." Danny picks up Anders' arm with one hand and fist bumps him with the other. Anders looks confused. "Primo won't know what hit 'im."

I smile at them. "Let's go kick his ass."

Once in the street, we split up. The roofs on the buildings facing the church are higher than I'd like, but the apartments facing it have balconies. I choose the best-positioned and have a word with the occupants, who quickly find somewhere else to be. They leave me a bottle of water, which I gulp down gratefully.

I unload half the bag's contents onto the balcony, staying low below the barrier.

Nothing's really changed since I looked down from the rooftop hours earlier. Primo's team are stationed at regular intervals around the church. There seems to have been no attempt at escape or attack from inside, though as I watch, I catch a flicker of movement at one of the windows high above the main door. But the figure is too distorted by the ancient glass for me to tell who it is.

My body's tense with adrenaline as I snap the small cap onto the end of one of the metal cans. I try and take steady breaths to slow my racing heart.

Stay calm. If this goes to plan you may not even have to fight.

I peek over the top of the balcony. Primo's talking to the guards stationed just inside the mangled metal gate to the churchyard. They haven't even moved the bodies of the two monks to one side. He looks around, surveying the surrounding buildings and rooftops, but his eyes don't linger on any rooftop in particular and they quickly return to surveying the church instead. Vihaan is nowhere to be seen.

My fingers curl around the metal can and I weigh it in my hand, judging how hard I'll need to throw it. Primo turns suddenly and glances up in my direction. I drop down behind the balcony, my heart hammering in my chest.

Did he see me?

My palm is sweaty on the metal can, and I swap it to the other hand to wipe my palm on my trousers. I feel suddenly light-headed.

I close my eyes and breathe deeply.

Stay calm. Think.

I wait another ten seconds then risk a peek over the railing. Primo is talking to the guard again, neither of them looking in my direction. He claps the woman on the shoulder and turns to move off.

I draw my arm back, raise my head to take aim and throw the can. It goes slightly wide, hitting the ground to the left of the guard. Fire blooms and I duck back behind the balcony, plugging my ears as the explosion cracks through the hum of the city.

Jeez, Danny didn't tell me they were that powerful!

Another explosion fills the silence left by the first, then a third. Anders and Danny are in position at least. I pick up the second can, more cautiously this time, and risk a glance over the balcony.

The female guard lies sprawled on the ground, motionless, her blonde hair stained red. The second guard is also down, twitching and moaning. I drag my eyes away from the woman's body and look around. Primo is nowhere to be seen.

My hands tremble. Three officers round the side of the church, one limping. I throw the second can, but either my aim is weak or I don't really want it to hurt them, as it falls short. The explosion this time is half the intensity of the first, and when I look over the balcony again, the officers are scurrying back around the corner. One of them looks up and meets my eye.

Time to get out of here.

I collect the third can and pack it carefully back into the backpack before leaving at a run. The dull thud of more explosions follows me.

My plan had been to duck into the street and move to another apartment block further up. But the street is deserted now, people having taken shelter when the bombs started flying. I go up to the roof instead, running as fast as I can while being careful not to jolt the backpack. By the time I get down to the third floor of a different apartment block, the explosions have stopped.

I retrieve one of the bombs from the backpack and crawl out onto the balcony. Smoke rises from around one corner of the church and there's the sound of fighting but the area at the front of the church is deserted.

Have Anders and Danny closed in already?

A movement at the front of the church catches my eye. The main doors are opening. Light flashes on a shard of mirror poked out on a stick. A hidden figure pulls it back in. Then the doors are flung wide and my people spill out.

Some clutch knives, others batons or sticks made from chair legs. There are even a few monks, brandishing metal candlesticks that flail dangerously near the heads of their companions. Tommy and the other kids rush to the front.

Something inside my chest swells and blooms like a flower in the spring sun.

I turn to run down and join them but a hoarse shout stops me in my tracks. Rogue appears around the corner. He's limping, and one arm hangs awkwardly at his side. His face is bloody and lined in pain.

He waves his hand frantically. "Get back inside! It's a trap!"

But his shouts are lost in the cheers and whooping of the gang as they stream from the church to beat off those who dared to attack their home. Only Tommy sees him and yanks at the robe of the monk next to him.

Rogue shouts again and begins to hobble toward them. This time the monk picks up his cry and takes a step backward, looking around. His gaze falls on the street that leads away from the entrance to the church, out of my sight, and the colour drains from his face. He shouts something and points a shaking finger before stumbling backward, pulling Tommy with him. Others halt and turn to retreat.

But they are all too late. Figures spill from the street, running toward the mangled gates. Tall and broad, they're dressed in the black undersuits of the Metz. I stand, frozen, as they fall upon those who had led the charge out from the church, and who are now at the back of the group trying to get back in.

Around the opposite corner of the church from where Rogue had emerged strolls Primo. He twirls one of the Metz batons in his hand, drops of blood flying from its tip, and wears a smile of satisfaction.

It's then that I realize that we've underestimated Primo's cunning. The suits and guns *were* all for show, but not in the way we'd thought. He's been baiting us, waiting to lure us out before bringing the rest of his forces in to finish us off. He knew he couldn't break into the church by force, so he set a trap.

And we walked straight into it.

22

Trey

"Darwin? What are you doing here?"

I stand frozen behind Louis's desk, my hand still outstretched in mid-air. I open my mouth but no words come out. My brain is screaming at me to run but my feet are rooted to the floor.

"I … I needed to speak to you," I get out, lowering my arm. "Elaine let me in."

"She's a peach." Louis walks over to me and claps me on the shoulder. "How are you doing? Have you been waiting long?"

My heart pounds, so loud that I'm sure he must be able to hear it.

Did he see the holo screen?

I try to pull myself together. "Just a few minutes. I was having a look at your family photos." I gesture to the photo frame. "Though I think I may have knocked your screen into life – I hope I haven't messed anything up."

I hold my breath as Louis brings up the map. But it seems to have reverted to the default display and looks the same as when I'd first opened it. Louis snaps his fingers to minimize it again. "No worries. I really should have a password or something on it. Security is always on my back." He grins ruefully. "But I'm terrible at that kind of stuff. Besides, it's much easier if Elaine can access my system when I'm not here."

Air rushes from my lungs and I feel suddenly light-headed. "I guess that makes sense."

Louis picks up the photo frame and studies it. The image of him with his father and the two older men appears and Louis freezes the reel. "That's my grandfather and his brother. At one time they pretty much ruled Britannia, you know. My great-uncle became President for a time, and Grandfather took over a languishing food company and turned it into the second biggest corporation in the country. Now Father's trying to make it the biggest. One day I guess it'll be down to me, though I don't know they'll be anything left for me to achieve."

He gives a short laugh and replaces the photo frame on the desk. "Father is determined to put off that day for as long as possible though. Anyway, what can I help you with?" He gestures to the chairs in the corner of the room. "Take a seat."

I hesitate. "Actually, I was wondering if you fancied going for a drink. I wanted to ask you about an issue that's been raised by quality control." I lower my voice and glance meaningfully at the ceiling. "Not sure if you want them listening in?"

Louis looks puzzled, then throws his head back and laughs. "Oh, good Lord! You don't think I let them put cameras and recording devices in here, do you? That is definitely one privilege I exercise from being my father's son. Don't want anyone listening in on my private meetings with my assistant, do I?" He grins and wiggles his eyebrows suggestively.

I try to stop the heat rising to my cheeks and fail miserably. Louis laughs again at my discomfort. "Come on, Darwin, handsome boy like you should have his pick of the women!

Emilie looked pretty keen on you, from what I could see. Bet she's a lively one between the sheets – the quiet ones always are."

"We've got a bit of a problem with the production line," I say carefully. "Wanted to ask your opinion on it."

Louis's face falls. "Oh yes, you said. Well, every problem is better faced with a beer. Come on, let's go get a drink."

We take a pod to Soho, then walk to a small bar tucked away up a narrow side street. There are only a few patrons inside, mostly solitary drinkers nursing a pint of beer or a whisky. The man behind the bar nods to Louis. "Usual?" he asks, his hand already on the pump.

"Yes, please." Louis turns to me. "I can recommend the pale ale."

"Sounds good."

I try to pay for the drink, but Louis waves my hand away. "You can get the next round."

I follow him up a narrow flight of stairs that leads up three floors to a small roof garden. The scent of lemon trees fills the air and water trickles down a tall water feature into a pool, masking the noise filtering up from the street below.

Louis takes a chair close to the fountain. "So, what's the problem?"

I take a sip from my glass and tell him about the visit from the quality control officers, the missing androcibus nanite and Barnes's insistence that she'd reported it up to Louis.

"I've had a run in with Davies before." Louis makes a face. "I think she has it in for me. Or perhaps she just has it in for everyone. Don't think she ever smiles."

"Do you remember getting a message from Barnes about it?"

"No, though, to be honest, I could have missed it. She knew

to come and speak to me if it was anything really important." He frowns. "I wonder why she didn't."

I'd been wondering the same thing.

"I don't think she thought it *was* that important. Do you know what the ingredient actually is? Why it's necessary for those products in particular?"

Louis shrugs. "No idea, mate. I leave that sort of stuff to the scientists. Some kind of stabiliser maybe? Or a flavouring? That low-grade stuff tastes like shit." He takes a gulp of his beer. "Nice up here, isn't it?"

I nod agreement. "Quality control want us to get rid of all the food that's gone through the system without it."

"Stands to reason. Don't want to be selling something that's not quite right."

"Sure. But if it didn't have the ingredient in before, surely there's nothing *wrong* with it?"

Louis eyes me with curiosity. "What are you suggesting?"

I shrug. "It just seems a bit of waste, that's all. You're in charge of distribution, right? Maybe you could keep the marked packages to one side for a few weeks. Philips just said to keep them separate, not destroy them. I'd like to try and speak to the scientists to find out if it's safe to eat. We could give it to one of the children's homes Outside or something."

My heart thumps in my chest and I take another sip of beer to wet my mouth. The bitter tang doesn't help. I'm pretty sure suggesting something that's directly contrary to the orders given by the quality control department is a sackable offence. If Louis were to report me …

But I also sense that Louis is a bit of a rebel himself. He chooses to obey the rules, but only when it suits him.

"You are an interesting one, Goldsmith," he says finally. "Still trying to help those poor buggers Outside?"

"Someone's got to."

"Hmm, well I'd be careful how far you go with that. There's a reason things are the way they are, you know."

I bite back a retort.

"But, I don't see any harm in storing a few boxes for a time. They can go in one of the reserve storerooms, no one checks there. I'll get one of my chaps to go and see Barnes tomorrow to arrange it." He stands, holding his empty glass. "Another beer?"

My glass is still half full. "I'll go," I say.

I return with a beer for Louis and a non-alcoholic beer for me. It tastes just as bad, but if I'm going to get Louis drunk without ending up on the floor myself, I need to do something. Fortunately, Louis seems happy enough at my insistence on buying him drinks. A couple of hours later, he's had four pints and a tumbler of whisky and has turned oddly maudlin.

"You know, being the son of a business hotshot isn't all it's cracked up to be," he says, staring into his glass. "There's so much *pressure* to be good at everything, particularly when you know you've been given the best genes available. I came second in my university class and Father didn't speak to me for a week. My sister, of course, came top in her class. Grandfather's just as bad. Still can't keep his fingers out of the company pie. Drives Father mad."

"Oh?"

"Yeah. Grandfather and his brother – they're twins you know – are supposed to have retired. They've got this big country mansion in what's left of Kent. But Grandfather still comes back to London every week to check up on what's going on. And most of the board are in his pocket."

I file away this information to pass onto Milicent.

"You know, I almost envy you, having all that excitement." He sighs.

"Well, being chased as a wanted criminal isn't all it's cracked up to be." I sip at my whisky, wondering why anyone drinks this stuff. Feels like it's stripping my throat raw.

"Oh, come *on,* it must have been! Hiding out, dodging the Metz, fighting Outsiders." He becomes suddenly animated, his eyes sparkling. "I heard a rumour that you broke into the government headquarters. That you were working for a rebel gang trying to overthrow the government, like … like Guy Fawkes or something. Gunpowder, treason and plot!" He raises his glass in a mock toast and downs the amber liquid.

I stare at him in incomprehension. *Gunpowder, treason and plot? What century is he in?*

He leans in, nudging me conspiratorially with his elbow. "Come on, spill the beans. What was it like?"

I think about running through the woods away from my school, the agony of cutting my chip out, the fear and danger of walking around in Area Four. The emaciated figures that line the streets, starving children, the Metz cutting people down. The streets covered in blood.

That's what I want to tell Louis about, but I know it's not what he wants to hear. He wants me to be like his other friends, one of the lads. And perhaps if I can pretend to be like that too, he'll be more likely to confide in me in the future.

"It was pretty gripping," I say. "There are all these gangs Outside, each with their own tattoos and colours. Blue are the Snakes, purple the Dragons …" I try to remember what other gangs Aleesha had mentioned. "Red, the Shanksters, I think. The city Outside is divided up into different patches, and when one of them wants to challenge the leader of a gang, they organize this big contest, like a boxing match or something, but with weapons."

I carry on, my stories of the city Outside the Wall getting wilder and more imaginative. Louis interjects with the occasional exclamation or comment, slapping me on the arm at one particularly outrageous part.

Finally, I run out of words.

"Wow, that sounds incredible," Louis says, his face flushed with excitement. Or perhaps that's just the alcohol. "I think I need another whisky – one more for the road?"

"I'm good, thanks."

"Suit yourself." He staggers over to the door and disappears.

The final rays of the setting sun reflect off the glass towers, bathing the lower rooftops in red. Around me, solar lights flicker to life and insects click and chirrup as the heat of the day begins to ease. It's peaceful up here, so tranquil you could almost forget there's a city below you. A city Outside the Wall that is so very different from what is in here. And I think I understand now why it is impossible for people like Louis to really comprehend what life is like Outside. Why, even when they see the fighting and protests on the news screens, Insiders don't really *know* what it is they are seeing. They can't put themselves in the position of the people who live Outside because they haven't experienced that life for themselves.

What they see on the screens is a different world to them. Like watching videos of extinct lions chasing gazelles across a barren plain. A world that is totally and utterly separate from their own.

And I know that if fate hadn't forced my hand and chased me Outside the Wall, I wouldn't have understood either. I'd have just accepted that this was how things were. Outsiders and Insiders. Them and us. That there was a *reason* for the divide, even if it was never really explained. I would have been like Louis and his friends, laughing and joking, oblivious to the suffering and injustice in this city.

I glance down at the barely touched whisky in my glass and pour it into the pot of the plant next to me. *Perhaps not totally like Louis.*

Louis brings me another drink despite my protests. "Y'see!" he slurs, looking at my empty glass. "I thought you'd need one."

He places the glasses down on the table with exaggerated care. "So, I've been thinking that I should take you to some of the bars Outside. In the better areas, of course – show you a few places you won't have seen." He claps me on the shoulder. "Good fun. Outsider girls can be so much more relaxed than girls in here."

I get a sinking feeling in my stomach as Emilie's words come back to me.

"I-I'm not really into anything like that."

"Come on, it's only a bar. Music, dancing." He wiggles his hips. "What do you say? This weekend?"

How do I refuse without offending him?

"I'm not really supposed to wander around Outside." I shrug. "One of the President's conditions on letting me back in."

Louis frowns. "Well that's a ball-ache." He leans forward and whispers conspiratorially. "Look, I might have something that'll help you out with that. Doesn't seem fair that you can't have fun. But you gotta promise *never* to tell anyone about it."

"What do you mean?"

"Here." Louis fumbles in his pocket and pulls out what looks like a transparent tube of plastic wrap. He rolls up the sleeve of his shirt and begins to pull it over his arm. I reach out and touch it. It feels slightly rubbery, but once it's on his arm, you barely notice it's there.

"Chip blocker. Mate of mine invented it as part of a university project. Got into some trouble for that, he did. It blocks the tracking signal and everything else from your chip. You disappear off *their* radar just like that." He clicks his fingers.

I frown. "Doesn't that look suspicious?"

Louis shrugs. "Not really. There're always a few blips in the system. As long as you're not gone too long and you turn up back where you're supposed to be, you should be okay. Of course, you need to leave your comm band at home – that's got a tracker in it too – but if it's night time and your comm band is tucked up in bed, they'll assume you are too."

My heart begins to race and I reach out again to touch the plastic sheath. *I could go Outside, go to see Abby and Bryn, help Aleesha, without any of them knowing.*

A thought strikes me and I fight to control the excitement in my voice. "So, would it let you pass through the Wall?"

"And why on earth would you want to try to do that?" Louis looks at me incredulously. "You just use a cheap replica chip to take a pod Outside. There are a couple of good places in Six. But the best places are in Ten and Twelve. There's a girl I meet there, sometimes, Rosie her name is—"

"Can you get me one of these?" I interrupt before he can get started on women again.

Louis winks. "Sure can." He finishes his drink and looks at my still-full glass. "Come on, drink up. It's past closing time."

I down the whisky in one. The alcohol burns the back of my throat, nearly making me choke.

"Good man." Louis pulls the chip blocker off his arm and shoves it back into his pocket. Unsteadily, he gets to his feet. "Y'know, I thought you were a bit of a prude at first, Darwin.

One of those boring, scholarly types." He staggers and I reach out a hand to support him. He responds by flinging his arm around my shoulders. "But you're alright, y'know? Maybe we'll be friends. Don't have many of them, whatever you might think."

Together we make it down the stairs and out onto the street. I hail a taxi pod and bundle Louis into the back of it.

"See you tomorrow!" he calls as the pod door slides shut.

"Tomorrow," I echo as it rises and shoots off up the street.

Despite the late hour, I decide to walk back home. The night air would help clear the alcohol fog from my head and the walk would give me time to think. And today's events have given me a lot to think about.

23

Aleesha

I stand, transfixed, for what must be a full ten seconds. My heart pounds a dull rhythm in my head, my chest constricting as I watch Primo's officers swarm into the churchyard. They move silently, efficiently. My people pause, confused. Some try to retreat, but their way is blocked by the people behind them. Their war-like cries of triumph turn to screams of pain as Primo's men and women strike them down, lashing out with their batons. My hands clench the railing of the balcony as if, somehow, this could stop what's unfolding below me.

I've failed them.

They looked to me as their leader, but I've let them down at every turn. I wasn't there when Primo came. And now, I've played right into his hands. And they are screaming, dying.

No.

My hands clench tighter as, with a jerk, I snap out of my daze. I cast my eye around. My eyes meet Primo's and his lip curls. He raises a hand in a salute, his cold eyes taunting me.

I tear myself away from the balcony and run, the grenade still in my hand. Adrenaline courses through my body, sharpening my thoughts as I burst out into the street.

I aim the grenade at the ground just behind the last of Primo's people and duck back inside the building, covering my ears.

The bomb detonates, shooting dust past the open door. Reaching into the backpack, I pull out two of the glass firebombs, holding the bottles by the necks as if they were clubs. Apart from my knives, they're the only weapons I have. Leaning back against the wall, I close my eyes and suck in a breath.

In and out. Keep breathing.

And as I breathe out, the fear that makes my body taut leaves with it. We can't win, not against so many trained killers. But we will give them a fight they hadn't bargained for.

Time slows.

I stride out into the chaos. Black-clad bodies lie scattered on the ground, some moving, some still. Primo's people, not mine. Others are bent double, hands over their ears.

I break into a run, wielding the bottles like clubs against the first people I find. The bottles smash, spraying their contents over the faces of the men and women around me, who turn away, clutching their eyes and howling.

Keep moving, don't stop.

Batons find their way into my hands from the officers who have fallen. I weave through the disorientated fighters, a whirlwind that smashes their kneecaps and jabs at their stomachs.

My height is an advantage – I can slip under their arms, almost invisible in the confusion. Each movement comes naturally, like a dancer completing a memorized routine, twisting and turning, never staying still long enough for one of their weapons to hit me.

Slowly, I carve a path through Primo's fighters to the steps of the church.

A blow glances off my shoulder, but I barely feel it. I'm lost in the dance, my body moving by instinct, not by direction. My batons bounce off them, not hard enough to kill, but hard enough to hurt.

Then the black-clad figures in front of me have gone and a hand grabs my arm and yanks it down before my baton cracks open the head of a cowering monk.

My head snaps around, my trance broken.

Anders lets go of my wrist. "Plan B?" he asks quietly.

Shaking, I glance at the fighting around us. We're still outnumbered. It's chaos. I can barely tell who's on my side and who isn't. It feels as if we've been fighting for hours, but I know it can only have been a few minutes at most.

I think of the monks – unarmed and unprepared, hiding inside the church – and of Tommy and the other children who looked to us for protection.

"We fight," I say simply.

There is no other plan.

He nods, resigned, and we turn, back to back, to face the next onslaught.

I lash out with my baton, hitting a man on his shoulder and catching the back of his knees with my return swing. There's a flash of movement above my head and I duck, hearing Anders' baton colliding with my attacker's in the spot where my head had been.

The man in front of me sways slightly, his eyes closing for the briefest of seconds. He shakes himself and raises his baton again, his face set in determination. Sweat trickles down his face and he sucks in a breath before steadying himself again.

They're like stone statues – however hard you hit them, they refuse to topple.

Quickly, I lash out, cursing for having missed an opportunity, but he's back on his guard and our batons collide with such force that my whole arm rings from the impact. My fingers lose their grip and the baton falls from my hand.

I stagger back up the steps, breaking contact with Anders. For a split-second, I can see over the tops of the officers' heads and spot a mass of people running toward us. They're brandishing clubs, knives and bottles, and many have strips of yellow cloth tied around their foreheads.

Yellow – the colour of the Bigland Boys.

I catch a glimpse of Danny at the front of the pack before a dark-suited man looms up in front of me and slams me back into the stone wall of the church.

The breath is knocked from my lungs. The man's hand presses against my right shoulder, pinning me against the wall. I try to squirm away, but his weight presses into me. He raises his gun, intending to use it as a club. In the split-second before he brings it down, I twist my head to the side. The gun smashes into the wall. Fragments of stone catch in the collar of my jacket.

The fingers of my left hand brush my leg, finding the handle of my short-bladed knife.

He raises the gun to strike again, but I've pulled the knife from my pocket and stab it blindly at his stomach. The blade pierces the man's black suit, sliding through to find the flesh underneath.

He grunts and stumbles back, tripping down the steps. Blood shines on the quivering knife blade. I turn to prepare for the next attack, but there's no one left to fight.

The tide has turned.

The Bigland Boys swarm over the few black suits who are

still upright, taking them down by sheer numbers alone. Danny runs up the steps, pausing uncertainly in front of me. He looks down at the ground. "Sorry. Found them waitin' a couple of streets back." He raises his head. Shame fills his eyes. "I didn't know what else to do."

I drop the baton and raise my arm to pat him on the shoulder, forcing a small smile onto my face despite the pain that's tearing me apart inside. "You did good, Danny. Did the right thing."

The shame is mine.

I look around for Primo but he's nowhere to be seen. Pushing Danny to one side, I stumble down the steps, but a shout stops me. Rogue sits on the ground, his back to the church wall, clutching his shoulder.

I kneel beside him, searching his body for the source of the blood that covers him. "Your shoulder …"

"Dislocated, I think. I need to put it back in but I'm too much of a wimp." He sees my face. "Most of the blood isn't mine."

I nod, reassured that he isn't going to die on me any time soon, and get to my feet. "Primo?"

Rogue shakes his head. "He's gone. Ran off as soon as *they* came." He jerks his head toward the Bigland Boys, who are milling around the entrance to the church.

I wipe the blood off the knife in my hand and sheath it, picking up a baton from the floor.

"Aleesha …" Rogue's voice carries a trace of warning. "Don't. He abandoned his people – are you going to do the same?"

"He can't get away with this."

The voice doesn't sound like mine. It sounds colder. Harder.

"Not yet. Not now. We need you more."

His fingers close on my ankle, his grip weak. I could break free easily and kick him away.

But just like that, as if he'd switched off the supply of adrenaline to my muscles, my body fails me. My knees buckle and I fall to the ground, my whole body shaking uncontrollably. Then the ache from my overused muscles and the pain of my injuries hits and every movement makes my nerves scream.

Around me, people are beginning to move. Slowly at first, helping each other back into the church. Monks emerge and carry away the people lying on the ground. Some are taken inside, others are laid out in a neat row behind the church wall.

Still, I cannot move.

How did this go so wrong?

I search for some flaw in our plan, search for someone else to blame. Anders had been the one to suggest it. *Has he been on Primo's side all along? Was he manipulating me the same way he had manipulated Danny into helping him?*

I snap my head up, but as my eyes find Anders, I know I'm wrong to even think that of him. His face is an open book, devastation written on every page. Tears run down his cheeks as he cradles the body of a boy a few years older than Tommy and lays him out as carefully as if he were a baby.

No, he didn't know. Primo tricked us both. Anders was an officer, after all, like Rogue. They were trained to follow, not lead; to kill, not to plot and plan. He's smart, but he doesn't have Primo's cunning.

But I should have seen through this. *I* should have realized that it all seemed too simple. There's no one I can blame for this but myself.

I wonder what his next play will be, because there will be one. He won't give up until we're dead or surrender to his command. And a small, traitorous part of me wonders if, perhaps, surrendering wouldn't be so bad. Surely it's better to live than to die.

But a life under his rule would be no life at all. It would be worse than being a hobie on the street, worse than the harshest gang rule.

Heavy footsteps come to a halt in front of me. Scuffed, worn boots, laced tight up bulging calves. My heart sinks.

I force myself to my feet, not letting the pain this causes show on my face. The leader of the Bigland Boys looks smug, as well he might.

I've never had much to do with the Bigland Boys before and have to search for his name. Denzel, I think. He's a big man in his late twenties. Acne dots his pudgy cheeks and his clothing is encrusted with dirt as well as blood. For an Outsider he's huge, but next to Anders, Rogue and the other Metz officers, he looks almost average.

"Were you the leader around 'ere?" He looks me up and down disparagingly.

"I *am* the leader around here." I meet his gaze steadily. We both know he was waiting on the sidelines until there was no chance of him losing. Still, I wonder what the price of his help will be. "Thanks for lending a hand."

He grins wolfishly. "Don't want them lot taking over our patch." He twirls a thin blade expertly between his fingers. "But I do believe you owe us. We could do with a bit of extra muscle. And some new girls." He eyes me again.

I resist the urge to bring my knee up between his legs.

"Primo escaped," I say through gritted teeth. "Which means you still have a problem."

"Oh?"

"He's still leader until someone challenges him."

The blade stops spinning. "Or until he dies."

"You don't have the people to attack the Snakes' HQ. Besides,

Primo would see you coming a mile off. He's not like the other gang leaders – you can't try a full-force attack and you can't outwit him. Face it, he's smarter than you."

His face turns ugly and he raises the hand holding the knife. "What are you suggesting?"

"Getting rid of Primo is the priority. Chop the head off and the body will crumble. It would be better for you – better for the Boys – if things return to how they were before. If you force us to join you, that's not going to happen. Plus you'll end up with people who don't want to follow you. Chances are you'll either lose them, or one of them will get leadership ideas of their own."

He doesn't like that. "Yeah, but I don't see what yer goin' to do about it."

I shrug. "As I said, Primo's only leader 'til someone challenges him."

He stares at me blankly for a moment, then throws his head back and laughs. It's a snorting, snuffling laugh, like his nose is blocked. "You? Beat that monster?" He wipes his eyes. "Go ahead. It's your funeral. If you can injure him a bit before he kills you, perhaps one of us fighters will have a chance."

As his laughter dies away, I can see him thinking it through, mulling that possibility over. Perhaps he's seeing himself at the head of two of the three gangs in Area Four.

That's right, think about the power that would give you, the possibilities.

Finally, he nods. "Fine. You lot can stay here for now. But remember, you owe me one."

He turns and stalks off, calling to his boys to follow him.

I let out a breath and my shoulders sag. As long as he doesn't see us as a threat, that buys us some time.

This can't go on.

* * *

Rogue finds me sitting with the dead in the crypt of the church. The room is long and thin, with a low, curved roof, reminding me a little of the tunnels Trey and I had explored when we'd broken into the government headquarters.

It's cool down here. Candles burn at intervals, but their yellow light can't warm the waxy faces of the people laid out in front of me. There are twelve of them – eight of mine plus four monks who'd died defending their home. The monks brought them down here after the fighting, washed the bodies and laid them out. Tomorrow we'll decide what to do with them.

They're arranged roughly in order of age. The youngest is a boy with dirty blond hair and an angular face that has seen too few proper meals. I don't remember his name.

He died because of me and I can't even remember his name.

What kind of leader does that make me?

Rogue sits down beside me. For a moment, neither of us speaks.

"How's your shoulder?" I ask finally.

"Painful, but much better now it's back in place." He grimaces. "I've never felt pain like it. Even missed my Metz suit for a bit. Get injured in it and you'd get a stim shot and painkiller before the pain even hit."

"Has Amber arrived?"

"Here before Tommy could even get out the door. I think she heard what was going on and was just waiting until the fighting had stopped." He glances over at me. "Abby's here too. She's been asking for you."

I nod. "Good. They should be able to fix people up."

Those who are still alive.

The silence between us drags on.

"Anders told me about the plan," Rogue says. "It was a good plan. It should have worked."

"Primo saw through it. He *planned* it that way. I should have known ..."

A pause.

"Anders blames himself, you know. You should go and talk to him."

"And what good would that do?"

Rogue sighs. "It would make him feel better." He gives me a sideways glance. "You're our leader. You can't hide down here forever."

"Perhaps I shouldn't be the leader. I didn't *ask* to be. And so far, all I've done is fail you all and get people killed." I scratch at the stone floor with my nail. "You could lead them better than me."

Rogue shakes his head. "No."

"Danny, then. He was one of Jay's seconds."

"Danny doesn't have the strength."

"He—"

"I mean the mental strength, Aleesha." Rogue's voice has a rough edge to it. He takes a deep breath. "You may not want to lead this group but you *are* the leader. Everyone looks to you. *I* look to you."

He turns to face me and I smell the soap on his freshly scrubbed face. "You freed us. For some of us, that was too much to come to terms with." He hesitates for a second. "Not everyone wants to be free and to have to accept what they might have done. But for me ..." His hand closes over mine. It feels warm, comforting. "You made me remember what it is to feel joy and sadness, and anger and pain. It's confusing, and sometimes I don't know how to respond to these emotions."

I shift uneasily, remembering the last time we had spoken and fearing what he'd been about to say. It must be overwhelming to go from feeling nothing to feeling everything.

"Don't think too badly of the officers who stayed with Primo. I … I think most of them are good people. But having all these memories of our lives and what we've done forced on us, well, it's a lot to come to terms with."

"Amber said that they … you … might have mental trauma." I stare down at our clasped hands, not wanting to ask the question but needing an answer. "Was I right to free you?"

Rogue runs his thumb gently along mine. His touch makes me want to lean into him and, at the same time, pull away.

"I wouldn't want to go back to feeling nothing," he says quietly.

My hand tingles, sending a shiver up my arm.

"Did you feel that? Like electricity running over my skin."

I nod, my mouth suddenly dry.

"When I'm around you, I feel warm inside. And when you're angry at me, there's an ache in here." He places his other hand on his chest. "I remember my mother telling me off when I was a boy, and it feels a bit like that, but different." He frowns and turns to me. "I'm not explaining myself very well, am I? I guess I was wondering … is this love?"

I don't know how to answer him. Don't know whether I should pull my hand away or let it stay there, covered by his. Like a child, he wears his emotions on his face for all the world to see. Whereas I keep everything locked inside.

If I'm honest, I don't know the answer to his question. There's a physical attraction between us, but that's all it is, I think. Like a ripple that moves the surface of the water but can't affect the deep swirling currents underneath.

But does he feel more? Does he even know what he's feeling?

I try and remember how I felt about my mother before she left, but it's a distant childhood memory. After that, there was just darkness, coldness, survival. Until Jay. But even then, what I had with Jay was not love. Attraction, yes. Fondness even and an element of mutual respect. But he only found love when he found Beth.

And what about Trey?

I push that thought away, realizing that Rogue is still waiting for an answer. "Well, I guess you must have loved your mother, that's why you felt hurt when you disappointed her. But that's not the same as, um, loving someone in a relationship way."

Heat rushes to my cheeks. This isn't a conversation I was planning on having.

"And then there's physical attraction, which is different to love. Like …"

Like what I feel around you.

I give up trying to explain.

Rogue's face wrinkles. "So how do you know which one you feel?"

I sigh and look away. "With love … Well, I think that when you experience that, you'll know what it is."

"Do you love Trey?"

Irritation flashes through me and I pull my hand away. "It's complicated."

Rogue turns away but not before I catch the look of hurt on his face. His hand lies open on the stone slab, where it fell. I take it and give it a squeeze. "I guess trying to figure out all these feelings must be difficult?"

He gives a wry smile. "Yeah, it is."

"You know, you can care about someone as a friend without being in love with them," I say quietly. "And friendship is just as strong and important as love. Did you have many friends at the compound?"

"I think I had friends when we were training. But when we became officers everything was erased. Memories, feelings, friendship. They told us we were family. But I don't remember ever feeling what I feel now. This … being here …" He shakes his head and looks down. "It probably sounds crazy, but this feels more like having a family than I ever remember feeling before."

I open my mouth, then close it again. He's right. The gangs have always been a family for those who have had none. A tough family, for sure, but still, there's always been a bond between members of a gang. Loyalty to their leader, even if that leader doesn't deserve their loyalty. That's why I never really felt at home in the Snakes before – never really felt as if I was one of them.

But now, perhaps, I have the chance to build a new family.

We sit in silence, hand in hand, each lost in our own thoughts.

"You should go and see Abby," he says after a while. "There may even be water to wash – if Tommy hasn't used it all." He shakes his head. "I've never known anyone take such delight in *water*."

"That's because you've never gone thirsty. Or had to choose between drinking and washing."

He frowns. "I don't understand why there isn't fresh water out here. I mean, there's plenty of it Inside. And we have the technology to hold rainwater and purify it."

"If that's the case, Insiders don't like to share with us."

Another pause.

"Do you know much about Primo? Who he is, where he comes from?"

Rogue shakes his head. "No, I'm not sure anyone does. From what I remember of the compound, we didn't see the captains when we weren't on duty. We didn't even talk to each other that much. Work, train, eat, sleep – that was our lives." He shrugs. "I don't know if Primo was any better or worse than the other captains. But he's the only one who chose to stay out here."

I stare at the body of a young dark-haired woman dressed in the black officers' suit. *She died for us. For Outsiders. Because she believed what the Metz had done was wrong.*

"Did you see the leader of the Bigland Boys'?"

Rogue nods and wrinkles his nose. "Seemed like a nasty piece of work."

"He's fairly typical of the gang leaders out here. Those who are stronger rise to the top. But you have to be smart too, or at least, smarter than the other people around you. Maybe tronk has something to do with that. The stronger you are, the more you can fight for better food – the stuff the government haven't drugged. Maybe it gives you an advantage."

"Tronk is a drug?"

"Yes." I suddenly wish I hadn't brought it up. My fingers curl into a fist. Rogue must feel me tense as he flashes me a puzzled look. "Anyway, my point is, life in the gangs is bad. Most of the time you're fighting others to curry favour with the leaders. As a woman, it's even worse. You're not seen as a proper gang member, most of the time, just a tool for pleasure. Though one of the gangs does now have a woman as their leader – she challenged and won the fight. So maybe things are changing.

"But even in the gangs, people care about something. They'll fight for their leader or their mate, or to defend their girl. They care about eating and keeping the Metz away. Some of them have families outside the gang that they look after with whatever chits and food they can scrounge. But Primo … he doesn't seem to care about *anything*. And that's what's so scary. There's nothing we can threaten him with. I … I don't know how he can be beaten."

Rogue squeezes my hand gently. "There's always a way."

I climb the steps behind him, taking one last look at the bodies lying in their stone coffin. Something wrenches inside me. My family. And I let them die.

I can't let that happen again.

24

Trey

I leave work early the next day and take the pod back Inside. The air in the streets is stifling and I'm sweating by the time I reach Milicent's house, despite my heat-regulating clothes. Summer has barely started and already I'm longing for the rains to come again.

Milicent's waiting for me in the large sitting room at the back of the house. I walk to the window and look out over the garden. A monkey puzzle tree towers over smaller shrubs and a pair of gnarled apple trees. Birds flutter to the feeders that hang from their branches.

"I take it from your message that you found something that couldn't wait until tomorrow?" she asks, joining me.

I'd comm'd her that morning using the code phrase we'd agreed and she'd invited me round to dinner. "Yes. We had a visit from quality control yesterday. Some ingredient has been missing from the production line for the past few weeks. We can't sell the food without it so they ordered us to throw it away, but I managed to persuade Louis to store it for a few weeks. Do you think there's any way we can get it Outside? I'm sure it's perfectly good and there must be a fair bit of it. It'll keep too, even in this heat, as most of it's dehydrated. We could give it to some of the children's homes or the hobies on the streets."

As soon as I'd got into the office this morning, I'd messaged Louis to remind him what we'd agreed. To my surprise, a holo message popped up from him a few minutes later saying he'd already instructed someone to deal with it. He looked remarkably chirpy given how much he drank last night. Barnes had nodded stiffly when I'd told her that someone from Distribution would be getting in touch to remove the low-grade products and had completely ignored me for the rest of the day.

"Perhaps." Milicent looks thoughtful. "Though it would be a drop in the ocean really. And we wouldn't want to risk them finding out about us – not if we have a chance of accessing the distribution centres."

I bite my lip, feeling a little disheartened at her lack of enthusiasm. "I managed to access a map of the distribution centres on Louis's computer."

Her eyes light up. "That's more like it." She walks briskly over to a low table, beckoning me to follow. The marble tabletop disappears to reveal a standard black holo table. Milicent brings up a map of the city and smiles at my look of surprise. "I may be old and like old things, but I'm not a total luddite. Now, how much can you remember?"

I spend the next ten minutes attempting to recreate the distribution map on the holo. It's tricky – the base map of buildings is different to the outline map that had been on Louis's computer and my memory of it isn't as clear as I'd thought. After a while, I straighten. "I think the details for these ones here in the east part of the city are all correct." I indicate the scrawled figures next to distribution centres in Areas Three, Four and

Five. "The others I'm not totally sure about. There's at least one centre in each area, more in the bigger areas."

"That's very helpful. We know where most of them are – they're well defended for one thing – but knowing the access codes is key."

I hesitate. "Are you thinking of trying to take one over?"

"Possibly. It could be an option." She doesn't sound very convinced. "If you're able to access Louis's computer again, grab some images so we can complete the picture. But only if it's safe for you to do so. Did you find out any more about the Coleman family?"

"Louis said his grandfather still holds the reins, even though he's supposed to be retired. He lives with his brother in some country house in Kent. I didn't realize anyone actually lived down there."

Milicent stares out the window. "If you have a private pod it makes a change from the city. My parents used to have a place out there where we retreated to during the Flood."

"The Great Flood?"

I didn't realize she was *that* old.

"Yes ... I was a young girl at the time. It wasn't safe in London – wasn't safe anywhere really, but we managed."

She seems about to say something more when there's a knock on the door and the butler announces that dinner is ready.

We eat in silence, but after the butler clears the plates away I ask Milicent the question that's been on my mind since we last spoke. "I tried looking up the Rose Rebellion but couldn't find any mention of it in historical records or records of significant events."

Her lips tighten into a thin line. "You're unlikely to find the truth in official records. It was all covered up, a bit of an embarrassment really, to most people."

"But not to you?"

She places her coffee cup carefully down on its saucer. "I was proud of my son, Trey. He was a good man and tried to do the right thing."

I get the sense that she doesn't want to talk about it, but I press her anyway. "You said last time that he died. That they all died. What *happened*? What was the Rose Rebellion?"

We sit in silence for a moment. Milicent takes another sip of her coffee. When she places her cup back down, it clatters slightly against the saucer.

"William fell in love with a girl called Rose," she says eventually. "She was a sweet girl, polite, pretty. But she was an Outsider. Relationships between Insiders and Outsiders today are discouraged, but back then they were forbidden. Any Insider who showed any intention of marrying an Outsider was thrown Outside the Wall and left to fend for themselves." She lets out a small sigh. "And perhaps if that was all William wanted, he would have lived. As an Outsider of course, but at least he would have lived."

There's another silence. "So what happened?" I venture.

"He didn't like what he saw and got this notion into his head that society was wrong. He felt that the Wall should never have been put up in the first place and that we were just using it as a barrier so we could ignore what went on outside it. Which was quite true, I suppose, but you couldn't *say* things like that then." She takes another sip of coffee. "You still can't now, really, not unless you want to get a visit from the Metz. But William was never one to stay silent. And he was quite the orator – got all his friends riled up and formed an organization they called the 'People's Alliance'. His father and I warned him to drop it. His father even threatened to cut him off financially, but William didn't care. He was so *passionate,* both about Rose and his cause.

"He had several warnings from the government, which he ignored. We even had a Metz raid here one night when he was away, but they didn't find anything. My husband nearly lost his job because of it. But it all came to a head when Rose was caught. They charged her with plotting to overthrow the government and a few other things and executed her. That's where Rose Square got its name from – the Outsiders named it after her. I think they meant it as a warning for William and his friends. But if anything, it made William madder. He was crazy about Rose, and after her death, well, I think he possibly lost his mind a bit."

A solitary tear trickles from the corner of her eye but she doesn't appear to notice. I shift in my chair, her distress making me uncomfortable. She seems frozen in a past she can't escape.

After a long minute, she sniffs and dabs at her cheek with a napkin. "Oh dear, I am melancholy today. But when you've lost a child, the pain never really goes away. Anyway, to finish the story, William rallied his friends to fight against the government in Rose's name. They called on Outsiders to join them, to rise up against oppression." She sighs. "All that foolish stuff that young people believe. I think they were planning to assassinate the President while he was giving his mid-year speech, but something went wrong. The Metz were waiting. They tried to fight their way out – they'd managed to get guns and some grenades – but they didn't have a chance. They shot them all, right there in the park where the President was due to speak. No trial, no chance of escape. The fires burned the bodies and a good part of the city. The government said later that the rebels had started the fires and they were too busy trying to stop them to extinguish the flames. But there's no way they could have done so much damage. The next year they built a new apartment block on top of the park. There was never even a memorial to them. And that was the failed Rose Rebellion."

She pushes back her chair and stands, placing a hand on her stomach. "Now, if you'll excuse me, I'm afraid I need to retire for the evening. The rich food, you know."

I stand, not sure what to say. But as she reaches the door, I find my voice. "I'm sorry. About your son and his friends. I always wondered why you were helping the Chain. Thank you for telling me."

Milicent pauses and turns toward me, a faint smile on her face. "It was the one thing I could do for him – finish his work. It's been decades since he died, but I hope I'll see the London he dreamed of before I die."

She leaves, closing the door behind her.

So that's what happens when Insiders try to help Outsiders. I think of Ella's demands for me to introduce her to the Brotherhood, of her friends who want to help, and for once, I know I've done the right thing. At least I can protect her – them – from getting involved in something they don't understand.

* * *

"Barnes has just called up to say you're needed on the floor," Emilie says, smiling her thanks as I hand her a mug of coffee. "Some delivery that needs signing for?"

I nod and take a gulp of the tea I'd made for myself before setting it on my desk and heading back out the door.

One of the white-suited technicians directs me all the way to the back of the factory floor. It's a five-minute walk through the production lines that chop, shape and package the fake meat, and past the humming dehydrators that suck the moisture from the long-life products. I find Barnes with a stiff-faced man who's clutching a small box to his chest as if afraid Barnes is going to grab it from him. She stands with her arms folded, one foot tapping a rhythm on the floor.

"Sorry to drag you out here, Mr Goldsmith," she says as I approach them. "But apparently, *you* have to sign for this delivery." She shoots the man a look that is pure poison. "I did tell him you were busy and that it's usually the foreman's job to take in deliveries, but he insisted."

A muscle twitches in the man's cheek. "Please press your hand here, sir." He nods to a data pad set into the box. I press the back of my hand to it to let it scan my chip. There's a bleep and a small green light blinks twice. "Thank you, sir."

He hands the box to me. "It's programmed for you to open and close it. No one else." His eyes flick to Barnes. "Someone will be back to collect the empty box this afternoon."

"Thank you."

The man nods and turns to leave.

"I guess this is the missing androcibus nanite," I say, looking for a label on the box.

"Must be." Barnes's voice is oddly tight.

I glance up at her. "Look, if you're worried about calling me down here, don't be. Stands to reason they want me to sign for it. That's my job, right? To keep them off your back."

The smile falls from my face; Barnes looks anxious. She glances around to check there's no one about, then steps closer so that we're almost touching. "The data pad should tell you what's inside. Here, let me hold it for you." She grips the edge of the box and adds in an undertone. "I need to talk to you."

My pulse quickens. *So she does know something.*

But they'll be cameras watching us, voice recorders tuned to pick up our words over the background hum of the dehydrators. "Why don't you show me where this stuff needs to go," I say, locking eyes with her.

She nods and drops her hands from the box, then turns to lead the way. She doesn't take the shortest route to the vats but weaves through the humming dehydrators until she reaches one that is making a loud rattling noise.

Barnes pauses and steps close, pointing up at the towering silver box, which seems to be trembling ever so slightly. "I was about to shut this one off when the delivery man came. Bloody thing's malfunctioning again."

It's certainly noisier than the usual low hum. Which, I realize with a start, is why she's brought me here.

"I don't think we should add the nanite to the line. I think it's—"

She breaks off at the sound of running footsteps. A dark-haired female technician rounds the corner of the dehydrator, panting. "Quality control … here," she gasps.

Already I can hear the click-clicking of heels getting closer.

I curse inwardly and lean in closer to Barnes, whispering urgently. "What do you mean? Is it poisonous?"

Her eyes flick to the technician, then back to me. "Not exactly. I don't know. I—"

"Mr Goldsmith." The clicking heels stop.

I straighten and turn around, the box still in my hands. "Ann. I didn't expect to see you again so soon. Is there another problem?"

Her dark hair is pulled back into that same tight knot that seems to pull her skin back from her face, making her sharp nose and cheekbones even more prominent.

"It's Miss Davies," she says curtly, eyeing the box in my hands. "And there's no problem. I was just coming to check the androcibus nanite was inserted into the system correctly." She raises the data pad in her hand and gives a cold smile. "Final checks so that I can close off the issue."

Right. My mind races, trying to find a way out of this situation. But I can't. She's going to be watching us like a hawk, every step of the way.

I plaster a smile onto my face. "Well, we were just on our way to do that, if you'd like to follow us."

Barnes falls into step beside me but I dare not speak or make any other acknowledgement as I know Ann Davies is behind us, watching.

The vats of lower-grade meat are clustered at the back of the factory floor. Each vat is part of a series of tanks that grow in size. In the first, the muscle cells are grown in a nutrient-rich serum; in the second, the cells form strips that are then attached to a scaffold in the main tank; it's in this tank the muscle tissue is stretched to increase its size. Barnes stops at the main tank.

She types a command into the screen set into the tank and a mechanical arm swivels from the vat, lowering in increments until the end of it is at chest height. A box extends from the end of the arm.

"They bolted this on to add the androcibus nanite into the nutrient mix," Barnes says, pulling a screwdriver from her belt and using it to turn a screw on either side of the box. "If this is going to be a permanent addition to the recipe, we could do with coming up with a better system."

"And what makes you think it isn't going to be a permanent addition?"

Barnes gives the woman a sardonic smile. "Well, I thought you might be testing it in these vats before adding it to the rest." She shrugs. "I don't know how these things work. My job is to keep these lines running and this is an inefficiency in the system, that's all."

"Noted," I say as Miss Davies opens her mouth to reply. "I'll discuss it with Phillips."

I place the box I'm carrying on the floor and press my hand to the pad to open it. There's a click and the lid splits in two, both sides pulling back to reveal the contents. Inside is a set of vials, capped and laid out in neat rows. There are twenty-eight altogether.

"Four weeks' supply?"

Barnes nods. "One vial is injected into the nutrient mix every day."

"And they're all full?" Ann Davies peers over my shoulder into the box.

"If they aren't, then it's nothing to do with us," I reply, a trace of irritation entering my voice.

I take a deep breath. *Don't let her get to you.*

Barnes hands me a pair of thin gloves. "It'll be quicker with two of us. You need to remove the cap from each vial and place it in here." She indicates to the empty cage system in the metal box.

I follow her instructions, and a few minutes later all twenty-eight vials have been transferred from the box to the machine. I close and seal the box and Barnes does the same with the container. She types a command on the screen and the metal arm rises and clicks back into place.

I straighten and turn to Miss Davies, who is typing something into her data pad. "All done. Is there anything else you need to see?"

She looks up. "No, that will be fine. We will, of course, be testing the products that come off the line to make sure the nanite is being inserted correctly."

The warning hangs in the air.

I incline my head toward her. "Of course. Let me see you out." I gesture for her to lead off down the line of vats. But before I turn to follow, I catch Barnes's eye. "Later," I mouth silently.

She ducks her head briefly before turning back to the vat.

Back in my office, I sink down in my chair. "That woman is …" I bite my tongue, remembering that *they* are probably recording everything I say.

"Ann Davies?" Emilie grimaces. "I went to school with one of her assistants. Sandy's only been there a couple of months but she's desperate for a transfer." She comes over and hands me a thin packet. "This came while you were out."

I turn the packet over in my hands. It's got my name on it, but no other indication of what it is or who it's from. When I don't immediately open it, Emilie returns to her desk.

I wait until she leaves the room, then press my chip to the seal and pull it open. A transparent sheath spills out onto the desk followed by a tiny golden chip and a thin piece of film with a few words scrawled on it.

Figured you might need the chip too. Tomorrow, 10 pm at The Flower Garden, off Primrose Square, Area Six.

Louis had been as good as his word. I wipe the film, shove the chip blocker and chip back into the packet and put it in my pocket, glad it's nearly the end of the day. Finally, I can go and see my friends.

25

Aleesha

"Oww!"

"Sorry," Abby murmurs, dabbing at a long slash on my side.

"If I didn't know better, I'd think you were doing it deliberately," I mutter under my breath. "Is that alcohol?"

"Yup, acts as an antiseptic. We only had a few packets of the anti-infection pills and they've gone to people worse off than you."

"So I get to smell like a drunken hobie?"

"You've smelled worse."

I scowl at Abby's smile. "Why isn't it healed yet?"

"Because it was a deep cut and it's only been two days. Have patience. You got off lightly compared to some."

We both turn to look at the two beds that are curtained off from the rest of the room by a pair of sheets hung from the ceiling. There are a couple of former Metz officers still cooped up in the room Amber had claimed as a makeshift hospital and an older man who's been in the Snakes for years. The three of them grumble and moan, but no noises come from the beds in the corner.

"How are they doing?" I whisper.

"Not great. I think Adi might pull through despite losing his leg, but Krishna has internal injuries. Without a medic unit ..." Her voice trails off but I can read between her words. Abby's medicines and skills can help heal minor injuries, but it's not the same as proper drugs and the medic units Insiders have that can cut a person apart and sew them back together good as new.

I try and bring their faces to mind. They'd been friends of Vihaan, once, had the same light brown skin and dark hair that so many people in that part of Four have. But they'd left Vihaan to follow me.

"I'll stay here and do what I can for them at least," Abby says. "It's pretty quiet up in Five at the moment, and Bryn knows where to find me if I'm needed. Amber has a much busier job down here trying to keep up with the fights and birthings in Three and Four."

A cough from behind makes me start. Abby stiffens, then pulls away. In the doorway stands my father. He surveys the makeshift hospital, a disparaging look on his face.

I stand, trying not to wince as aches and pains shoot through my body, and walk over to him.

"What are you doing here?"

"I came to talk to you. Though it looks as if you might need my help." He waves a hand around.

"Your help would have been more useful a few days ago." My voice is bitter. I peer around him. "Is Katya with you?"

"No." His voice is placid. "But I do have a portable medic unit waiting out front."

Abby's head snaps up. "You have a medic unit?" Hope lights up her eyes. She looks to me, a trace of a plea in her voice. "It could save them, Aleesha."

Even now, I hesitate, not wanting to accept his help. But I can't let any more of them die. "Of course," I manage. "A medic unit would be great."

My father nods and beckons for me to follow him. We walk down the corridor to the main entrance to the church. Two men I don't recognize stand by the door. They're dressed in combat gear and hold large guns. My father nods to them and they pull back the doors.

I gasp. Outside the church, about a dozen men and women, all dressed in the same combat gear and holding the same weapons as the men by the door, stand around what looks like a small pod hovering a metre or so off the ground.

"Bring it in!"

The team parts to let through the pod. A woman with pale skin, black hair and hooded eyes walks up the steps into the church, the pod floating behind her.

"You won't make it into the hospital room, Mika," my father says to her. "Leave it here and bring people to it. They're in the second room on the left." He points down the corridor. "Lady named Abby is in charge."

"Yes, sir." The woman gives him a nod and me a curious look before heading off down the corridor. The rest of the team have fanned out into a semi-circle outside the church entrance, all facing out.

"Walk with me."

I'm not sure if it's a request or a command, but I follow him all the same, down the steps, through the line of guards and around the side of the church into the graveyard.

"I think I owe you an apology," he says finally. "When I first saw you, it was a shock, to say the least. You probably don't know this, but outside of this country, I'm quite well-known. Famous, you might say. And I have money, which can attract the wrong kind of attention. I've had all kinds of kids come up to me, claiming I'm their father. Assuming that because I'm rich and often have an attractive woman on my arm, I'll sleep with anyone. Some of them want attention, but most just want money. There's still a lot of poverty in the world."

I study the ground around us, not sure what to say. He stops and turns to me.

"I swear if I'd known … If I'd had any idea that Maria had had a child, I would never have left you here." He raises a hand to life my chin, forcing me to meet his gaze. "I can't turn back time, or change what's been done in the past. But if I can make up for it now, I will."

I tear my eyes away and jerk my head back, embarrassed by the intensity of his words and intimidated by the power that radiates off him. He doesn't *feel* like my father. I always thought I'd know, when I met him, that I'd feel something inside. But his touch feels strange and unfamiliar.

I continue walking.

"What's it like, in the world outside?"

He chuckles.

Why is that such an amusing question?

He catches the scowl on my face and his laughter dies, his face sober again. "I'm sorry. I wasn't laughing at you. It just seems crazy that you know nothing of the world. Britannia has isolated itself for decades, and in the meantime, the world around you has grown and developed. There are cities with buildings that make the tallest of your glass towers look like matchsticks. I can travel halfway across the world in the time it would take one of your pods to cross the city. And outside the cities, there are still snow-capped mountains that stretch into the sky, hot jungles full of life and vast deserts devoid of life."

He points up at the sky. "Half the stars you see are not stars at all but satellites and space stations. The colony on the moon is making progress and there are plans to begin terraforming Mars."

My mouth falls open. "People live on the *moon*?"

"Yes." He grins. "I can take you there, if you'd like. Earth looks so beautiful from space."

I sink down on a nearby bench. My world is no more than a few square miles. It's all I've ever known. And he comes here talking of cities and deserts and space. Space! My fingers curl into a ball and I hug my knees to my chest, suddenly feeling very small indeed.

My father sits down beside me, looking worried. "Have I said something wrong?"

I shake my head, unable to speak.

He reaches out and tentatively rests a hand on my shoulder. "You don't have to live here anymore. I'll pay for you to go to school. In Paris maybe, or Stockholm – it's cooler up there in summer. I've got apartments in most cities that you can stay in …" His voice trails off uncertainly.

An apartment. School. Safety. Everything I'd dreamed of on those nights I'd sat up on my rooftop, staring at the tops of the glass towers Inside and fantasizing that one day I would live there. He's offering me everything I've ever wanted.

But is it still what you want?

I try and push away the voice in my head but it niggles at me, refusing to budge.

Would you leave them all behind? Run away to pretend at being an Insider?

Who would blame me? I owe them nothing. All these years I have struggled. And now, a door opens to a new life, a better life. The life my mother would have wanted me to have. A life in which I wouldn't have to worry about getting enough clean water to drink and food to eat. A life in which I could truly leave the past behind.

You can never truly leave it behind. The past is what made you who you are. If you leave, nothing here will change.

"What about my gang? Primo's taken over ... He's destroying Four."

My father pulls back in surprise. "That crazy Metz officer?" He shrugs. "I'll get my team to get rid of him if you want."

My pulse quickens. He makes it sound as easy as swatting a fly.

"How?" I manage.

"I had to leave my larger weapons behind – only just managed to smuggle the medic pod in – but my teams are still well-armed. Your weapons are antiquated compared to what's available now. We'd storm the building, probably at night to minimize casualties on our side."

"On your side? What about them?"

He shrugs again. "Depends how much they resist."

My mind works through the scenario. They'd blow open the doors, or smash the skylights perhaps. Armed men and women in combat gear running through the headquarters. Confusion and chaos. People running, reacting by instinct to defend themselves. People being shot, the screams of the injured, the silence of the dead.

Primo wouldn't stand a chance ... would he?

But if there's one thing I've learned, it's not to underestimate him. He's cunning enough to escape any situation and wouldn't hesitate to get others killed doing so.

I look down at my hands. "That's not how things are really done out here."

"Well, we could just blow up the whole building. But I'd rather not. Don't want to give away our tricks before the main battle."

"The main battle?"

"We came here to take down the government. To transform this city into a modern democracy."

I remember what Bryn had said to me, after Andrew Goldsmith's death. *For the Leader, this was never just about the city. London is personal. This was personal.*

"To transform the city or get revenge for my mother's death? Which would you put first?" I ask.

"What's that supposed to mean?"

I look at him steadily. "You know what it means."

Irritation flickers in his eyes, then he looks away, letting his hand fall from my shoulder. "Look, do you want my help or not?"

I let my feet drop to the floor and stand, stretching my sore back. "I'll think about it."

My father raises an eyebrow. "Think about it? I offer you the life you want on a platter, everything money can buy and you want to *think* about it?"

I can sense the anger and confusion building in him. *Perhaps we're not so different after all.*

"Yes. This is a lot to take in and I'm tired. I had friends die today. I need some time to think."

He nods, tight-lipped. "Fine. I'll leave a team with you to guard the building. None of you are in any state to defend yourselves."

I bite back the refusal that jumps to my lips, knowing that

he's right. We do need his help.

"Thank you," I manage. I take a deep breath, trying to banish thoughts of apartments and food and fine clothes and bring myself back to reality.

* * *

"I really think this is a bad idea," Rogue says, surveying the open space in front of us.

"Shut up. You don't know who might be listenin' round 'ere." Danny's eyes are constantly on the move. He's trying to hide his nerves, but his shoulders are tense and his knuckles pale as he grips the thick, nailed club in his hand.

His fear is well-founded. Even the gangs stay away from the concrete jungle and the people who live in it. And when people do venture into it, they don't always return.

Rogue twitches, sensing Danny's fear. "Remind me what we're doing here, again?"

"I need to speak to a friend. He may be able to help us."

"An' what will he ask for in return? Makin' a bargain with these lot is askin' to have your throat slit."

"They're not all like the Boots Brothers."

"No, some of 'em are worse."

Rogue looks from Danny to me, his eyes wide in the dim light of dusk. I'd asked them to come with me, partly so they don't think I've run off again, and partly to help me deal with any trouble we run into. I might have saved the Boots Brother from the Metz officer who attacked them, but I'm under no illusion that they'd repay the favour.

Tension thickens the air around us, seeping through my skin and chilling my bones. "Come on, it's about dark enough. If someone is looking out for us, they'll be able to see us anyway with that moon."

"That's what I'm worried about," Danny mutters under his breath.

We cross the open area between the rows of half-derelict buildings and the pile of rubble quickly and silently. Rogue's shadow looms in front of us. Having him and Danny with me makes me feel safer, but I hope that having three of us rather than one doesn't just make us a more tempting target.

"Wait here," I whisper as we reached the first of the concrete blocks.

"Not likely," Danny replies, hauling himself onto the first block after me.

"You don't know your way through here and it's loose underfoot. Don't be an idiot, I'll be fine from here."

Somewhere to our right, a stone falls, collecting others as it tumbles before it hisses to a stop. Rogue tightens his grip on the baton he took from one of Primo's men. "You sure about that?"

"Fine. Just follow exactly where I go and don't kick any rocks down. We don't want to draw attention to ourselves."

To their credit, they do just that. Even Rogue steps from rock to rock with a lightness that I wouldn't have expected given his size. I hold up a hand when we get nearer to the entrance to Giles's home. "Wait here."

The tunnel is black compared to the moonlit night outside and I feel my way along slowly, waiting to see if my eyes adjust to the dark. I find the drop-off, and lower myself down feet first.

"What are you doing here?"

The voice makes me start, and I'm glad it's dark so he can't see my surprise. At least, I don't think he can see in the dark. With Giles, I never really know.

"Can I come in?"

He hisses in reply and for a moment I think he's going to refuse. But then a light comes on further down the tunnel and I see him silhouetted in the doorway, holding the heavy curtain aside for me.

My eyes water as they adjust to the brightness and I look around Giles's home. It looks the same as last time I was here, though the pile of gadgets and tools on the table has spilled onto the floor.

Giles is hunched over, his eyes red-rimmed with dark bags underneath that stand out against his chalk-white skin. He's holding a small ball of putty and rolls it over and over in his hand, his fingers constantly reshaping it.

"What do you want?"

"Are you okay, Giles? You look sick." I glance over at the bench that forms a makeshift kitchen but can't see any sign of food. "Have you been eating?"

He ignores the question and stares at me almost malevolently. "What do you want, Aleesha?" He extends the vowels in my name and I wonder if he really is sick or if I've just come at a bad time.

Perhaps I should just go. But not if there's any chance he can help us.

"Do you know what's going on outside, in the rest of Area Four? One of the Metz captains, Primo, h—"

"I've seen." His fingers pinch the putty, blood draining from them as the putty squeezes out between them. "You were supposed to protect them."

"I tried, Giles. I thought it was the right thing to do, giving them a choice about their future. I didn't realize this would happen." I stare down at the floor. "I thought they would be grateful."

"You made them face who they really are."

He turned his back on me and shuffles across to the table. Sticking the putty against one of the legs, he begins to sort through the junk piled on top of it.

"Did you know Primo? From your time in the Metz compound?"

His hand freezes on top of a small metal lockbox.

"Do you not find it interesting that he's named himself Primo?"

I'm taken aback by the question. "I don't know. Does it mean something?"

"Primo, from the Latin *primus*, meaning 'first'." Giles places the lockbox carefully on the floor. He seems calmer now. "Yet, when he was a Metz captain he was X4, not X1."

"That's what Rogue said. That he was the captain of the fourth unit. But why wouldn't he just use the name he had before he became an officer?"

"He may not have had one, or at least, not one that he wanted. Did you know that most of the officers who become captains were either born in the Metz compound or taken as babies? It's what makes them so committed to the Metz cause, unquestioning of their role in society and what they have to do. They are bought up as killing machines. They don't know any other world, any other way to be."

I stare at him. "But they must have had friends, people to look after them when they were young. They must have known what it was to *feel* before they were implanted with the chip."

"Friends? No, they never had friends. Those who came when

they were older had friends but the Metz younglings were different. They didn't even have proper names – even then they were given a number." He opens a small box and begins to pick electronic chips from the table to pack into it. "The professor taught me that what we learn at a young age stays with us for life, that it shapes us into the person we become. That is why they treat them like that, and why it's usually only the younglings who become captains. Other officers may be strong enough and brave enough and have the leadership skills, but when they're faced with the facts of what they're being forced to do, even the strongest of them quails."

I walk over to the other side of the table. Giles gives me an agitated look and I hold my hands up. "What are you saying?"

"It was right to give the officers a choice, most of them at least. But the captains … The captains would never choose what you believe to be right. They are not really human, just weapons in human form. The government created them to be monsters, and you … You have let the monster loose."

"You're saying I could have stopped this? Why didn't you tell me this before?"

He jerks his head up, anger flashing in his eyes. "You can't expect me to think of everything, tell you every single thing I know in case you need the information."

I swallow down my irritation and eye the devices scattered across the room. Giles follows my gaze. "You came to find out if I could reverse it, didn't you?"

I nod.

His lips tighten to a thin line. "The answer is no … Or at least, not yet. I've been working on it night and day, but I still haven't figured it out."

Frustration echoes in his words as if he's personally affronted by this challenge to his intellect. And with his words, the tiny flame of hope that had flickered within me dies, leaving behind an emptiness I don't want to face.

I turn and walk away.

"Aleesha?"

I glance back at him. His face is twisted with indecision. He seems about to ask me something, but then his mouth snaps shut and he shakes his head.

"Good luck."

"Thanks." I step through the curtain and let it fall back behind me, cutting off the light.

I need more than luck to get rid of Primo now. I need a miracle.

26

Trey

As I push open the door of the underground bar, I immediately get the feeling that this is a place I don't belong. Music pumps from hidden speakers, almost deafening after the relative quiet of the alleyway outside, and coloured lights pulse across a deserted dancefloor.

Not the kind of place I imagine Barnes frequenting either. So why did she want to meet here?

The bouncer doesn't bother to check my chip, just frisks me for weapons and gives me a curious look. I guess I'm not their typical patron.

Half a dozen people sit on plastic chairs at tables scattered around the bar. There's no sign of Barnes.

I head to the bar and order a tonic water.

"You want that with gin or vodka?" the bartender asks. An intricately patterned skullcap is tattooed onto his shaven head, and his stocky build and black uniform makes me wonder if he doubles as a bouncer.

"No, j—" I catch the bartender's frown. "Gin, please."

He nods and makes my drink, adding ice and a twist of lime. I take it and walk over to a vacant table to wait.

I've finished my drink and am wondering if Barnes has stood me up when she walks in, nods to the bartender and heads straight over to sit down opposite me.

"Sorry to keep you. What are you drinking?"

I glance down at the slice of lime over a rapidly melting ice cube. "I'm fine."

She shrugs. "Suit yourself."

I lower my voice, though it's doubtful that anyone can hear us over the thumping tune blaring from the speakers. "What is this place?"

"Bar by day, club by night. A friend of mine owns it. It's popular with people who feel they don't fit in at the usual places." She eyes me. "Not the kind of place your lot come to, I bet?"

I'm saved from answering by the arrival of the bartender, who places a lurid green cocktail down on the table in front of Barnes. He looks at me quizzically. "You wanna refill?"

"No, thanks."

He nods and turns to Barnes. "Want me to put it on the boss's tab?"

She nods.

"His too?" He jerks his thumb in my direction.

"Better had. Thanks, Bobby."

The bartender ambles off.

"Who's your friend?"

Barnes flicks her fingers. "Oh, he's just a guy I've known for years. Owns a few of the clubs and entertainment centres out here."

I think for a minute. "So if these drinks are being paid for by your friend, they'll be no record that we were here?"

She smiles. "Exactly. Unless they're tracking you, obviously, but this place is underground, it disrupts the tracking signal.

Besides, we're in Area Six – even Insiders are allowed out here, right?"

I nod, belatedly realizing that I should probably be wearing the chip blocker Louis gave me.

"So have you always lived Outside?" I ask casually.

"Yes. Outsider born and bred."

Higher-class Outsider though. She's smart. Smarter than me, at a guess. The address on her file was in Area Seven, but I don't know if that's a good area or a bad area. I'll have to ask Aleesha next time I see her.

We fall into silence. Barnes seems to be waiting for me to make the first move.

"In the factory today, before the quality control woman arrived … you were going to tell me something."

"Yes." She frowns, toying with the plastic cherry that floats on top of her drink.

"About the androcibus nanite," I prompt. "You were trying to keep it out of the food."

She doesn't answer, just keeps twirling the cherry. I get the feeling that she's ended up in a situation she didn't want: she has to tell me something but isn't sure whether to trust me with the truth.

"I've done some research, to try to find out what it is," I say after a moment. "Phillips doesn't know, neither does Louis. I asked Philips if I could speak to the lab directly, but he just gave me the brush-off. There's no number for them in the directory. But it's not just in the meat products – it's in the ingredients list for all the lower-grade food lines."

It's only because I'm watching her closely that I catch the brief spark of interest in her green eyes.

"Anyway, I've asked Louis to keep the products rejected by

quality control to one side for now, rather than destroying them. If we can prove they're safe to eat, I don't see any reason why we can't give them away. Might be good PR for the company to look charitable."

Another silence.

"Do you know what the androcibus nanite is?"

Barnes removes the plastic cherry from her drink and places it on the tabletop. She takes a sip of the green liquid. "No. At least, not exactly. I have my suspicions."

My pulse quickens.

But Barnes pauses and looks up at me, her eyes searching mine. "Are you sure you want to know? Really sure? Because this isn't a game, you know. If they find out we're having this conversation, we'd lose our jobs at best. At worst …" She shrugs. "Well, you've already had a taste of the Metz."

I raise my glass to my lips, forgetting I've finished my drink. *Maybe I should have got another.*

"I know what the consequences are." I hesitate, wondering whether to confide in her about Milicent's request and my own snooping around the factory, but decide against it. I'm still not sure what to make of her, and while I don't think she's working for Coleman, there's still a lot I don't know about her.

Barnes gives me an appraising look, then sighs. "Fine." She takes another sip of her drink and lowers her voice so I have to lean forward to catch her words. "You know I used to work in the government food factories?"

I nod.

"I was in charge of one of the production lines there. Their machinery was pretty shoddy compared to the lines at Coleman's. Stuff was always breaking down. Sometimes I got the feeling I was a bit too efficient at fixing things. Anyway, that's beside the point. I overheard my manager talking with his boss one day about one of the ingredients that went into the government food. Co-tronkpretine."

Barnes nods, seeing the expression on my face. "I made the connection immediately. My … my sister was a tronk addict, and my mother. Stuff killed 'em both." Her eyes harden. "But I wasn't *sure*. I'd never really looked at what went into the food before – my job was to keep producing it, and I'm a mechanic, not a biochemist. But I managed to get into the computer system and over the next couple of weeks memorized the ingredients for most of the product lines. It's all just chemicals at the end of the day. But I couldn't find anything more about the co-tronkpretine."

She falls silent for a moment before continuing. "To cut a long story short, I ended up getting it out of one of the senior managers. He thought I was … interested in him. He didn't know exactly what it was, but he admitted it was some kind of drug to control the population. That confirmed it for me. I threatened to go to the press and tell them what was in the food, spread the word around Outside." She gives a small smile. "Which, in retrospect, was a pretty dumb thing to do. I should have just gone to the press without asking them. But I thought … I thought they actually cared about giving people decent food. That the limitations on quality were related to the cost of production, not their ideology. I was wrong."

"What did they do?"

"They gave me a choice. Take a promotion and go and work at Coleman's and keep my mouth shut, or get hauled off by the Metz to the Farms."

"So they bought your silence."

Anger flashes in her eyes. Then she sighs and shakes her head.

"That's one way of putting it. But if I'd been dragged off to the Farms I wouldn't be able to do anything with what I knew. At least if I took the job at Coleman's and made myself useful, I could bide my time and look for another opportunity."

"Why didn't you go to the press anyway? You could have done it without leaving proof that it was you."

"You think they'd need proof? Don't be an idiot. You should know how things work by now."

I grit my teeth and lift my glass to my mouth. A trickle of lime water sours my tongue.

"Sure you don't want another drink?"

"So that explains why you came to work here, but what's the link to the androcibus nanite?"

Barnes frowns. "When I started at Coleman's, I checked out all the ingredients that go into the meat products. Just to make sure there was no tronk in *them*. Which there wasn't. Then there were all those news stories about how the government were poisoning everyone with tronk, and the hunger strikes and riots." She looks up at me. "It was pretty bad out here for a while."

I nod. *Don't I know.*

"Then, a few days later, the androcibus nanite arrived, and we got told to insert it into the production line for the lower-grade meat." She leans forward, the end of her ponytail almost dipping into her drink. "You see? It was only to go into the products that go to Outsiders. The products Outsiders were buying because they were afraid to eat the government rations."

She drops her voice to almost a whisper and I have to lean in to hear her next words. "Androcibus nanite was one of the ingredients in the government rations. I'm sure of it – I memorized every chemical. But it wasn't in the food produced at Coleman's, not until people were no longer eating the basic rations."

Her words hang in the air, her breath warming my ear. She smells clean and fresh, of soap and citrus trees. I draw back slightly, needing space to think. "You think there was something else in the government rations? Something else ... to what, affect people's brains?"

Barnes looks troubled. "I don't know. I've been trying to find out what it is, but there's nothing on it anywhere. All that information is confined to the labs, I guess. But I wonder ..." She hesitates. "We know tronk is addictive, but maybe it isn't the tronk that's really the problem. The tronk takes away the hunger people feel, but we've only assumed that it's also responsible for affecting people's brains and their ability to learn and retain knowledge. What if that's what the nanite does? The two work in combination. No one's eating the government rations anymore and the government can't risk putting tronk in the normal food supply, not now the President's been forced to commit to eradicating it, but no one's raised any issues about this androcibus nanite. They can sneak that in and people won't be any better off than they were before. Their brains will still be poisoned!"

"And we let it get into the production system." I rub my fingers against my temples.

Barnes grimaces. "We didn't exactly have much choice, not with Miss Spiky standing over you. And you can bet they'll be keeping a sharp eye on us from now on. I knew I couldn't get away with leaving it out for long before they noticed."

"So what do we do now?"

She sighs. "I don't know. I'm not sure there's much we *can* do until we know for sure what it is. I thought you might be able to find out more than me."

"I've tried. As you say, there's nothing."

"Have you not got any Insider friends who work at the labs? I haven't come across anyone who works there – I guess they must have cleaners and other low-level workers, but they must recruit from a different area, or have them live on-site."

I shake my head. "I don't really have any friends, at least, not anymore."

And not Insiders.

But Ella had mentioned her group included people who worked in the government and in the labs. I shake my head again. *I'm not getting her involved.*

"What?" Barnes looks at me quizzically.

"Nothing. I guess you're right though. All we can do is stay quiet and not draw attention to ourselves until we can find out more." I shrug. "I'll see if I can get Louis drunk again. I'm pretty sure he doesn't know anything, but he may know someone who does."

"You? Get Louis drunk?" A smile tugs at her lips.

"Well, he mainly gets himself drunk, actually. It's preventing him from buying me drinks that's the hard part."

She leans back in her chair and laughs. It transforms her face, and her normally cold eyes dance with mirth. "There's more to you than meets the eye, Mr Goldsmith."

"It's T— Darwin," I say with a smile.

"Fine, *Darwin*." She lifts her glass and I clink it with my empty one. "To secrecy."

"To secrecy," I echo.

So many secrets. Sometimes I wonder if we'll ever find the real truth.

* * *

The next morning, I wake and stare at the ceiling, trying to connect the jumble of facts and rumours and the different gangs and factions who seem to be fighting for control of the city. At least I have the weekend to mull over my conversation with Barnes before I have to go back to work.

I wonder whether to comm Milicent and report this latest development but decide it can wait until our regular weekly meeting.

Wasn't there something else I was supposed to do?

My brain still feels fogged with sleep. Yawning, I sit up and stagger from the bed to the small hygiene cubicle in the corner of the room. Ten seconds in that and I feel clean if no more awake. I get dressed and retrieve the small packet Louis had given me from its hiding place under my mattress.

Louis. Damn, I was supposed to meet him last night.

I check my comm. Sure enough, there are several messages from him asking where I am. I message him an apology, saying I wasn't feeling well and went straight to bed, suggesting we meet up after the weekend. Then I close the comm and stare at the tiny microchip on my bed. If Louis is right, this and the chip blocker will allow me to move around Outside without the government tracking me.

Perhaps even go through the Wall?

But I'm not sure I'm brave enough to test that yet. Still, the thought of being able to visit Aleesha is tempting. I brush my fingers over my lips, remembering the brief touch of her lips on mine. The thought makes me shiver.

I shove the chip and the blocker into my pocket and head out into the living room. Mother's talking to Ella. On the sofa beside her sits an overnight bag.

"Are you going to the hospital?" A flash of alarm shoots through me. *Has she got that much worse?*

But though she's thinner than ever, her eyes are bright when they turn to me. "Morning! I'm going away for the weekend. Dan and Carol have invited me to their home in the New Forest. They thought it might do me some good."

"Sounds lovely." I walk over and drop a kiss on her forehead. "Do you want me to carry your bag down?"

"Would you? I've got a taxi waiting downstairs."

I follow her down with the bag and place it in the pod in the street outside. When I return to the apartment, Ella's drinking the last of her coffee and studying a table of figures on her holo pad.

"Ella." I hesitate, wondering how much to tell her. "I'm going out. Maybe just for a few hours, but I might be away overnight. If anyone asks, will you tell them I'm sick in bed?"

She looks surprised. "Why? Where are you going?"

"Just going to try and catch up with some old friends."

She narrows her eyes at me. "Trey ..."

"Please, Ella. I'm not doing anything dangerous. I just need to test something out, that's all."

"Well, okay. I was actually going to spend the night at Dexter's, so I won't be around anyway." She shuts down the holo pad and rubs her eyes.

"You okay?"

She doesn't answer me, just stands and returns her coffee cup to the kitchen. "We've just had the latest bill through from the hospital. Are you able to ask for an advance on your pay?"

I nod. "Is it ... Do they think the treatment's working?"

"No." She shoves the holo pad roughly into a bag and slings it over her shoulder. "They're saying they need to do more tests, but we can't afford them at the moment."

"When I get my p—"

"Not even with your pay, at least not for a few months." She squeezes my arm. "Don't tell Mother – I don't want to worry her even more. Comm me if you need anything." She pushes past me toward the front door.

I stand there, alone, feeling as though I've been punched in the heart.

She's going to die.

My job isn't highly paid, but it's not bad. I earn more in a month than my workers earn in six, and more than most Outsiders earn in a year. And yet, it still isn't enough. The irony would make me laugh if it wasn't ripping me apart.

I can't lose her too.

I sink down on the sofa, running through options in my head. First thing Monday, I'll ask Phillips for my first month's wage in advance. But that doesn't really solve anything, it'll just help us pay this bill.

I wonder about asking Louis for a loan but discount the idea. I don't want to feel beholden to him for anything. Milicent, on the other hand ... She's got more than enough money. And I've been helping her and the Chain out. Why shouldn't I get some compensation for the risks I'm taking? I need to be more like Aleesha, demanding something in return for the information I'm giving them.

I send her a quick message, asking to change our weekly dinner from Thursday to Tuesday next week, then return to my bedroom and remove my comm band, tucking it under the sheet. I pull the rubber tube from my pocket and tug it up my right forearm. It's surprisingly elastic, and once in place, fits snugly but isn't too tight. The golden microchip I shove into the front pocket of my jeans.

Returning to the kitchen, I raid the cupboards, shoving packets of food and bars into my rucksack, making a mental note to replace them when I come back. Moping around here all weekend isn't going to do anything to help Mother.

I leave the apartment and walk to the nearest pod station, feeling free for the first time since moving back Inside.

* * *

Abby's in the garden, tending to some seedlings inside a small plastic polytunnel. She looks up when the back gate creaks open.

"Trey!" She closes the distance between us and gives me a hug, then pulls back, holding me at arm's length while she looks me up and down. "You're looking well. How's life Inside?"

I shrug. She pulls off the dirt-covered tunic she's wearing over her clothes and leads me inside the house, setting the kettle on the hotplate to boil. Almost every surface, bar half the kitchen table, is covered with pot plants at various stages of growth.

"Garden doing well?"

She nods. "Everything's growing, thank goodness. Another few weeks and I'll be able to start making remedies again. If we get some rain." She sighs. "It's been so dry, even the extra tanks I have are pretty much empty. Still, I think we're due a storm soon." She looks up at me. "Anyway, that's enough of my wittering. What are you doing here? Aleesha said it was too dangerous for you to come Outside?"

"I didn't want them tracking me here. But now I have this." I show her the rubber sheath on my arm and hold up the gold microchip. “It blocks the signal from my chip. Tested it on the pod over to Six – the pod only picked up the signal from this chip, which is registered to a fake name.”

Abby runs her finger over the rubber. “Hmm, Bryn will be interested in that.”

“Where is he?” I look around.

“Down at the church with Aleesha, I think. Oh, I forgot, you probably don’t know what’s been going on.”

“I know her father turned up, and she nearly got caught by the Metz. She came to see me,” I add in response to Abby’s raised eyebrow.

“Ah, well, since then, Primo and his gang attacked the church Aleesha and the others have been staying in. It was quite a mess.”

“But she’s okay?” I realize I’m digging my fingers into the back of the chair I’m holding onto.

“Yes, she’s fine.”

Some of the tension drains out of me. I swing the backpack off my back and place it on the table. “Brought you some food.” I begin to pull packets out and pile them on the table.

Abby’s eyes widen. “Trey, you didn’t have to … It’s too much.”

“You fed me for weeks, shared your own rations, it’s the least I can do.”

“No, I mean, really, it’s too much. Take it to Aleesha. They need all the spare food they can get down there. There’s only me and Bryn here now, and he can get his hands on most things.” She smiles warmly. “Thank you, though. I appreciate the thought.”

She places a mug of herbal tea beside me as I repack the bag. “How’s your mother?”

I shrug. “They still haven’t found a cure for whatever it is that’s wrong with her. She’s getting weaker.”

Abby clucks sympathetically. “And the job?”

I place the backpack on the floor and sit down. “Actually, it’s pretty interesting. I’ve been doing some snooping around and reporting back to Milicent.” I tell her about what I’d found out about the distribution centres and my conversation with Barnes the previous night. “I just don’t know what I can *do* about it though.”

Abby frowns, her eyes full of worry. “Are you sure you should be reporting to Milicent? What if you get caught? They won’t give you a reprieve again.”

“I think we’re safe enough. She’s pretending to take an interest in me since I lost my father. Besides, I can’t just do nothing.”

Abby smiles. “Well, just be careful, okay?”

I nod. “So, where would I find Aleesha?”

Abby reels off a set of directions. I pull a roll of film from my pocket and make her write it down. There’s no way I’d remember otherwise. “The Leader’s put one of his teams outside the church, to guard it. Ask for Bryn and he should be able to vouch for you.”

She accompanies me to the door where she gives me another hug. “Don’t be a stranger, okay? And stay safe … please.”

I smile and kiss her on the cheek. “Always.”

27

Aleesha

"You're mad." Anders slams his fist down on the table, unusually aggressive. "There's no way you can beat him in a leadership fight."

I cross my arms. "You haven't seen me with a knife. I'm good."

"But you have to get through two rounds before you're even allowed a knife," Danny objects. "And the first one is wrestling. There's no way you can beat 'im at that."

"That's why I need you to help me figure out a way to survive through that bit."

Anders' face creases in a frown. "Impossible. I thought my suggestion was bad, but this is a terrible plan. You'll just get yourself killed for nothing."

"What's a terrible plan?"

Trey?

I shoot up out of my chair, turning to the door. He stands with his shoulders hunched, his hands in his pockets. His blond hair has been cut shorter. Something else seems different about him too, though I can't put my finger on what.

"Sorry for interrupting. Do you want me to come back later?" He cocks his head to one side, a smile playing at his lips.

I feel a sudden urge to run to him and throw my arms around him and bury my face in his chest. Instead, I grip the back of the chair and shake my head.

"No, come on in." I manage to find some words. "We could do with an extra brain."

I introduce him to Anders and Danny.

"Where's Rogue?" he asks.

Good question.

"He went off with Tommy to find out what Primo's getting up to," I say, not mentioning that Tommy had returned two hours ago, saying he'd lost Rogue.

Trey glances at Anders whose face is a picture of concern. Danny is frowning, though I'm not sure whether that's out of concern for Rogue or because of Trey.

There's a tap on the door and Bryn sticks his head in. "Apparently lunch is ready? Figured I'd let you know before it gets demolished."

I turn back to the others. "Go eat. Let's come back in an hour."

Anders and Danny file out, but I pull Trey back. Bryn raises an eyebrow, then leaves, closing the door behind him. Trey's face is oddly unreadable.

"You're looking better than when I last saw you," he says after a moment.

"My father brought a portable medic pod. It's miraculous, I've never seen anything like it. Ten minutes in there and I felt as good as new." I touch my side briefly, still not quite able to believe that the slash Abby was so worried about getting infected is fully healed.

"Your father? So you made up with him?" Something flickers across Trey's eyes, too fast for me to catch.

I shrug. "Kind of."

What do I tell him? That he offered me everything I've ever wanted?

My father's words keep running through my head, keeping me awake when I try to sleep. The thought of leaving London is terrifying, but at the same time it tugs at my core. White cities of towers and platters of fresh food fill my dreams.

I shake myself and eye Trey again, trying to put my finger on what feels different about him. "How did you get out here? Are they still tracking you?"

"Nope." He rolls up the right sleeve of his shirt and holds his arm out.

For a second I wonder what he's showing me, then I look closer and realize that the hairs on the back of his arm are plastered to the skin. His entire forearm, from wrist to elbow, seems to be wrapped in some kind of clear plastic. "What is it?"

"Chip blocker. One of the guys I work with gave it to me. I left my comm band at home and asked Ella to cover for me. If anyone asks, I'm hungover in bed."

"Hungover?"

Trey grimaces. "I don't understand why people drink alcohol. It makes you feel weird and the next day you feel like hell. Makes no sense to me."

His mention of Ella jolts my memory. In all the confusion of the past few days, I'd forgotten that I'd agreed to speak to Samson on her behalf. And now Samson is missing.

Should I tell him? She didn't want him to know but ...

"What's wrong?"

He touches my arm, startling me. I realize I've been chewing my lip. "Um, nothing."

Trey frowns. "What is it? You can tell me."

His hand lingers on my elbow and I find myself taking a step forward so we're inches apart. He ducks his head to stare down at me. Then it hits me – what's different about him. He has a confidence, a sureness in himself that he's never had before. It was the same with Jay, except his confidence was mingled with arrogance. But there's no arrogance with Trey. He still has that boyish innocence that lights up his face, but he moves and speaks more confidently now, with no hint of the stammer that plagued him before.

Should I tell him?

I told Ella I wouldn't, but I didn't promise her. And I know all too well how secrets can tear people apart. I don't want Trey to lose his family, now he's found them.

"I think you need to talk to Ella. A—"

The door flies open and Tommy runs in. I pull back from Trey, then freeze as I see the look on Tommy's face.

"Tommy, what's happened?"

"Rogue's back," he pants.

I run for the door but haven't gone two steps before it opens again and Rogue limps in, cradling the limp body of a woman in his arms. Blood runs from a deep cut on his forehead and the trousers and shirt the monks had given him to wear are torn and stained with blood and dirt. There's a wild look in his eyes. Behind him, Bryn and Anders pile into the room.

Rogue heads to the sofa set against one wall and gently lays the woman down. He kneels beside her, his head bent over hers, murmuring something too quietly for me to hear.

I move around him to see who it is. "Megan?"

Her face is mottled purple and yellow with bruises. One eye is swollen shut and her lips are cracked and bloody. For a moment, I think she's dead, but then her head turns slightly, toward Rogue and his lips part as she tries to speak.

"Water. Someone get me some water!" Rogue's voice is harsh

and urgent. His eyes never leave Megan's face and I feel a spark of irritation at his obvious concern.

Me, jealous? Of Megan?

But this is a battered ghost of the Megan I knew.

Rogue always wants someone to save.

Tommy runs from the room and returns a minute later with a bottle of water. Rogue holds it to Megan's lips and lifts her head so that she can drink. She gives a slight nod and he lowers her head back down tenderly as if any sharp movement could break her.

I shake myself and turn to Bryn. "Can you get the medic pod back? Quick?"

He nods and leaves the room. I kneel beside Rogue. "What happened?" I whisper.

He rocks back on his heels. Megan's fingers are curled around one of his, like a baby's hand clinging to its mother's finger. "I was watching the headquarters like you asked, when she ran out the building. Two thugs followed her and started laying into her, so I intervened and managed to knock them both out. She didn't say much but kept repeating your name, so I brought her here. She ..." His voice breaks. "*He* did this to her. I'll kill him."

I can feel the anger boiling off him and place a hand on his shoulder. "First, we need to get you both healed."

He shrugs me off. "I'm fine. She's badly hurt though, and not just from the beating those brutes gave her."

"'Leesha," Megan's eyes flutter, her voice a cracked whisper.

"I'm here, Megan. It's me, Aleesha."

"Aleesha," she repeats a little more clearly this time. Her swollen eye remains shut but she manages to open the other one. "Need to speak to you ... alone."

I glance behind me. "Everyone out." They don't move. "Now! Someone get a bowl of warm water and some cloths."

Rogue hesitates until Megan turns her gaze on him. "Please?"

Reluctantly, he pulls his finger from her grip and stands. They exchange a look and the faintest of smiles blooms on Megan's battered face. Then Rogue turns and walks from the room. The door closes behind him, leaving me alone with Megan.

"More water?"

She nods weakly. I lift her head as Rogue had done and let a trickle of water flow into her mouth.

"Did Primo do this to you?" I ask, setting the bottle down on the floor.

"Yes. And others." Her hand fumbles weakly at her waist, two of her fingers twisted at awkward angles. "In my pocket … for you."

Hesitantly, I find the pocket in her jeans and slide my hand in. My fingers close around a small familiar object.

My amulet.

The green glass twinkles in the sunlight from the windows. I rub my thumb over its familiar edges, feeling a sense of comfort at having it back.

"It's important to you?" Megan's words are slightly slurred.

I tear my eyes from the amulet and pocket it, looking at her again. She's a mess. I feel a stab of pity, though she's never been anything but hostile toward me until now.

Then why did she bring me the amulet? A peace offering?

"D'ya think things'll ever be different, Aleesha?" Her eye closes and when it opens again, it's clouded with the weariness of years of gang life. Of being used and abused, of knowing that the only reason she was wanted – the only use any of us had for the gang – was for our bodies and company.

I see myself reflected in her eyes, as I was a few months ago. The despair of hoping, again and again, that something would change. And the eventual realization that this was life. That it was this or …

Or tronk.

And Megan had never given in to that, as far as I know. In that, she was better than me.

She wheezes painfully, rallying herself to speak again. "I used to think p'rhaps I'd meet someone, y'know? Someone who liked me … for being me. Who lov—" She clamps her mouth shut and a bitter smile twists the corner of her lips. "Silly, isn't it?"

I sit down beside her, curling my legs under me, and take her uninjured hand. Her skin is smoother than mine. Megan isn't a fighter. But she's tougher than she looks, and when I glance at her again there's a spark of life behind the clouds of misery in her eyes.

"No, it's not silly. *That* shouldn't be our lives. Perhaps we can change things. Build a different type of gang, or leave the gangs behind altogether." I sound more confident than I feel.

"You can stop him … stop this." It feels like she's trying to convince me, but the uplift in her voice betrays her uncertainty.

"I … I will try."

Hollow promises. She needs more than that. Deserves more than that.

"You need to stop him. He … he will destroy everyone … everything."

Her words strike a coldness into my heart. The urgency in her eyes tells me that she's not just referring to herself.

"What is it, Megan? What's he planning?"

"The food depot … He's going to raid it, break in …" She gasps and whimpers in pain. "Take it as the new headquarters … Hold

… the area hostage …"

Her eyes roll back in her head as the pain becomes too much for her. *When will that damn pod get here?*

The coldness in my heart spreads, radiating outwards until it feels as if my bones are carved from ice. The food depot … I would have said it was impossible to take, surrounded by a tall barrier as lethal as the Wall itself. But if the Snakes had managed it when Dane had been in charge, they'd certainly manage it with Primo in charge.

The door slams open and Anders walks in. "The pod's here."

I glance down at Megan, who's conscious again.

Anders takes a step toward us, but Rogue pushes him aside and limps forward. "Kian," Megan whispers, loud enough that only I hear. Her fingers reach up and brush his arm as he bends over, obviously in pain, and lifts her into his arms.

"Wait." I pull him back, ignoring the furious glance he gives me, and lean over Megan. "When, Megan? When's he going to raid the depot?"

Her eye flickers. "Next week … five days maybe."

As they leave the room, Trey walks back in, his face set in grim determination. Anders leaves us and I turn to Trey. "Will the medic pod be able to heal her?"

"I don't know. The more advanced medic centres can heal pretty much anything, but I don't know what a mobile pod can do. Did you say your father brought it from overseas?"

I nod. "It sounds like they have even better technology than us, so maybe …"

I sink onto the sofa and rest my head in my hands.

This is what it's been coming to all along. I've known it since the moment I heard Primo had challenged Jay for the leadership. I had hoped that someone else would come forward to stop him.

But no one has.

And no one else can. Not without fracturing the politics of the gangs and the areas.

My father would destroy them all. Raze the headquarters to the ground if I asked. But that wouldn't solve anything other than killing more people. But Primo won't refuse a leadership challenge – he's far too arrogant and sure of himself.

What if I lose?

Then at worst, I'll have delayed his plans for a few days and given others the chance to figure out a plan to stop him.

"Anders said you're thinking of challenging Primo," Trey says, sitting down beside me.

I nod. "Are you going to tell me it's impossible too?"

"Nothing is impossible. It just depends on how you look at it. How long do you have to prepare?"

"Not long." I explain what Megan had told me.

Trey frowns. "You know, I have the access codes and details for that depot memorized. I told Milicent about them. We could beat him to it."

I stare at him. "You can get into the depot?"

"Well, not exactly. I guess you'd need to hijack a pod, scramble the codes, and once you've landed take over from whoever's running the place. But I imagine the Chain could help with that part."

I slump back. "No. My father doesn't want to do anything that'll attract the government's attention. Not yet."

We sit in silence for a moment.

"You know, Jay suggested I should be leader. Before his fight with Primo. He asked me to promise to look after the Snakes."

"And did you?"

I look down at my hands, twisting together in my lap. I tug at my fingers, bending them back until a warning pain radiates down the back of my hand. "No, I didn't. I didn't think they'd want me as their leader. I've never been part of the gang, not really. They tolerated me when I was with Jay, but they didn't like me." I shrug. "And I'm a woman. Women aren't gang leaders."

"I thought you said there was a gang who had a woman in charge?"

"Yeah, well, she's the only one."

"They see you as their leader." Trey points toward the door.

I sigh. "That's the problem. They do. Even though all I've done is get them hurt and killed … They still look to me as if I know what to do."

My hands ball into fists and I thump the sofa beside me in frustration. "But I don't know what to do, Trey. I know I need to stop Primo, but I can't work out how, other than throwing a knife in his eye, and how on earth do I get in a position to do that? And even if I can win, what happens then? Then I would be the leader of the Snakes. And I don't know *how* to be a leader." I rub my fingers over my eyes, feeling emotion well up in me. "I don't even know if I *want* to be a leader," I whisper into my hands.

Trey's arm wraps around my shoulders and I lean into him. He wraps the other arm around my back and I sag against his shoulder, inhaling the smell of him.

"It'll be okay," he mumbles into my hair. "Whatever happens, it'll be okay."

And somehow I believe him. In his arms, I feel protected from the world outside. Like I can finally let my guard down and be me.

Is this what love feels like?

I don't know, and in that moment, I don't care. I lift my face to his, feeling his hot breath on my cheeks. Then his lips brush mine, hesitantly at first, then firmer. And as I sink into him, I forget about Primo and Megan and everyone else. There is just him and me.

And that is all I need.

28

Trey

There's a firm knock on the door, and Bryn walks in. Aleesha and I spring apart, blushing furiously.

"Sorry to interrupt," Bryn says with a wry smile. "There's a messenger for you, Aleesha. I asked him to wait, but he wasn't keen – was going to barge in here himself if I didn't come and get you. Says he's from Samson."

"Samson?" Aleesha leaps to her feet, our kiss apparently forgotten. "Send him in."

I sigh inwardly and shift awkwardly on the sofa. *Always some interruption.*

Bryn beckons and a lean, weasel-faced man sidles into the room. He wears one of the oddest hairstyles I've seen Outside – the front part of his head is shaved smooth, the back gathered into a single thin braid that hangs down to below his waist.

Dark eyes look at Aleesha, then move to me. "Boss says I was to speak to you alone."

"I trust Trey. He stays. Samson won't mind." Aleesha looks at Bryn, who leaves, closing the door behind him.

The man looks me up and down, then shrugs. "He won't be happy. But it's your funeral."

"Is he back? Where's he been?"

Samson's been gone somewhere?

"He's back. A bit beaten up. Got into a bit of a scrap. Anyway, you can ask him yourself – he wants to see you."

Breath hisses through Aleesha's teeth. "At his headquarters?"

The man looks at her suspiciously. "No, at a safe house in Three. You coming?"

Aleesha nods and turns to me. "Want to come along?"

"Sure." I shrug casually, though my heart begins to pound a little faster. I'm not sure I'd risk messing with Samson, but Aleesha seems confident that he won't mind.

The man shrugs. "Whatever. As I said, your funeral."

In the vaulted entrance to the church, Abby is standing beside what looks like a small pod, talking to an Asian woman dressed in combat clothing.

"How is she, Mika?" Aleesha asks as we approach. "Can you fix her?"

The woman turns to her and shows her a data pad covered in rows of squiggly lines. I suspect it makes as little sense to Aleesha as it does to me. Her eyes slide over it and she looks up at the woman. "What does that mean?"

"She's pretty badly hurt, and there's internal bleeding. The pod's still going, but it looks certain that she'll survive. She'll need to rest at least a week to build her strength back up." The woman's accent is lyrical and thick as if English isn't her first language.

Aleesha's shoulders relax slightly. "Thank you."

"Once she's out, we'll run the other guy through – he shouldn't take too long. But will you tell him to stop getting into fights? We can't come down here every time he messes himself up."

A smile twitches the corner of Aleesha's mouth. "I'll tell him."

Samson's messenger shuffles impatiently by the door. "You coming or not?"

We follow him out the church and through a part of the city I haven't been to before. If anything, it's worse than Area Four. I have to resist holding my nose as we pass hobies lining the streets two deep. As we walk, Aleesha fills me in on what's been happening.

"Samson was going to talk to the President, to see if the government would intervene to stop Primo. When he didn't come back, I thought ..."

"He'd been captured by the President?"

She nods.

The man veers sharply off the main street down a side alley. I kick trash to the side and hold my breath until we make it to a small door set into the building to our left. Inside, there's a steep flight of stairs that opens into a large room that's part of a first-floor apartment. Half the room contains a battered table surrounded by chairs, and the other half, two rows of beds packed close together.

A couple of people sit at the table, talking. Others lie on the beds, more people milling around a bed in the far corner. I catch a glimpse of auburn curls and a long black overcoat, then Amber pushes herself out of the group.

She spots us and walks over.

"What are you doing here?" I blurt out.

Amber smiles. "I go where I'm needed, don't ask questions." She shrugs. "That's my job."

Aleesha glances over at the mob of people and drops her voice. "Is he alright?"

"He'll be fine if that lot stop fussing over him. Strong as an ox, that one." She smiles ruefully. "Hard part's going to be keeping him resting long enough for his body to heal. Anyway, I gotta go. Duty calls." She pushes past us, out the door.

There's a shout from the corner and the people clustered around the bed pull back. The messenger darts in and speaks in a low voice. There's a rumble from Samson, then a gasp from someone as he heaves himself up into a sitting position.

He turns to look at us, still swaying slightly, and his eyes are glassy as if he's drugged. He seems to be naked under the white sheet, his bare chest crisscrossed with thick bandages. Blood oozes from a cut on his forehead that's been stitched up and he holds some kind of compress to his jaw.

"Get out of here. Can't a man get some rest?" He flicks his fingers at his entourage, who all scurry away. Aleesha's eyes alight on a brown-haired girl who gives her a hesitant smile. I've seen her somewhere before, but can't put my finger on where.

Samson awkwardly shuffles himself back on the bed and the messenger arranges his pillows to prop him up. Samson glances at Aleesha, then me and scowls. "I thought I said her only."

The messenger shrugs, unrepentant. "She wanted him to come. Told her you'd be pissed."

Samson's expression relaxes. "Trey, isn't it?"

I nod.

"Well you're here now," he says gruffly. "You still working for the Chain?"

His eyes seem to look right into me and I swallow nervously, feeling the power that exudes from him, despite his incapacity. "Sort of."

"Sort of? You either are or you aren't."

I think of Milicent and wonder whether to deny it. But I get the feeling that this is a test. "Yes."

Samson nods. "Fine. Well, no going telling the Chain about any of this, okay?" He indicates himself and then the room. "Or you'll get a nasty surprise in the night. Being Inside won't help you – I have people *everywhere*."

He gives a short laugh, which turns into a cough. His face creases in pain.

"Cracked a rib," he gasps.

"Them lot have got a healing pod at the church." The messenger jerks his thumb toward Aleesha and smirks. "Not sure it'd fit you though, big man."

Samson swats at him good-naturedly. "Haven't you got somewhere to be, Petal?"

Petal?

I stare at the man, who glowers and takes a step toward me, his fists clenched. "You got a problem, posh boy?"

I raise my hands and shake my head. "No problem."

He gives me another scowl then walks off across the room.

"Petal?" Aleesha asks in disbelief, trying to keep the smile off her face.

"Dad was drunk when he named him – thought he was a girl. Don't tease him about it. He'll only fight you and he's got a mean right hook."

"Why didn't he change his name if he hates it so much?" I ask.

"I don't know. Perhaps he's sentimental at heart. Either that or he likes having an excuse to pick a fight with people." Samson rolls his eyes. "Probably that."

"So, your chat with the President didn't go well then?" Aleesha asks, surveying him.

"It was a trap. He was waiting for me with a handful of Metz. Managed to take them down and took him as a hostage but they must have discovered my secret entrance as there was another load of them waiting. Bastard pulled a knife on me and stabbed me in the leg." A grudging respect enters Samson's voice as he looks down at his thigh. "Didn't know he had it in him. Never underestimate an enemy."

"Don't I know that," Aleesha mutters under her breath.

Samson glances at her. "Heard you had some trouble with Primo."

"Just a bit."

"Bigland Boys got their eye on you, you know."

"I know."

Samson nods. "Well, that's probably a secondary problem for now. There's going to be no help from the government to get rid of Primo. I think the way the President sees it, Primo will get rid of us, and *then* he'll send the Metz in to knock him down." His face twists into a grimace. "Which doesn't help much, I'm afraid."

I look at Aleesha. She's staring off into the distance, as if thinking about something.

"You were afraid to challenge him after he killed Jay," she says eventually.

Samson bristles. "Not afraid. But it wasn't the right time. You can't just go into a fight with someone like that on a whim. You have to study him, know his weaknesses, figure out what you can do that he can't. You have to have a *plan*."

"A plan …" Aleesha turns her head to look at him. "And what *are* his weaknesses?"

Samson's eyes narrow. "You're going to challenge him."

Aleesha juts out her jaw defiantly. "Yes."

But if she was expecting Samson to laugh or mock her, he doesn't. "You're so different to him that you might just have a chance," he says thoughtfully. "What are your strengths? How will you kill him?"

Aleesha hesitates.

"If you don't tell me, I can't help you," Samson snaps. His dark eyes bore into her. "Your choice."

"Knives. I can throw a knife into any point you choose at twenty paces." She shrugs. "Bit less accurate in a fight, but good enough."

"Show me." Samson points to a dartboard set into the far wall. "See how close you can get to the bullseye."

Aleesha slides a knife from her pocket and weighs it in her hand, staring at the board. It's perhaps ten metres away, but at an angle from us. There's no one nearby – the other occupants of the room are sitting around the table, occasionally shooting curious glances in our direction.

Aleesha flicks the knife into her grip and pulls back her arm, her eyes never leaving the dart board. The tip of her tongue sticks out in concentration. In a blur of movement, she throws, the knife wheeling through the air. The point sticks in the small circle at the centre of the board, the blade vibrating.

There's a stunned silence. Aleesha walks over to the dartboard and retrieves her knife, pocketing it as she returns to us. I catch Petal watching her, surprise and respect mingling on his face.

Samson just nods. "Good." He winces. "Damn jaw." He blinks and focuses on us again. "Well, that's how you can kill him. Get that in his eye and even he won't be standing back up."

"I don't want to kill him, just make him yield."

Samson looks at her darkly. "Men like him don't yield. If you're not prepared to kill him, you'll die."

Aleesha shrugs. "Whatever. I figure if I can get through to the knife round, I've got a chance of beating him."

A twist of fear tightens my gut.

"What do you mean, get through to the knife round?" I say.

"Leadership contests are a series of rounds. You keep going until one person yields or is too badly wounded to continue. There are no weapons in the first round – just fists and wrestling. The second round is clubs. Then knives. Doesn't often go beyond the third round."

"So you have to wrestle with Primo and fight him with clubs before you can even use your knife?" Now I understand why Anders and Danny were so against the idea. It sounds like a suicide mission. "There has to be another way. You can't fight him."

Aleesha gives me an irritated look. "We've been through this, Trey. There's no other way." She turns back to Samson. "The officers are trained mainly in baton use and guns, with some hand-to-hand fighting and wrestling. Anders says they almost never use knives, so I have the advantage there. And I'm smaller than him – I figure I just need to keep out of his way for the first round so he can't grab me."

"He'll be fast though," Samson warns. "Enhanced genetics."

Aleesha nods. "That's why I need to do something to slow him down. Or tire him out. I don't think their stamina is so great."

Samson looks thoughtful. "You've seen him fight more than me. Did he have any obvious weakness?"

"Nothing obvious ... He walked all over Jay. But they're not used to the heat out here. Their suits help keep them cool, but he can't wear it for the fight, at least, not if he's following the rules."

"He'll follow the rules. That's one of his weaknesses – his arrogance. He doesn't believe anyone can beat him, let alone a slip of a girl. No offence meant."

A smile ghosts across Aleesha's face. "He downed two bottles of water during a rest break in the fight with Jay – more than I'd drink in a day. He was sweating buckets, and that was weeks ago – it's much hotter now."

Samson nods. "And he's been desperate to get water. Half of Area Four is suffering because of it – there's nothing liquid left in the shops. So if we can cut off his water supply in advance, he'll be dehydrated before he starts."

"But surely he'll take whatever water his gang has? So if you stop him getting water, you're stopping them all getting water." I frown at Aleesha. "All of them will suffer."

"But not all of them are going to have to fight. Besides, the Snakes will be okay – they're used to not having much to drink."

"Do the officers not matter then?"

Her shoulders stiffen. "Of course they matter," she says in a low, controlled voice. "But what do you expect me to do, Trey? They chose to follow him. Besides, it's only for a few days." She turns to Samson. "Can you do something? About their water supply?"

Samson smiles. "I reckon I can help you with that much, at least. Oi, Petal!" The man turns from his seat at the table. "Get Rae for me, will you?"

Petal nods and gets to his feet, pushing past us to a small door at the end of the row of beds.

"It'll be easy enough to cut the supply from the tanks on the roof," Samson continues. "If they've got a stockpile inside, that'll be tough to get rid of, but I doubt they're that organized. Seemed to be living in squalor when we broke in to rescue you."

A door clicks open and there's the sound of footsteps.

"You wanted me?"

The hairs on the back of my neck prick up at the voice. That odd accent, part-Insider, part-Outsider. The ever-present trace of sarcasm. I look across and meet her green eyes.

"Barnes?" I can barely get the word out. "What …?"

Barnes looks amused. "Something got your tongue, Mr Goldsmith?"

Aleesha looks from Barnes to me. "You know each other?"

I recover myself. "Barnes works for me. At the factory. I … I thought you were working for the Chain."

"What, that group of wannabe politicians?" She smirks. "That lot couldn't organize a piss up in a brewery. Too busy fighting among themselves about how they're going to save the city to actually *do* anything. Though I hear the new guy in charge has got some fancy tech." Her gaze falls on Aleesha. "Is this your girlfriend? And I thought Emilie was going to woo you over."

"Who's Emilie?" Aleesha mutters out the corner of her mouth.

"No one important."

"Rae …" Samson's voice carries a warning note.

Barnes turns to him, smiling brightly. "Yes?"

"Aleesha is looking to take care of a problem for us. We're going to help her out. What's the weather doing over the next few days?"

Barnes is suddenly serious. "Hot tomorrow, even hotter the day after before it breaks. They're forecasting big thunderstorms."

Samson frowns. "That doesn't give us much time." He looks to Aleesha. "Can you be ready to fight him on Monday?"

Aleesha nods. "Get it over and done with." Her voice carries a faint tremor. "Besides, he's bound to have spies. The less time he gets to figure out what we're up to, the better."

Barnes gives her an appraising look, then looks back at Samson, one eyebrow raised. "*She* is fighting Primo?"

Samson meets her gaze levelly. "Yes. But first, we have to cut off their water supply. If we can disable the tanks on top of his headquarters tonight, then he's got a couple of days to dehydrate." He looks at Aleesha. "Make sure you state a specific time for the challenge. Mid-afternoon will be hottest."

"Won't he just go out and raid the other apartment blocks for water?" I ask, looking from Samson to Aleesha.

It's Aleesha who answers. "Won't be any use. With the dry spell we've had, they'll all be empty. The HQ tanks are big, but I doubt there's much left even in them. Everyone'll be suffering."

"We can provide distractions in case they go out looking for more," Samson adds. "Rae, ask Petal to get a team together. If they're able to empty the tanks without drawing attention to themselves, we can redistribute the water tomorrow night. See if we can get any intel from our contact inside as to what supplies they've got bottled. We may have to break in, but I'd like to avoid it if possible."

I glance over at Barnes to find her looking at me. She pulls me to one side as Aleesha and Samson carry on talking. "I presume you've removed your chip?" she says in a low voice.

I pull up my sleeve and show her the rubber sheath around my forearm. "Chip blocker."

"Where did you get that?" It's the first time I've heard her sound surprised.

I smile, feeling a little bit smug that I finally know something she doesn't. "You have your secrets, I have mine."

Barnes rolls her eyes.

"What about you?"

She twists her arm, showing me a thin scar. "It's in a biobox. I carry it with me when I'm at work or out in public. But according to my chip, I spend most of my non-working hours in a dingy leisure building playing VR games. Samson runs the place so there are plenty of people who'll swear blind I was there if anyone asks."

"What's a biobox?"

"Just a small box. You set it up to mirror your vitals – pulse, breathing rate, that kind of thing – then you pop your chip in it and it thinks it's still in you. You can even set it up to simulate workouts and stuff. Pretty neat. Samson's got a contact in the labs who makes them. The only downside is that you can't buy anything or use the pods when you don't have it with you." She shrugs. "But that's not really an issue for me."

She glances back at Aleesha. "You're not going to the fight, are you?"

"What do you mean?"

"Monday is a work day."

My heart sinks. If I don't turn up, it'll look suspicious. But I can't be at work, not knowing what is happening. Not being there to support her …

I meet Barnes's eyes. "Cover for me?"

She shakes her head, her ponytail swinging behind her. "Don't be an idiot. No one misses work. You'll blow your cover."

"It's just a day. My sister's covering for me at home – she'll tell them I'm sick or something."

"You're an Insider. Insiders don't get sick."

"I'll tell them I need to go with my mother to a medical appointment then." I feel a twist of guilt at bringing Mother into this. "I'll go back tomorrow and comm Emilie. She'll cover for me, even if you won't."

Barnes sighs. "Fine. Just be careful. If the Metz come to break things up and you get caught with that on …"

She doesn't have to finish her sentence.

"I know."

Her brows knit in a frown and she lowers her voice. "Can she beat him? She's so small and thin ..."

I nod firmly. "She's fast and smart. If anyone can, she can."

But I sound more confident that I feel. I know Aleesha can fight, but this Primo sounds superhuman. I only have a vague memory of the captain we'd met in the Metz compound, but I remember he loomed even taller than Rogue.

Barnes turns away but I grab her arm.

"How did you get involved with Samson? How long have you been working for him?"

"A long time." She glances over at the big man and her eyes soften. "I've been with him a long time."

As if he can sense her watching, Samson looks up and smiles.

"Damn man thinks he's invincible," Barnes mutters under her breath as we walk over, but there's no anger or irritation in her voice, just concern.

So she is human, after all.

A look of relief passes over Aleesha's face as Samson nods and frowns in response to some question she's asked. "Fine. But after the fight."

I look at her quizzically but she just shakes her head in response.

More secrets?

"I'll send Petal to you tomorrow to let you know how the raid on the water tanks goes," Samson says. He sounds weary and sweat beads on his black skin. "You'd better send your challenge to him tonight. Distract him from his other plans."

Of course. I'd forgotten about Primo's plans to take over the food depot.

What would the government do if they found out? Or Coleman? I could let slip to Louis ...

They wouldn't care. They'd probably just cut off supplies to that depot, and by extension, the whole of Area Four. I think of the stick figures on the streets, the scrawny street children begging for food that no one has to give. They will die before Primo dies.

There's more riding on this leadership fight than I'd thought. If Aleesha loses, the people of Four will starve. A sick feeling spreads through my stomach. I want to believe she can win. But doubt threads through my mind. How can Aleesha possibly hope to defeat that giant?

Have faith in her.

I push the doubts back down. I can't get rid of them entirely but I can keep them inside. Because more than anything else, she needs to know I believe in her. She needs to believe that she can win.

Otherwise, she'll have lost before the fight even begins.

29

Aleesha

Bright morning light filters through the high windows, blinding me. I blink, still in that stage of sleepiness where nothing quite feels real.

Still, at least that means I did sleep a bit.

I yawn and stretch, feeling others begin to wake and move in the room around me. Sitting up, I press my hands into my lower back and roll my neck.

"How did you sleep?" Trey asks from the roll mat next to me.

Well, when my brain wasn't racing at a million miles an hour trying to figure out the odds of me surviving today, I was running through various scenarios in which I end up dead. Oh, and interspersed with that were a few glimpses of Jay's broken and mangled body. But apart from that, I slept great, thanks for asking.

I shrug. "Okay."

There's an atmosphere of tension and anticipation in the room. People look at me as if they're not sure whether they're ever going to see me again. I should probably say something, give a speech perhaps. But I can still remember the last time Jay forced me to speak to the Snakes, and I don't think a repeat performance is going to make me feel better.

Not today.

I force down some food and a bottle of water and pull on my boots. My fingers linger on the amulet that's tied around my ankle. I'm glad to have it back, but I don't feel the same attachment to it that I used to. I once thought it was my ticket to a new life. Now, it's just a piece of cheap jewellery. But it does remind me of her.

Maybe I'll be seeing you sooner than I thought, Mother.

I head to the long, narrow room where the monks sleep. It's empty, the sheets on the beds neatly folded back. At the far end of the room, a wooden post stands against the wall. Rogue had torn it down from one of the old sheds at the back of the graveyard and brought it in for me yesterday. The abbot reluctantly agreed when I explained that if I practised throwing outside, one of Primo's spies would surely see me and give away any advantage I have.

The only thing I can't control is whether the officials will let me use my own knives when we get to that round.

If I make it to that round.

I shake the thought from my head.

Usually, the knives are provided, but Samson said he'd have a word with the head official. I just have to hope she's happy with the two I have. They're regulation length, at least. Throwing knives accurately is hard enough. Throwing ones I don't know the weight and balance of is much harder.

I pull the blades from my belt and toss them at the beam. They land where I'd intended them to, one at head height, one at heart height.

I walk forward to retrieve the knives from the beam and hear the click of the door opening behind me.

"You've got a good aim."

I freeze with my hand on the handle of my best blade.

Yanking it from the wood, I turn and pocket it. "What are you doing here?"

I don't need this. Not now.

My father walks slowly toward me.

"It's not too late, you know," he says quietly. "You don't have to do this. I can ... deal with him."

I feel a flash of irritation. "I don't need you to fight my battles for me."

"I never said you did," he answers mildly, a smile tugging at the corner of his mouth. "But having only just found out that I have a daughter, I'd quite like to keep her alive for a bit longer."

I stare at him, then turn and pull the second knife from the beam.

He doesn't think I can do it.

I stiffen as his hands rest on my shoulders. "Come on, Aleesha. You don't have to do this. You could leave today – I'll ask Katya to take you out on one of the boats."

I resist the urge to whip around and press the tip of my blade into his belly. It would almost be worth it to see the look on his face.

Instead, I blow out a breath and shrug his hands away, trying to damp down the anger sparking inside me. "You don't know me at all, do you? You look at the people out here and see beggars, thieves, murderers." I scratch a thin line in the beam with the tip of my blade. "I see friends, allies, people who need my help. I can't *leave* them. Not when Primo is still around."

"And if he were not around?"

I close my eyes and swallow. "I don't know."

"Let me deal with him. I don't understand why you have to go through this stupid charade anyway."

The tip of my knife digs into the wooden beam.

"It's how things are done here. It's how the gangs work. You have to *earn* your right to be leader."

"And that's what you want? To be the leader of a group of half-starved vagrants?" He grunts out a laugh. "I can't believe you'd choose them over family."

The spark ignites into flames.

I whirl around, the knife still in my hand. "They *are* my family. The only family I've known for the past twelve years."

He steps back, taken aback by the emotion in my voice.

"You left me here!"

He steps forward, gripping my arms. His hands are strong, almost as strong as Samson's. "I didn't know you existed."

I whip my arms up between his, breaking his hold. "You can't come here and expect me to give everything up for you."

"What are you giving up?" He gestures around us. "A hovel in a church? A half-starved group of people who look to you to save them from a gang leader? If Primo falls, someone else will take his place."

"That's what you think of us? Of me?"

His shoulders sag and he runs a hand across his forehead as if realizing he's gone too far. "That's not what I meant."

No, it's exactly what you meant.

He sucks in a breath. "Look, I'm just offering you an alternative. I'd have thought you would be happy to be given a chance to start over. That's what Maria would have wanted for you."

How dare he bring her into this.

"And what about what I want? Or what Katya wants? I saw you two together, and if you think I want to go anywhere with *her*, you're mistaken."

His face darkens. "Look, Katya and I—"

"Shut up!"

I close my eyes and take a deep breath. I can't do this now. I need to save my energy for the fight.

"I don't want to talk about this. The best thing you can do for me right now is leave."

I keep my eyes closed, not opening them until I hear his footsteps move off across the stone floor and the door click shut behind him.

Strangely, the knowledge that he doesn't believe I can win makes me even more determined to prove him wrong.

I shove the knife into my belt and follow him from the room.

It is time.

* * *

The sun blazes down on the square. The arena has already been ringed off when I arrive. The jury's table is set up, ready for the fight to begin. The head official comes to meet me as I make my way over to my corner, flanked by Trey and Rogue.

"Stop and search," she snaps.

I raise my arms, submitting to the request. She runs her hands down me, paying close attention to my legs, seeking out hidden weapons. Her search is thorough but she finds nothing. The amulet is back around my ankle, inside my boot. I hope it'll bring me luck.

She stands and tugs at the loose vest I'm wearing. "You know the clothing rules?"

I nod and lift the vest to show her the tight cropped top I wear underneath. Men have to fight bare-chested so there's no clothing to grab or tear. Or protect your skin. But when the current leader of the Dragons had her leadership contest, the official had to come up with a new rule for women, so we're allowed a minimal covering for modesty.

The woman meets my eye. "Good luck, Aleesha. I hope you have a plan."

As she returns to the jury's table, I walk through the gathering crowd to where Anders, Danny and most of the rest of my gang are waiting.

My gang.

Funny how I think of them as that now.

On the opposite side of the arena, Primo is laughing and joking. He's already stripped to the waist, his dark snake tattoo stark against his pale skin. He seems in high spirits as he takes a swig from a bottle of Chaz.

"I thought they'd taken all their supplies?" I hiss to Rogue.

He follows the direction of my gaze and frowns. "Perhaps it's just the one. They must have picked it up on the way down here. I'll see if we can do anything about it."

When Petal had come to see us the previous evening, he'd looked exhausted but triumphant. "Got the tanks emptied last night. Wasn't much in them, as you'd said. Some of the kids managed to sneak in and empty the water bottles they had in the building. Took their food too, not that they had much of it. Then we hung around the entrances to the building – anytime any of them popped their heads out, we took a pot shot at them. They soon got the message."

"Are you sure you want this on your skin?" Trey studies the unlabelled bottle of oil Petal had handed me last night.

"Yes. It'll make it harder for him to get a grip on me." I hesitate. "Would … would you mind rubbing it in for me? I don't want to get the oil on my hands."

Trey nods and I pull my vest over my head. I feel naked without it and cross my arms over my cropped top. My stomach is pancake flat and my arms twigs compared to Primo's bulging figure.

How can I hope to beat him?

Gently, Trey lifts my arms away, one at a time, and rubs oil into my skin before moving to do my back. His breath heats my neck and a shiver trickles down my spine as his fingers massage my tense muscles. It feels strangely intimate given that we're surrounded by people, and when his hands finally leave my body, I ache for them to return.

"The square's full and people are still trying to get in," Anders comments, bringing me back to the present with a jolt.

Danny offers me a protein bar, but I shake my head. Even the thought of eating is enough to make me nauseous. My pulse quickens and I force myself to take long, slow breaths to slow it down.

"Leadership challenges are always popular," Danny says, pocketing the bar. "Everyone's rootin' for you, y'know."

He says it to make me feel better, but his words just remind me of how much is at stake. The bookies will be weaving through the crowd now, taking bets on the outcome of the fight. I wonder what the odds are and decide I probably don't want to know.

I take a glug of water, though I don't really need it. I drank my fill this morning, and normally that would be enough to see me through the day, but even I'm feeling the unrelenting heat. The air is muggy and thick with the tension that comes before the rain. In the distance, south across the river, dark storm clouds gather. I hope they hold off long enough.

I find myself hoping a lot of things.

A bell rings and the babble of the crowd fades to silence.

Trey cups my face, turning it to his and looking into my eyes. "I believe in you," he says quietly.

"I know."

He releases me and I duck under the rope into the arena.

The concrete ground is covered in a thin layer of dust. Guards stand just outside the roped-off arena, their backs to us, keeping the crowds at bay. Behind them, hundreds of faces are turned to me and the man who walks toward me.

I look past Primo, to his supporters waiting on the far side of the arena. Vihaan stands to one side. He catches me looking at him and a sneer appears on his face. He jerks his thumbs down and mouths something that I don't catch, though I can guess the gist of it.

Primo's officers stand stiff and silent, many of their faces creased in worry. They haven't learned to hide their emotions yet, but they will.

But are they worried about what happens if he loses, or what happens if he wins?

That I won't know until after the fight.

If I survive.

Stop being so negative.

Winning is all in the mind. That's what old Davie used to tell me when he was teaching me to fight. You have to imagine you alive and them defeated, and then you let that feeling bury your fear deep inside you. Show them that you *know* you're going to win. That's half the battle.

But as hard as I try, all I see when I close my eyes is Jay's crumpled and bloodied body.

I reach the centre of the arena, where the official is waiting. Primo comes to a halt two metres from me. A murmur of apprehension ripples through the crowd and I wonder what this looks like to them – a child next to a giant, my head barely reaching his chest. He could probably encircle my leg with one of his hands.

What had seemed like a good idea in the safety of the church now seems like a hopelessly idealistic plan.

The first round. Just get through the first round.

I breathe slowly through my nose and clench my hands to stop them trembling. Adrenaline surges through my veins and I fight to control it – to use it rather than let it overcome me.

Sweat beads on Primo's upper lip and forehead, and the small triangle of hair on his chest is dark and slick. I count the rise and falls of his chest. His breathing is shallow and fast, quicker than I would have thought for someone with his fitness and genetics. His tongue flicks out repeatedly to lick his lips.

So he is thirsty.

And he's sweating. It's a good start.

But when I lift my eyes to his, an icy chill quenches the heat in my body. They are the eyes of a snake. A snake who has its prey in his sight and is just waiting to strike.

"You both know the rules. Fifteen minutes. Any blow or tackle after the bell has rung and you forfeit the contest. Any assistance from outside the arena and you forfeit the contest. If either of you want to give up, you just have to slap the floor and say 'I yield'. Otherwise, you fight until your opponent overpowers you."

Or kills you.

"Do you both wish to proceed?"

She looks to Primo and then to me. We both nod.

"Then let the fight commence."

The bell tolls.

For a moment, neither of us move.

Then Primo attacks, lunging toward me in a blur of movement. He's fast, but I'd caught the flicker of his intention in his eyes and spin on my toes to dodge his outstretched arm.

We circle one another, each trying to guess the other's strategy. His eyes never leave mine, waiting for me to move so he can assess how fast I am. I wonder if he watched me when I fought at the church, how closely he studied my movements during my brawl with Vihaan.

He can't know about my knife skills. Not even Vihaan knows I can throw.

It's the one opportunity I'll have to take him down. Of course, that's only helpful if I can make it to the third round.

Nerves claw at my stomach.

Primo darts forward, a feint intended to draw me out. I ignore it and keep circling.

He runs at me again and I'm slow to react, not sure if this is another deception. Just in time, I spring to the side, but he's already there in front of me, having anticipated my move.

So fast.

I barely see his arms move before his hands are on my waist, lifting me and swinging me around as easily as a bag of flour. But his hands slip on my oil-slicked skin, and I fly through the air as his grip fails.

The crowd gasps.

I hit the ground, instinctively rolling away. Dust rises around me, coating my mouth and choking my throat.

I lie there, the breath pounded from my lungs. My brain screams at my body to move.

Slow footsteps make the ground beneath me tremble.

I scramble to my feet, ducking as Primo's arm slices the air above my head. Sucking in the dry air, I dig the toes of my boots into the hard ground and launch myself forward, diving under his outstretched arm, my hands brushing against his chest as I slide past him.

I don't stop until I'm at the far side of the arena, my chest heaving from exertion.

Calm your breathing. It's all about the breath.

I push air out, trying to make the fear leave with it, as it had at the church. If I can find that same state of flow, perhaps I'll have a chance.

But I'm given little opportunity to do that.

Primo charges toward me and I'm forced to run. We race around the outside of the arena, his long legs eating up the distance between us. The crowd murmurs in discontent. They came to watch a fight, not a man chase a skinny girl around a ring.

A moment before he catches me, I veer into the centre of the ring and turn to confront him. Dust coats my oiled body but I'm not sweating, and despite the heat, I feel fresh.

Primo stops five paces away. He's panting heavily and sweat trickles down his chest like rain on a windowpane. I tense, waiting for his next attack.

"You know, we don't *have* to do this. I don't like killing pretty girls. You could give up now. Join me." He gives me a cold leer. "I'm in need of some female company."

He wants to talk?

"No, thanks. I saw what you did to your last girlfriend."

"Megan?" He spits in the dirt. "She was a pathetic creature. Stupid like the rest of these Outsiders. But not you."

He tilts his head to one side but I'm not fooled. He's taking a moment to recover. Already, his breathing has slowed.

"Do you know how long I was a captain in the Metz?"

I shake my head.

"Fifteen years." He pauses and I wonder where he's going with this. "After I saw you in the compound, I looked up the records you'd accessed." A smile spreads in a hard line across his face. "You do look like her, you know. Your mother, I assume?"

It feels like a punch to my heart.

Primo nods sagely. "She was very beautiful. I'd have rather fancied her for myself if I'd been permitted. Such a shame she had to die." He takes a step toward me. "As you will die."

"You killed her."

The words pass from my lips though I barely remember thinking them. My mind is numb, my body unresponsive. Inside me, anger flares.

"You killed her," I repeat, more strongly this time.

"Just doing my job."

"Where is he?" A harsh guttural voice. The baton coming down on my mother's elbow, her scream of pain. The shot. The shot ...

I tear my eyes from his and clutch at my chest.

At that moment he strikes, moving so fast that even my instincts can't get me out of the way in time. His fist slams into my chest. I'm on the ground and he's kneeling over me, his hand pinning my shoulder down.

Pain wracks my chest, making it hard to breathe. I wonder if he's cracked my breastbone.

He killed her.

Primo's breath is hot on my face. Sweat drips off his forehead onto mine.

Silence surrounds us. I think of Trey's face and wish he wasn't here to see this.

"Like this position?" Primo jams my shoulder a little harder against the concrete. "Get used to it."

I close my eyes. From somewhere deep in my mind, something Samson had said comes back to me.

He's used to fighting fair. So fight like an Outsider.

"All you have to do is yield ..."

I bring my knee up hard between his legs. My eyes fly open as he grunts in pain, his body jerking back reflexively. I knee him again and punch his nose with my free hand for good measure.

He tilts sideways, off-balance. I shove him, twist my legs out from under him and shakily get to my feet. I cradle the hand I'd punched him with across my chest.

Reckon it hurt me more than him.

Primo lies on the ground for just a little too long.

Surely it can't be long until the bell?

I glance over to my corner. Rogue holds up three fingers.

Three minutes. I can last that long ... I think.

Primo takes his time getting up, brushing the dirt off him. His body is as tense as a coiled spring. I swallow, trying to moisten my mouth. So far he's been holding back, wanting to see what I can do. But now he knows how weak I am, how my blows fall like a child's fists against his body, he won't hold back.

The pain in my chest throbs relentlessly.

He seems to grow even taller as he walks toward me. His head blocks out the sun, casting his face in shadow. I back away, trying to judge how far I am from the roped boundary of the arena.

Not far.

I feint to one side, then the other, arching my back as his fist whistles through the air above me.

I flip backward but he's already on me, his arm closing around me, trapping me to his side. The oil on my body slides against the sweat on his as I try to wriggle free. He brings his other hand around to grasp me, but he's too late. Like an eel, I slither from his grasp and fall to the ground.

My relief is short-lived.

He lashes out with his foot, catching me in the stomach. I fly through the air, the landing knocking the air from my body once again, and I don't have time to move before he's on me. This time, he rests his knee on my chest.

I can't breathe.

My lungs gasp for air. Black spots dance in front of my eyes and pain radiates from my chest as his weight presses down.

I bang my fists against his leg but it's like beating an iron bar. Futile.

The dark marking on the inside of his arm proclaiming his Metz rank hovers in front of my eyes, the numbers blurred. His hands pin mine to the ground

My nostrils flare, trying to suck in air, but there's no room for my lungs to expand. My vision darkens.

"Yield," he says quietly.

My ribs bend under the pressure on my chest. It's almost unbearable. Soon they will break and I don't think I can face the pain.

He could have killed me already, but he chooses to play with me, like a toy.

"Yield and be mine."

But surely a short pain is better than a lifetime of torture? I think of Megan's battered body, her spirit almost broken.

"No," I gasp out through my teeth.

Anger flashes in Primo's eyes as he pulls back his arm.

"Then y—"

A bell rings out, loud in the hushed silence that surrounds us.

"End of round one. Return to your corners!"

For a second, I think Primo is going to disobey and kill me anyway. But slowly he lets his arm fall to his side. The weight lifts from my chest and I'm left there panting as he stands and walks away.

Saved by the bell. And Primo's arrogance.

For now.

30

Trey

My shoulders relax as Primo rises and stalks to his corner of the arena.

"That was too close," Anders murmurs.

"But she made it."

No one answers me, but Danny and Anders exchange a worried look.

Aleesha lies still for a moment, then rolls onto her side and gets awkwardly to her feet. She wraps her arms protectively around her chest and hobbles over to us.

"How long's she got to rest?" Rogue asks.

"Fifteen minutes," Danny replies.

My limbs feel frozen in place and it's Anders who helps Aleesha under the rope barrier and sits her down in the chair with a bottle of water. He pulls a small box from his pocket and opens it revealing a pair of small syringes.

"Pain meds. The medic woman gave them to us." He selects a syringe and jabs the needle into Aleesha's arm.

She winces. "Thanks. Did the official clear them?"

Anders mutters something inaudible.

Aleesha glances over her shoulder at the jury's table, then

shrugs.

"That's the worst round out of the way." I try to control the tremble in my voice. "Good idea getting him in the balls. At least that's one disadvantage he has."

"He won't fall for it again," Rogue says darkly.

Shouts rise above the background murmur of the crowd, and I look up to see what the commotion's about. A widening space is growing around Primo, who seems to be in a fury about something.

"Guess he's just found out that his Chaz is gone," Danny drawls.

Aleesha glances at him. "You took it?"

"Tommy did. Kid sneaked in while they were watching the fight and grabbed it from under their noses."

"It's handy being small," a brown-haired boy pipes up from behind him, his chest swelling with pride.

Aleesha gives him a fond smile. "Good work, little man."

He beams at her.

The bell rings once. Five-minute warning. When they're fighting, time seems to slow down, whereas the rest breaks go past in a flash.

I pull bandages from my pockets and begin to wrap them around Aleesha's wrists to give her a bit of extra support in the next round, but my hands are shaking so much that Rogue has to take over.

Once finished, he glances across the arena at Primo with such hate in his eyes that, for a moment, I wonder if he's going to run over there and take him on himself.

Anders places a hand lightly on his arm. "Rogue ..."

I help Aleesha to her feet. "Try and use the weight of the club to your advantage."

Great advice, Trey. Tell her something she doesn't know.

She nods, flexes her wrists and ducks under the rope again. Her movements are less awkward and I thank the stars that Anders had managed to get hold of some painkillers.

The official waits in the centre of the arena, her fingertips balancing two clubs beside her. They're about half a metre long and made from smooth wood.

They look heavy.

Sweat gathers under my arms and at the back of my neck. The sun blazes down and I wish I'd thought to bring a hat. It doesn't seem to bother Danny, Tommy or the other Outsiders, but Rogue's sweating freely and Anders keeps glancing up at the sun as if by doing so, he can hide from it.

But if I could do anything to make the sun's heat stronger, I would. Because as much as we're suffering, Primo is suffering more.

The bigger they are, the more they sweat.

In the arena, the official inspects Aleesha's bandages and nods, convinced that the added support won't make a significant difference to the fight. She hands one of the clubs to Primo and one to Aleesha. The muscles on Aleesha's back tense, her shoulder blades drawing back as she hefts the club, testing its weight.

The official says something and looks from Primo to Aleesha. They both nod.

The bell tolls.

Aleesha raises her club and pulls back so there's about ten paces between her and Primo. She uses both hands to lift it, and though her arms are steady I can see the strain in her muscles.

Primo twirls his in one hand like a baton. If I didn't know better, I'd have thought his club weightless. He strolls confidently toward Aleesha. In this round, with his superior strength, I guess he thinks he's already won.

"Keep moving, Aleesha," Rogue murmurs by my side.

Aleesha drops the club to the ground, her shoulders slumping in tiredness. One hand clutches at the side of her chest and I damn well hope she's feigning, because if not, this round isn't going to last very long.

I lick my lips, feeling the sun burn the back of my neck.

Primo attacks from above, bringing his club down in an arc aimed at Aleesha's shoulder. She sidesteps out of the way and swings her own club at ankle height across the ground. Primo dances back out of reach, surprise registering on his face.

Aleesha launches into another attack. She brandishes her club, aiming for Primo's exposed side.

No, he'll see that coming.

One second Primo is there, the next, he's gone. The momentum of Aleesha's swing carries her forward into his path. He thrusts upward and the tip of his club catches Aleesha's arm.

Aleesha stumbles back, dragging her club one-handed along the ground. They're just a few metres from us now. Dust rises, biting at my eyes. I blink furiously and wipe my sleeve across my face.

"Come on Aleesha ..."

When my vision clears, I catch Danny scanning the crowd. His gaze lingers on those gathered in Primo's corner.

What does he think they're going to do?

There's a collective intake of breath and my eyes dart back to the arena. Aleesha's club rests on her shoulder, but it's Primo who the crowd is staring at. His eyes are closed and sweat glistens on his bare chest and back. He takes a hand from his club to wipe it against the fabric of his trousers.

The sun beats down.

"Move, Aleesha, this is your chance." Rogue's words are a whisper between gritted teeth.

But Aleesha doesn't move, and a second later Primo's eyes are open and he's walking toward her, squinting against the glare of the sun. Aleesha backs away, but he follows, blocking her path.

Her eyes flick from side to side, then she darts forward, letting the club slide off her shoulder and slam into the back of Primo's knee. She stumbles away, just in time to miss his flailing club, and drags her weapon back up to her shoulder.

Primo's leg buckles and he falls to one knee.

Now!

This time, Aleesha takes advantage of Primo's moment of weakness. The club in her hand trembles as she struggles to raise it over her head. She lets the weighted end fall toward Primo's back.

Crack. Wood meets wood as Primo blocks the blow.

Aleesha staggers back and drops her club. It lands with a thud on the ground in front of her. She shakes one arm awkwardly, then the other before stretching down for the handle.

Before she can recover, Primo's on his feet, swinging at her again. She tries to bring her club up, but she's so slow …

I blink and in my mind's eye see the club connecting with her head, her body crumpling to the ground.

I taste blood in my mouth.

There's a crack and my eyes fly open.

Somehow she managed to get the club up in time to block Primo's blow. But her club is on the ground between them now and she's shaking like a leaf, her chest heaving. Her eyelids flicker as she forces air in and out of her lungs. Fear is etched into her features.

My stomach clenches.

Five minutes, Aleesha. You just have to last five minutes.

Then something changes.

The fear on her face fades and her eyes narrow. She ignores the club on the ground and backs away, drawing Primo with her.

His club whips through the air toward her, but she's no longer there. He strikes again but she weaves around him like a cat, pulling him further and further from where her club lies. The two of them are locked in a strange dance that neither quite controls.

Then Aleesha breaks away, sprinting across the ring. Primo follows, but his momentary hesitation provides enough time for Aleesha's hands to close on the handle of her club.

She swings it as he approaches, putting her whole weight behind the movement, letting the club spin her around.

She catches Primo on his side. Her second swing follows it up with a strike to his elbow as he stumbles.

Primo howls in pain.

Aleesha wheels away, her long braid whipping around her head.

She's actually winning ...

I realize I've been holding my breath and let it out before sucking hot air into my lungs.

"They found 'im more water."

I glance around, then down to find the source of the voice. Tommy's tugging urgently at Danny's arm. "They stole it from a woman in the crowd."

Danny curses.

"I can get it back!"

"It's too dangerous, Tommy. They'll be on the lookout after last time."

"I can do it, I know I can!"

Danny nods reluctantly. "Well, okay, but be careful. Don't take any risks."

Tommy scurries off, disappearing into the crowd. Danny gives me a grim smile.

There's a gasp from the crowd and I feel Rogue tense next to me. My eyes fly back to the arena and lock on Aleesha.

She's on the run, dragging her club behind her, her eyes wide.

Behind her, comes Primo.

With a roar that deafens out the murmur of the crowd, he strikes. The tip of his club catches Aleesha on her thigh and she screams in pain.

Heat drains from my face.

Somehow she stays upright and turns, raising her club in defence.

I can see the hunger in Primo's eyes – his desire to crush her. My fingernails dig into the back of the wooden chair.

He slams his club down onto hers with such force that Aleesha loses her grip and the weapon hits the ground with a dull *thunk*. She snatches at it and staggers back, dragging it out of his reach.

I wait for Primo to close in and finish her off.

But he doesn't move. He just stands there, the veins in his arms bulging as he grasps his club even tighter. His face hardens into a snarl and he spits, throwing the club half the length of the arena.

The sound of the bell cuts through the dull thumping in my ears.

Air rushes from my lungs. Two rounds over.

"How are you doing?" Rogue asks as Aleesha stumbles back

under the rope.

She slumps into the chair and closes her eyes. "Been better." She presses a hand lightly to her thigh and grimaces.

"Can't give you another shot for the pain yet," Anders says. He makes an anxious face. "Sorry, you're going to have to make do."

I bend down beside her, wiping the sweat from her brow with the soft fabric of my sleeve. "You've done the hard work. Everything is going to plan. Primo is weak. Look at him."

She follows my gaze to where Primo is slumped on the ground in his corner. A woman tries to shade him with a jacket, but he pushes her away. They're all staring down at him, all apart from a thin man with greasy black hair and sallow skin. He looks at us and I feel a trace of unease pass over me.

I glance over at Danny. "Is Tommy back yet?"

"No." His forehead creases in a frown. But Primo doesn't seem to have anything to drink, so maybe Tommy's managed to get hold of the water.

"Where are these blades then?" The official strides toward us, stopping on the other side of the rope. She holds out her hands. Rogue pulls a pair of knives from his belt and hands them over. The official inspects them, though I'm not sure what she's looking for. Apparently satisfied, she hands them to Aleesha with a nod. "You've got five minutes."

Aleesha flexes her fingers then lifts a water bottle to her lips. The bottle trembles, betraying her fear. She takes two big gulps of water.

I kneel beside her and take her other hand, massaging her forearm with my thumbs.

"Thanks." She gives me a small smile.

"Do you want me to take the bandages off?"

She shakes her head.

"Rain is coming." I look up to see Anders staring south across the river. Broiling clouds scud across the sky toward us.

"It's time."

I pull back and let Rogue help Aleesha to her feet. His lips are set in a hard line and fire still burns in his eyes. "You have to end it this round. Remember who you're fighting for."

The bell dongs.

I raise my hand to Aleesha's face, turning it toward me. My thumb strikes a line through the dirt on her cheekbone. "You can do this."

I brush my lips across hers, tasting salty sweat and blood.

When I draw away her face is set in determination.

She turns without a word, ducks under the rope and walks across to the centre of the arena, one knife held lightly in each hand.

Primo is already waiting. He grips the six-inch blades tightly, his shoulders tense. The official's talking to them, explaining some rule or other.

Out the corner of my eye, I catch sight of a familiar face in the crowd. It's Tommy, and I lift my hand to wave before realizing that he's not alone. As I watch, a squat thug of a man with a bald head wraps an arm around the young boy's neck, pulling him up so Tommy's forced to stand on his toes. His eyes are wide with fear as they meet mine and he chokes for air as the arm tightens. Then the man pulls Tommy back into the crowd and out of sight.

It takes a few seconds for my brain to piece together the puzzle.

They're using him as bait. To distract Aleesha.

I push through the crowd, ignoring Danny's shout behind

me. Tommy is in danger. Which means Aleesha's in even more danger than she realizes.

She won't hesitate to save him, even if it means sacrificing herself.

I won't let her do that.

A dull dong sounds and the crowd falls silent.

I try to push the fight from my mind. Aleesha can look after herself. I just need to make sure everything goes to plan.

The crowd is packed tight and making headway is slow, but I manage to grab a short knife out of the belt of a skinny man while he's trying to look over the heads of the people in front of him. He curses and whirls around, but I'm already gone. I keep the blade pointing down, still wondering what I'm going to do if and when I find Tommy.

The crowd parts momentarily, giving me a glimpse of Aleesha and Primo circling one another, neither one attacking.

"Get on with it!" someone shouts from nearby.

My eyes seek out the voice, but instead, I catch a glimpse of the bald man who'd been holding Tommy.

He's twenty paces away.

I slip through the crowd as quietly as I can, grateful for the muttering and jeering that masks my movements. As I get closer, I see Tommy, his head bobbing up and down as he struggles to break free.

No one seems bothered that a man is quietly throttling the life out of a child in their midst.

Finally, there's just an old woman between him and me. I hesitate, then gently push her aside and dig the point of the knife blade into the man's back. His spine stiffens.

"Let go of the kid." I try to make my voice gruff and low to sound threatening, but my mouth's so dry that the words come out cracked and broken. I poke the blade a little harder to make up for it.

It has the desired effect. Slowly, the thug pulls his arm back and Tommy wiggles from his grasp.

Tommy's eyes meet mine, then dart to a point over my shoulder and widen. His mouth opens as if to give a warning.

Cold metal presses against my neck.

"I'd drop that knife if I were you."

My fingers open and the knife clatters to the ground. I mouth at Tommy to run, but the boy just stands there, gaping like a fish out of water. The thug makes a grab for him and finally Tommy moves, sliding from his grasp and pushing his way through the crowd.

The blade against my throat is sharp enough to nick the skin when I swallow, and a drop of warm blood runs down to my collarbone.

The thug turns and gives me a toothy smile. "Plan worked," he says to the man behind me.

"Course it worked." The man holding me sounds irritated. "Now, get his hands."

The bald man grabs my hands and yanks them behind my back. The man behind me grasps my sleeves and twists them, torquing my hands together. He yanks down, forcing my back to bend painfully.

A strand of greasy hair brushes across my forehead.

"Nice meeting you, Trey."

31

Aleesha

We stand in silence after the bell has rung, each trying to work out how much the other is suffering. Primo looks tired, his eyes slightly glazed and squinting in the bright sunlight. But his gaze never leaves mine and I know that despite the dehydration and the heat, he's still stronger than me.

In my right hand, I carry the blade Bryn gave me. It's my best throwing knife, though I've practised with both and can throw with either arm.

"You caused this, you know," Primo says finally. His voice is cracked and dry. "With that black box, you took everything from me. Everything!"

He takes a step toward me. I stand my ground.

"Do you have it? Can you … can you make us as we were again?" His voice is barely audible.

I shake my head, confused. "No. It only works one way."

His shoulders sag.

"You could have gone back to the compound, like the others. You didn't have to stay out here. You had a choice."

"You gave me no choice!" He drops his voice. "How could I

have gone back after that? The shame of it."

His eyes burn with rage.

My hand tightens on my knife.

He darts forward suddenly, slashing wildly with his blade. I dance to the side, poised on the balls of my feet.

"You killed my friends."

"You could have saved them if you'd given yourself up. *You* had a choice." His eyes narrow. "We didn't."

"You're wrong."

He's right.

My friends died because I wasn't smart enough to see through Primo's ruse. They died because I wasn't there when he surrounded the church. Because I did what I wanted, not thinking about the consequences.

My heart pounds, a dull ache in my chest, echoed in my ears. I shake my head but I can't clear it.

"Do you end up killing *everyone* you care about, Aleesha? Is that why you don't have any friends?"

A mist comes down over my eyes. Before I can stop myself, I'm surging forward, my knife flailing in front of me.

But Primo's not there.

A stab of pain shoots up my left arm. Dark blood leaks from the wound and slides down my arm. I sense movement and drop to my knees as a blade slices the air above my head.

I drop and roll, fury driving me to my feet.

My blade meets his in a clash of metal. Sparks rain down as metal slides over metal with a screech that makes my jaw clench.

I release my knife and dive to the side, managing to catch his chest with the tip of my second blade as I move.

In return, I get a slash across my back that causes me to scream in pain and stumble away. A thick rope blocks my path.

"What are you doing?" Rogue's voice cuts through my daze.

His hands are white on the rope. My eyes trace the line of the rope to the corner.

I'm trapped.

I whirl around, the knives feeling suddenly heavy in my shaking hands. Primo is strolling toward me, his face twisted into that familiar cold smile.

I've fallen into his trap again.

"Whatever he said to you, ignore it! It's not important," Rogue whispers in my ear. "Go!"

Blood trickles down my back and into the waistband of my trousers.

"Come out, Aleesha. Can't stay in your corner forever. No hiding behind your friends this time, letting them die for you."

His words cut me to the bone.

Control. Breathe.

I draw a breath, trying to grasp that control, the flow I'd had in the last round. But anger and fear make me jittery, and it feels as if I'm clutching at smoke.

I lurch forward just in time to stop him boxing me into the corner.

Our knives meet in the air. He presses his weight down on the blade, forcing me back, daring me to weaken. I whip my knife out from under his, slashing at his belly as I dance to one side.

I may be bleeding, but so is he. We both know this can't go on much longer. I just need a bit of distance to give me some throwing room and something to distract him. A breath of wind whips around me. It's warm and carries rain, and with it a memory of Jay's fight with Primo.

Use the dust.

I scuff my boot across the floor. A cloud of dust rises, enveloping Primo as he lurches after me. I back away. Five paces. Ten. He's coughing, scrubbing at his face with his arm, sweat caking the dust on his skin.

I draw my arm back. My blade has already tasted blood. It will taste more.

"Aleesha!"

My head whips around.

Vihaan.

He calls again and I follow the sound of his voice. My arm falls to my side. He's at the front of the crowd, mid-way between Primo's corner and mine. In front of him is Trey, his head bent back and his eyes wide with fear. A tiny trickle of blood runs down his neck from the tip of Vihaan's blade.

My body turns to stone.

He can't do this. It's not allowed.

I glance at the head official, but she just shrugs as if to say "it's outside the ring, not my responsibility". One of the guards makes a move toward Vihaan but he just shakes his head, pressing the knife into Trey's neck and the guard retreats.

"Your choice, Aleesha." He cocks his head. "What will you sacrifice to win?"

A distant rumble of thunder rolls over the square.

Primo's coughing has stopped. I've lost my advantage. But my eyes are still locked on Vihaan.

Trey's mouth moves in silent words. "Kill him."

But who? Kill who?

Trey's eyes shift to the side. He means Primo. Killing Primo would end the fight and end his control over Area Four. That's what Rogue and Anders would tell me to do. It's the logical thing to do.

But Vihaan knows what he will lose if Primo dies. And I know he won't hesitate to kill Trey if he has to.

I've already waited too long.

Footsteps pound toward me, Primo bearing down on me like a raging bear. Sunlight sparkles on the dust that rises around him, creating a ghostly halo. I draw back my arm. I still have time to throw. The balance is right.

It has to be a perfect throw.

I let the knife fly.

My aim is true. Fifteen paces away, the tip of the blade pierces Vihaan's eye. He doesn't even cry out as the knife tumbles from his hand and he falls back into the crowd.

Primo crashes into me, his weight and momentum carrying us both to the ground. I try and twist away but it all happens too fast. My left arm is trapped beneath him and I hear the bone crack as it's crushed under his weight.

A scream erupts from my lips as pain explodes in my arm.

Primo rolls off me, causing another wave of agony. I scream again, wondering how my lungs can produce such a sound.

Have to ... get ... away.

The concrete is hard under my knees as I push myself up and vomit, my whole body shaking as my stomach empties itself onto the ground. I try and get to my feet but my legs collapse under me. Blackness threatens to overwhelm me and I blink as another wave of nausea rides up my throat.

Pain is all in the mind.

The thought cuts through my dizziness as a breath of cool air caresses my face. Whoever said that was an idiot.

A drop of water tickles my neck. I glance up at the wind-whipped clouds moving across the blue sky just as the sun disappears.

My breath comes in gasps. Pain races through my body like a fever.

Primo.

I stagger to my feet and look around.

Primo stands to one side, his chest heaving. One of his knives is gone – in the dust somewhere, presumably – but he clutches his remaining blade in his right hand. He seems to be waiting for me to recover. Perhaps he's still waiting for me to yield, to submit to him. He knows I can't win this fight.

I look down at my hands, both knives lost in the dirt, and nearly fall to my knees in relief that it will soon be over.

I believe in you.

Trey's words come back to me. He believed I could win. Can I let him down? Let them all down?

My body sways, halfway between standing and falling, and through the fog of pain in my head, my mind begins to work.

I glance up again at the black cloud moving across the sun.

It's a crazy plan. Chances are, it won't work. But I'm out of choices.

I force my legs to carry me toward Primo. Blood pulses from my broken arm and I wonder how much longer I'll be able to stand.

Primo's in better shape, but as I get closer, I can see the pain lining his face. His breath rasps and he sways slightly, the effects of dehydration taking their toll.

"Giving up yet?" he manages.

I don't answer but limp around him, forcing him to turn to face me. The sun's rays begin to warm my back again.

A few more seconds.

"Ready to yield, or do I have to finish you off?"

The heat intensifies. Primo's eyes screw up, his pupils black pinpricks.

Now.

I jerk my head over my shoulder as if I've seen something. Primo's eyes instinctively follow my feigned line of sight, and at that moment, the sun emerges from behind the cloud, momentarily blinding him.

My legs close the distance between us. He blinks, stupefied by the light. He can hear me approaching and waves his knife helplessly in front of him.

I reach out with my good hand, not for his knife, but for his wrist. Sinking my teeth into the fleshy part of his thumb, I taste sweat and dirt and blood. I bite down harder until his thumb releases its grip on the handle of the knife.

It falls into my hand and I stumble forward, slashing at the back of Primo's knee. He screams as his leg collapses under him. I slam into him, my fragile weight enough to tip his balance, and we fall to the ground.

Blood fills my mouth. Darkness calls to me, but I force my eyes to stay open.

Primo lies under me. His skin is wet and slippery with sweat.

The knife is still in my hand. I press down on it to push myself up and feel it sink into flesh.

Primo wheezes, his body oddly still.

I straddle him and pull the knife from his side, place it against the vein bulging from his throat.

"Yield."

The word comes out cracked and half-formed. I clear my throat, my vision blurring as a fresh wave of pain shoots up my arm.

"Yield," I manage, more firmly this time.

Primo shifts under me and I feel like I'm trying to ride a whale who could topple me with one roll. I press the tip of my blade a little harder, trying to stop my hand shaking.

Primo closes his eyes and makes an odd sound, part way between a cough and a laugh. "Kill me then."

My heart thumps in my head.

"Yield!"

Don't make me kill you. Please don't make me kill you.

So much death. So much blood.

The tip of my knife scratches his skin. A thin line of blood runs down his neck to the ground.

His chest heaves as a hoarse laugh escapes his lips.

"You cannot take a part of someone ... and expect them to be whole." The words rasp between his teeth.

His body shudders and my leg slips on the blood that leaks from the wound in his side.

"You cannot take someone's life ... who they are ... and expect them to live as a different person."

His eyes open and find mine. They are the grey of the storm clouds that gather above us.

"I remember everything." The corner of his mouth twitches up then falls back. "Everything."

Tears spring to my eyes.

"How can you live with yourself? Knowing what you've done?" My voice is a whisper on the breeze. Silence surrounds us. My hand trembles on the knife handle.

If you're not prepared to kill him, you'll die.

But I can't do it. Can't plunge the blade into the throat of a man who lies at my mercy.

One stab is all it would take. But still, my hand falters.

Primo's eyes close again.

"Because I believe … that to protect the many, we have to sacrifice … a few. Without order and fear, society … falls. So it has always been. So it will always be."

A bloody tear leaks from the corner of his eye. His hand rises from the ground and finds its way to my fingers wrapped around thc knife. His fingers close over mine.

In the sky, another raincloud has joined the first. As Primo looks up at them, his face relaxes.

"We do not yield … do not bow … To anyone."

His hand presses on mine, pushing the blade down.

Blood gushes from the wound, covering my hands, mingling with the blood that flows from my broken arm.

Blood and bone and flesh.

Primo's eyes stare at the sky as the life fades from them. They look strangely peaceful. His body gives a final shudder, then lies still.

I release my grip on the knife, swaying as adrenaline seeps from my body. A drop of water falls, then another, and the smell of hot air just before the rain mingles with the scent of the blood that pools on the ground around us.

A cheer rips through the silence. Then another, and suddenly I am surrounded by overwhelming noise. I try and get to my feet, desperate to get away from it, but my head swims and there is so much pain, so much pain …

I look around, searching the crowd for Trey as my feet finally push me up from Primo's body.

Where is he?

A hand grasps mine, holding it high above my head. The woman shouts my name, pronouncing me the winner. When she releases my arm, it falls to my side.

Faces blur in front of me and I wish people would stop waving their arms – the motion is making me sick. But then I realize I'm the one swaying, and as the rain finally begins to fall and cool my burning body, darkness clouds my vision and I feel myself falling into emptiness.

32

Trey

"Wait, lad!" the man holding me back shouts in my ear, above the roaring of the crowd. "She gotta be announced the winner first. No help 'til then."

He releases me as the referee drops Aleesha's hand. Her eyes seem unfocused and she sways on her feet before collapsing over Primo's body.

I scramble past the guards and under the rope, my hand shaking and slick with sweat. Dropping to my knees, I gently roll her off Primo, so her head is in my lap. I lean down, straining to hear her breathing over my heartbeat hammering in my head. She lies still and, for a second, I think she's not breathing and my own breath catches. But then I spot the slight rise and fall of her chest and feel the warmth of the air leaving her body.

A crack of lightning splits the darkening sky, followed by an ominous rumble. The rain, light at first, gets heavier, hammering into my neck and back as I bend over Aleesha, trying to shelter her from it. The water runs red off her arm and chest.

"Is she alive?"

I look up at Rogue and nod. "I think her arm's bad though. I

... I don't know how to stop the bleeding."

"The pod's coming in now." Rain plasters Mika's hair to her head and drips off her nose, but she doesn't seem to notice. She glances down at Aleesha, then at Rogue. "Can you carry her?"

Rogue nods and bends down to lift Aleesha from me. I let her go reluctantly, carefully supporting her injured arm as Rogue lifts her body. The red medic pod lands in the arena, drawing curious glances from those who haven't been driven away by the rain. Rogue places her inside and the door hisses shut. Mika wipes the rain off her data pad and runs her finger over it.

"It's just analyzing her condition to find out what's wrong with her."

What's wrong with her? She's been beaten half to death, that's what's wrong with her.

I glance around, then back at the pod, then out at the crowd again, trying to distract my thoughts. A group of people are hunched over Primo's body, a makeshift stretcher beside them. It looks too small and fragile for his weight.

"What will happen to him?" Rogue says.

Danny wanders over to us with Anders and catches his words. "Probably get thrown in the river, unless someone wants to take him to the crematorium."

Rogue glances over my shoulder at Primo's followers, who are milling around uncertainly at the corner of the arena. "I don't see any volunteers."

"I'll go and talk to them," Anders says, moving off.

A bleep from Mika's holo pad jerks my attention back to the pod. She scrolls through different screens, her forehead creased in a frown.

"What does it say?"

"Left arm is broken, obviously, but repairable. She'll have to wear a bone healer for a week or so." She continues to scan the reports. "That's the worst injury. There's internal bleeding in her thigh and a little in her chest, plus heavy bruising to the ribcage and femur. Everything else is just cuts and bruises." She looks up at me and smiles. "Don't worry, she'll live. I'm going to take the pod back to the church though – don't fancy hanging around here much longer."

Her fingers fly over the data pad, then she steps onto a small platform at the back of the pod. It rises about eight metres into the air and moves off in the direction of the church.

We watch it go in silence. My body feels weak in the wake of adrenaline. Rain seeps through the collar of my jacket, soaking the shirt underneath.

She'll live.

Despite my faith in her, I still hadn't quite believed that she could do it. I'd tried to prepare myself for the worst and there had been times when I'd thought all was lost. But in the end, Primo's arrogance had been his downfall.

"For a moment, I thought she wasn't going to do it," Rogue says quietly. He's staring at the dark stain on the ground where Primo's blood and Aleesha's soaks into the dirt. He turns and spits on the ground. "And if she hadn't, I would have."

I stare at him in surprise, but Danny just nods and pats his arm. "He's gone now, at any rate. And we have a new leader. A girl. Times are changin'."

I can't tell if he's happy about that or not.

Anders walks back over to us, running his hand through his sandy hair. "I've told them to go back to headquarters for now. The tanks will be filling back up with this rain so at least they'll have water to drink. They're all pretty dehydrated and hungry. Seems like Primo hoarded most of the food and water for himself and his more loyal followers."

"No surprises there," Rogue mutters darkly.

"I think most of them will be quite glad to have a change of leadership," Anders continues. "Though it'll be up to Aleesha, of course, to decide what to do with them. What did the medic say?"

"She'll be okay. They've gone back to the church."

Anders' face breaks into a smile. "Thank goodness. She looked pretty bad." He glances around and lowers his voice. "We should probably head there ourselves. Seems like this might not be the best place to be."

I follow the direction of his gaze. A fight's broken out on the far side of the square and people are starting to look in our direction. "I'll second that." I pick at my sodden trousers. "Besides, I could do with drying out."

Rogue claps me on the shoulder and I try not to wince. "So could we all."

* * *

It's early evening by the time Aleesha emerges from the medic pod. The lower part of her left arm, up to her elbow, is encased in a bone healer and she's very pale, but she manages to walk from the pod through the church to a bed, only leaning on my shoulder for the final few paces.

Mika follows her in. "You need to rest in bed for a couple of days. Eat and drink as much as you can – your body needs calories to recover."

Aleesha raises her arm. "When can I take this thing off?"

"*You* can't. Come and find me in three days. I'll run a scan then and see if you're healed enough for it to be removed."

We crowd around her bed as she eats what seems to be her body weight in food. She doesn't speak until she's finished, then leans back and sighs. "You know, those medic things are bloody awesome. Thought I was done for."

"Don't suppose you can persuade your father to give it to us on permanent loan?" Anders jokes.

"Doubt it."

"So, what happens now?" Rogue asks. He's sitting on a chair between Aleesha and Megan's beds. Megan is sitting up, her fingers entwined with Rogue's on top of the sheet.

"I should get back to headquarters." Aleesha sighs. "There's supposed to be a party. It's traditional."

I put a hand on her shoulder as she starts to get up. "You need to stay in bed."

"B—"

"Trey's right," Danny cuts in. He shuffles awkwardly at the foot of her bed. "'Sides, people aren't, like, in the party mood. Not with all the fightin' and everythin'. It's not like normal," he finishes dolefully.

"Not like normal," Aleesha echoes.

"I sent all Primo's lot back to headquarters," Anders says briskly. "You can decide what to do with them later. How about a couple of us head over there now and try and clean up the place? Get things ready for when you return. From what that Petal chap said, it's a pig sty." He glances around at us. "Let's leave Aleesha to rest for a few hours, shall we?"

Reluctantly, people drift away from her bedside. Rogue turns to Megan and the two begin to converse in low voices, their heads bent together.

"Trey!" Aleesha calls me back. She pulls the sheet back from the bed, looking faintly embarrassed. "I need to … um, visit the bathroom. Can you give me a hand getting there?"

She directs me down a long corridor to a small room with a door in the far wall. She lets go of my arm and hobbles toward the door. "Wait here."

I look around the room. It smells like the rest of the church – slightly old and fusty. Two long pews sit against each wall, below arched windows. The rain has faded to a dull patter and the grey sky is darkening. I know I need to go back Inside, but I feel reluctant to leave this place. To leave her.

When Aleesha steps out of the room, her hair's hanging loose down her back and her face is damp. She flashes me a smile and reaches up to re-braid her hair, then scowls and looks down at the cast on her arm. "I didn't think this through."

"I'm not sure I can help with that." I step forward and take her hand. "But I like it loose."

I raise my hand to cup her cheek, but she tenses and pulls away from me, moving over to stare out the window.

"What is it?"

She shakes her head. "Nothing."

I move up behind her and touch her gently on the shoulder. The urge to wrap my arms around her and bury my face in her hair is almost overwhelming, but I can sense something's wrong.

"Hey, I thought we were being honest with each other? About everything?"

"It's just ... Jay used to say that. That he liked my hair loose. Just reminded me of him, that's all." She gives a slight shrug.

Jealousy punches me in the gut and I take a step back.

Still, she cares for him?

Sensing my movement, Aleesha turns to look up at me, a soft smile on her face. "I don't mean it like that. He wasn't very nice, most of the time." She turns back to stare at the rain streaking down the window. "But he didn't deserve to die."

I can sense her unease, her guilt. And I realize it's not just about Jay. "But Primo did deserve to die," I say quietly.

She doesn't turn around but her shoulders stiffen slightly.

"You know I believe everyone deserves a second chance." I shake my head even though she can't see me. "But not him. He was a monster, Aleesha. All he wanted was power. If he had lived, more people would have died."

She's silent for a moment. "I didn't kill him, you know. I wanted him to yield. He ... pulled the dagger into himself. Made it look like I did it."

Breath hisses through my teeth.

Finally, she turns to look at me. "He was too proud to fail. But I put him in that situation. If I hadn't deactivated them all, this would never have happened."

"You can't think like that. What he did is not your fault."

"Isn't it?" Her eyes are empty and hollow. "I ... I didn't think, Trey. Didn't think what it would really mean for them. Giles said that many of the officers were taken to the compound at birth. They have no other memories. All they know is what they've been taught to believe, and I stripped all that away from them. No wonder so many of them ran straight back."

Deep inside, a little part of me breaks. She looks so young and vulnerable, her shoulders rounded as if the weight of the responsibilities piled on her thin shoulders is too much for her to bear.

"But if you hadn't freed them, Rogue and Anders and all the others would still be under Metz control. You gave them a choice, the opportunity for a different life. A life that wouldn't be possible if Primo were still alive. Who cares if you killed him or he killed himself? You won and he's gone."

I move closer and rest my hands on her hips, giving her the time to pull away.

"I didn't win, not really," she whispers. "I just failed to lose."

I draw her closer and tentatively wrap my arms around her back. "It is better this way," I murmur into her hair.

Her body is stiff at first, but after a minute, she relaxes and her arms move up to wrap around my waist. I close my eyes, breathing in the smell of her, trying to memorize the feel of her arms, her head pressing against my chest and her sweet vanilla scent.

Let me remember this when I have to go back.

Eventually, Aleesha leans back and turns her face up to mine. The haunted look hasn't quite gone from her eyes – perhaps a trace of it will always be there – but it's masked by a familiar glint. "Better that he's dead or better like this?" She indicates my arms wrapped around her.

"Both."

Her lips part as she stands on tiptoe to bring her face closer to mine.

"Why are you so tall?"

"Why are you so short?"

She swats me playfully on the shoulder. I smile and bend my head toward hers. Her breath is warm on my face. Anticipation flutters in my chest.

Her lips are soft under mine. For a second, we are frozen, as if the touch of our lips turned us both to stone. Then the kiss deepens and I feel her tongue slide inside my mouth, and I follow her lead because it feels right, natural.

A shiver runs down my back and I pull her tighter to me, pressing my lips harder to hers, as all the emotion I'd been holding back – the tension of the fight, the fear that I'd lost her, and the relief that I hadn't – rush up through me and out into her.

I pull back, gasping for air. Aleesha's face is flushed and her lips are slightly swollen. Her eyes are on fire, not with anger or hatred, but with something else. I've barely had time to catch my breath when she pulls my head down to hers and our mouths meet again.

This time our kisses are more tender, like soft summer rain that follows a thunderstorm. She is the first to draw back, resting her head against my chest. I can feel her heart beating. Her body trembles slightly, though I'm not sure whether it's from tiredness or emotion.

"What happens now?" Her voice is slightly muffled.

"You need to rest. And I … I have to go back Inside." I sigh. "If I take another day off work, they'll be suspicious. And my position in there, it's too important to lose."

She pulls back and looks up at me in surprise. "What do you mean?"

"There's something going on with the food supply. I was going to tell you but didn't want to distract you from the fight. Since people started refusing to eat the government rations, they've added a new ingredient to the food Outsiders are buying."

"I—" Her eyes flutter and her body sags against me. She shakes her head woozily. "Sorry, I …"

"I'll tell you another time." I loop my arm under her shoulders. "It's not urgent. Come on, let's get you back to bed."

"Damn drugs," she mumbles.

"You've practically been brought back from the dead and you're moaning that you're a bit tired?" I give her a gentle squeeze and half carry her out of the room. "I thought you were dead, you know. You're like a bloody phoenix."

Aleesha smiles sleepily. "Swearing now, are we? Being around Outsiders is rubbing off on you. What's a phoenix, anyway?"

"A firebird. Not a real bird, a mythological one. The ancient Greeks saw it as a symbol of renewal and hope. When it dies, the phoenix bursts into flames, and from its ashes a new bird is born." I frown, trying to remember the quote from the poem we'd studied at school. "'When all seems lost, the phoenix burns. The cycle of birth begins anew. A new bird rises, stronger and brighter. From the ashes of loss, hope returns.'"

"Hope returns ..."

I glance down to see her eyes closing. "Come on," I say gently. "Bed."

* * *

I wake in darkness, disorientated. The bed under me is softer than I remember and my neck twinges in pain when I try to sit up.

Where am I?

Blinking, I look around, my eyes gradually adjusting to the dim light in the room. Arched windows, high above, are grey with pre-dawn light. Around me people sleep, the odd snuffling and snoring noises breaking the stillness.

I remember putting Aleesha to bed, then sitting down beside her. At some point, my head had dropped. I was just going to rest for an hour before heading back ...

And somehow I ended up on the sofa. I swing my legs around and push myself up off the squidgy cushions, rubbing my neck. My eyes fall on the two beds on the far side of the room. Megan lies in one. Rogue sleeps awkwardly next to her, half sat in the chair, head resting on the bed. But Aleesha's bed is empty.

My heart lurches and I suddenly feel very much awake. It seems to take forever to cross the room, stepping around and over the sleeping figures on the floor. I close the door quietly behind me and look around the corridor. It's empty.

I head back down the corridor toward the bathroom but find no sign of her. Worry nags at me.

Where is she?

In the main entrance chamber to the church, I find Bryn curled up on a stone bench. He starts awake at the sound of my footsteps.

"Oh, it's you." He yawns and sits up. "I'm too old to be sleeping on stone." He stretches his back out and rubs his shoulder.

"What are you doing here? Have you seen Aleesha?"

"Thought I should check in on you two." He gives another yawn and checks the band on his wrist. "Aleesha left a couple of hours ago to go to the Snakes' headquarters. Was muttering something about phoenixes." He frowns. "Do you think the drugs in that medic pod addled her brain?"

"She was supposed to be resting!"

Bryn shrugs. "Well, she looked better than when I last saw her. Said she'd sleep at HQ." He heaves himself to his feet. "I'm guessing you'll be wanting to go after her."

"Yes, but ..." I hesitate. "I also need to go back Inside. What time is it?"

"Five in the morning. Reckon you've got a couple of hours before you need to be home? Aleesha asked if you could stay until the morning. She's planning some big speech, I think."

I stifle a yawn. "Fine." *Not that I needed much of an excuse to stay.*

The streets are quiet, aside from the snores of sleeping hobies and the odd scuttle of a rat amongst the litter. It is the first time I've been to the gang's headquarters and I'm curious to know what it's like. But I can't see much in the dark, just a huge block of a building looming over us. Giant murals of snakes decorate the wall that surrounds it and a pair of the Chain's guards stand alert at the entrance. Bryn nods to them and they let us in.

Once inside, we follow the only noise toward what appears to be a large hall. But our way is blocked by Tommy, who appears from nowhere.

"Yer not allowed in there." He jerks his thumb toward the room behind him, then wipes the back of his hand across his nose. "'Leesha says so."

I glance around. "Where is she?"

"Sleepin'. This way."

We follow him past a series of closed doors to a small room. Mattresses lay scattered across the floor. Aleesha lies on one, up against the far wall, and on the other side of the room, Anders sleeps.

"Thanks, Tommy," Bryn says quietly.

"No probs," the kid replies cheerfully.

I sink down on a mattress next to Aleesha. Her jaw is slack, her face peaceful in sleep. Her chest rises and falls. I feel a flush of relief followed by an overwhelming tiredness.

Bryn was right. I've got a few more hours before I need to be back.

Curling up on the mattress, I stretch my arm out so my fingers are resting against Aleesha's back. Then I fall into a deep, dreamless sleep.

33

Aleesha

I stand on the platform at the end of the main hall, in front of the blackened brick wall. The toxic smell of paint fills the air.

"It were the best I could do in a few hours," Jax mutters, setting the spray paint down and shaking his hand to help the blood flow back into it.

"It's perfect." I turn to him. "Honestly, you've outdone yourself."

He mutters something unintelligible, but I can see that he's pleased.

"Are there some old sheets or something we can cover it up with?"

Jax nods and pushes a strand of grey hair back from his face. "I'll go 'ave a look." He gives me a brief nod. "Good to 'ave you back."

As he strides over to one of the side doors that leads off the hall, I turn back to gaze at the image in front of me.

Yes. It's perfect.

A faint footfall sounds in the empty hall. *Who else is up at this time?*

Not who I was expecting.

Samson observes me from part way up the hall. He's leaning on a thick metal pole and I can see the bulk of bandages under his tight long-sleeve top.

"How did you get in?" I scowl at him irritably.

He shrugs and begins to limp toward me. "I have my ways." He nods at the painting on the wall behind me. "Going for a change of branding?"

"Thought we might need a new start. Changing times, and all that." I step down gingerly from the platform and walk over to him. "So, why are you here? Come to demand that I follow your lead like the rest of the gangs? Come to threaten me if I don't obey, like you did with the other leaders?"

He gives me an appraising look. "*Will* you follow me?"

"No."

There's a flash of anger in his eyes, but as quickly as it's come, it's gone. He waits for me to continue.

"We won't follow you. But we will work with you, *if* we believe in what you're trying to do."

His lips twitch as if he's trying to hold back a smile. "Well, that's a start at least." He glances around. "I was hoping your father might be around."

"What do you mean my f—" I glare at him as a smile breaks through on his face. "Is there anything you don't know?"

"It's my job to know things. Information is power."

I nod thoughtfully. He's right, but information can only get you so far. You have to have the resources to act on it.

"Would you work with them? If it was for the good of the city? For Outsiders?"

White teeth flash in the dim light. "That depends on what he is offering."

They'd be stronger together, but would they ever be able to work together? It seems unlikely, though it may be the only way to change things in this city.

"I came to pick up our conversation from the other day. You said you had a contact Inside who wanted to help."

"Yes. Her name's Ella."

"And ..." Samson prompts when I don't continue.

Again, I feel torn. It feels like I'm betraying Trey all over again, getting his family into trouble.

But it was Ella who came to me. It was her decision.

"She says she's got a group of friends who want to work with you. Some of them have got jobs inside the government, labs and other companies. But they're quite young – they can't be that important."

Samson tilts his head to one side, his eyes boring into me.

Say no, say no.

"Good," he says finally. "Tell her to go to the Dancing Donkey on Wall Street, Area Six on Thursday night at seven. She's to ask to speak to the boss."

My heart sinks as Samson smiles. "Sounds like your friend could be useful."

A door on the other side the room opens and Jax enters, a bundle of stained sheets in his arms. Samson nods. "I'll let you finish getting things set up." He turns and hobbles off.

"Who was that guy?" Jax asks as I walk over to him. "Don't remember seeing him with all the Metz officers."

"He's not a Metz officer. He's an Outsider."

"No way. Not with that body."

I don't answer but pull the sheets from his arms. He's right though. Samson may call himself an Outsider, but no Outsider has those genes. The must have been some genetic enhancements somewhere down the line. Perhaps, now he seems to be opening up a bit more, I'll be able to find out a bit more about who the man behind the Brotherhood really is.

Outside, the sky lightens as dawn breaks across the city. Grey clouds still scud across the skylights and I can feel that there is more rain in the air. That's good. We have a lot of thirsty people. I'll have to get someone to look into whether we can build an extra storage tank on the roof.

We hang the sheets up to cover Jax's work. The paint is almost dry already. "I'll finish touching it up later," he says, yawning. "Might go get a bit of shut-eye."

As he leaves the hall, I sit on the edge of the platform and wait for my people to awake.

* * *

The hall is half full of people crowded in front of the platform, on which I stand alone. I'd wanted Trey up here with me, and Rogue and Danny, but they'd all refused. Said it had to be me. That I was the leader.

I'm not sure I feel like a leader. I feel small, standing here and this stupid cast on my arm does me no favours. But it doesn't hurt anymore and I'm grateful for that. Mainly, I just feel tired. So very tired.

Nerves tremble in my belly, a thousand baby snakes weaving around one another, fighting to get out. They surge up my throat and I gag and swallow, tasting bitter bile.

Their eyes are all on me, waiting for me to speak. But I'm struck dumb.

There are still divides between them, visible in their body language. Those who had followed Primo linger uncertainly around the edges of the group, still not sure what their fate will be. The Outsiders still keep their distance from the former Metz officers, fear still showing in their movements.

But there are exceptions. Danny mutters something to Anders, who breaks into a smile. Rogue has hoisted Tommy onto his shoulders so he can see above the heads of the others. Megan clings to Rogue's hand like a lifeline.

My chest tightens as another wave of panic washes over me. I don't know what to say. My mind is empty.

I close my eyes and take a deep breath. In and out. Just like before a fight, right?

Speak from your heart, Trey had said earlier. Give them hope.

I open my eyes and drop my gaze to the floor. Perhaps if I don't look at them it will be easier.

"I … some of you may remember the last time I spoke, when Jay pushed me up on a chair in front of you all. If you do, you'll remember that I'm not that great at talking to people."

A few titters. People shift expectantly.

I swallow. "Some of you have been in this gang a long time. Longer than me. And others are very new here, both to the gang and this world Outside. This is the first time a woman has been leader of this gang. Some of you may not like that, and you are free to leave. Some of you followed Primo and may not want to follow me, and you, too, are free to leave."

I look up at them then. "I will only have people in this gang who want to be here. And if you stay, I can promise you that things are not going to be as they have been in the past."

My words echo in the vast room. It's strange. I'm not thinking them in my head, not really planning what to say. They just appear on my lips, as if they're coming from inside me.

"We are not the Snakes anymore. Snakes slither in the dirt,

waiting in the shadows to launch themselves at their prey. We are better than that. We will not be like the other gangs. We will create something new, something different. Something better. Some of us have come from the grime and dirt of Area Four, others from the darkness of the Metz compound, but together, we will rise above both of these places. Together, we will have the skill and intelligence of Insiders *and* the grit and determination of Outsiders."

My voice rises, and within me, something swells that I didn't know existed and I have to fight to keep my voice from breaking as I see the sea of faces in front of me, all turned toward me, captivated.

"Many of our friends are dead. But from death comes life."

I reach behind me and yank down the sheets that cover the image that Jax had so skilfully painted while the rest of the gang slept. Mika had looked puzzled when I'd asked her to search for a picture of the creature so he had something to work off. Even so, what Jax managed to create is more impressive than any of the images she found.

Emblazoned on the burnt brick wall is a bird of flames. It rises from fiery letters, wings outstretched, each feather an individual flame to consume the darkness. It's long neck curves to end in a crested head, stretching up toward the sky. In the gloomy early morning light, the bird seems to glow, golds, reds and oranges setting the room alight.

A gasp ripples through the people stood before me. Most of them won't know what a phoenix is, but they don't have to. I close my eyes to remember the words I had made Trey repeat to me ten minutes earlier.

"When all seems lost, the phoenix burns. The cycle of birth begins anew. A new bird rises, stronger and brighter. From the ashes of loss, hope returns."

I open my eyes and look around at my gang. My family. "We are the phoenix that rises from the ashes to burn more brightly than before. Because there is *always* hope. Whatever is done to us, whatever they take from us, they cannot take that away. Today, we start a new life, every one of us. It doesn't matter who we used to be or what we've done. We've all done bad things ..." My voice chokes with emotion and I have to look away from them and up at the blank brick walls of the hall to be able to continue. "What matters is our future. I don't care who you were. What matters to me is the person you choose to become."

They are silent, hanging on my every word. Behind them, I catch sight of Bryn leaning against the wall, smiling, his eyes not focused on me but on Trey. On the far side of the wall stands Samson, his face expressionless as always. But it's a movement at the back of the room that catches my eye. Half hidden in a doorway stands a tall dark-haired man.

Father.

And I wonder what he thinks of me now. Now I have rejected him for these people he so despises.

But I don't care. Because his opinion doesn't matter as much as that of the people in front of me.

And Trey's.

My eyes stray to his. His eyes glisten with unshed tears as he smiles at me and nods.

It's time to finish.

I raise my voice even louder until it cracks under the strain. "Look at the person next to you and see not an Insider or an Outsider, not a Metz officer or a child of the gutter, but a sister or brother. You can choose to leave us. But if you stay, if you decide to join this family, know this. We will stand together, we will fight together, we will live together. And together we will be strong. Together, we are Phoenix."

The applause starts as a trickle. Then it grows and swells until it's a wave of noise that breaks over me, filling me, rejuvenating me, and I feel whole again, though I had not realized I was broken.

I close my eyes and drink it in, feeling it coarse through my veins, more powerful than the strongest drug. There are cheers, whoops and the sound of voices talking.

I know that this is only the beginning. That the wounds for many people cut deep and it will take more than few words and a new name to heal them. But for the first time, I have hope that maybe we can have a future where people will stand together rather than fight divided. Where women can be the equal of men, and Outsiders friends with Insiders. And if it can happen here, in this building, perhaps it can happen elsewhere.

A hand closes around mine and I turn to see Trey smiling. "I told you that you could be a leader," he says quietly.

"I don't think I believed it until now."

"You promised them a lot." His eyes search mine. "Too much, perhaps."

I shrug. "I promised them what they deserve. And hope – that's the most important thing of all."

"Do you think we'll ever have a city when there's no Wall between Insiders and Outsiders? When we released the government documents, I thought we could, but now I've experienced both sides ... I'm not so sure."

"A lot's changed since then." I nod toward the back of the room. I hadn't noticed him leave the shelter of the doorway, but my father stands next to Samson, the two men deep in conversation, sparing an occasional glance in my direction.

Their body language is cautious, like two alpha dogs sniffing around each other, but it is a first step.

Trey follows the direction of my gaze. "Together, they would be a force to be reckoned with."

"Yes. Samson has the gangs and—" I break off, realizing I still haven't told Trey about Ella. *I promised her.* But Trey should know.

Trey nods. "And the Chain has the technology and resources from outside Britannia. Together, perhaps they can change things."

"There's—"

"I—"

He smiles. "You first."

I take a deep breath. "There's something you should know."

He frowns at the look on my face. "Bad news?"

"Not exactly." I hesitate, wondering how to start.

"Can it wait until tomorrow? I'd hate for anything to break this moment." He glances out at the crowd. Someone has found a bottle of alcohol and is passing it around. Anders takes a swig and gasps, coughing, his face turning purple as Danny laughs and slaps him on the back.

Trey smiles ruefully. "I have to go. I'm supposed to be at work already. I at least need to get back home and call in sick or something." He makes a face. "I'm supposed to see Milicent tonight – there's a lot to update her on. I'll try to come back tomorrow, okay? Then we can talk properly."

I guess another day won't hurt.

"Sure."

He reaches out for me, but I pull back and nod to a small room, just off the hall. I don't want to say goodbye to him up here, in front of everyone.

As soon as I close the door behind us, he pulls me to him. A shiver of desire runs through me as he holds me tight, almost possessively.

"Where's shy schoolboy Trey gone?" I murmur.

His fingers trail across my cheek, his touch burning my skin. "He grew up."

He pulls my face up to his, his lips parting as they meet mine. His hands roam across my back and I can feel the heat rolling off him. Energy courses through me and I feel like I'm on the crest of a wave, and that if I let myself go, I could drown in the flood of emotion that threatens to overwhelm me. But I can't let go, can't give up control – not yet.

"I think I like this new version," I say as we part for breath. I wrap my arms around his waist, pushing my hand up under his t-shirt and pressing my body to his.

"Aleesha …" His breathing is ragged. He pushes me away and swallows hard. "Just, um, give me a minute. I really do have to go."

I bite my lip and turn away, but Trey stops me, turning my face to his and showing me in one look that if he had any choice in the matter, neither of us would be leaving this room.

I manage a small smile. "Come back soon."

"As soon as I can."

"And be careful out there. It's still not safe. I don't want to have to send the boys out to rescue you."

His face falls.

Damn, I always have to ruin things.

"I'm sorry, I didn't mean it like that. Just … stay safe, okay?"

I stand on tiptoe to kiss him again. He reaches for me, but I dance back, knowing that I have to let him go.

A smile tugs at his lips. "You're impossible, you know that?"

He means it as a compliment – I think.

I follow him out into the hall. In the few minutes we've been talking, a party seems to have started and no one seems to have noticed our absence.

There's so much to do ...

But the work can wait until tomorrow. I can let them have this day of fun, at least.

* * *

Ten hours after my speech and the party is still going strong. They ran out of alcohol a few hours ago, thank goodness, but a good two-thirds of my new gang are completely inebriated and the others aren't much better. There'll be a lot of sore heads when they wake up tomorrow. Fortunately, I'd managed to avoid the usual drinking challenges that await a newly appointed leader, the former members of the Snakes choosing to challenge the ex-officers to contests instead. They ended up fairly evenly matched; the officers have pretty much no tolerance for alcohol having never had it before, but their larger bodies absorb it more easily than the scrawny Outsiders.

Jax appears at my elbow. "You've got some visitors."

He'd been one of the few to remain sober and had dragged a couple of the older gang members off to form a light guard around the perimeter of the headquarters. I don't think any of the other gangs will try anything, but I haven't forgotten about Denzel, the Bigland Boys leader.

I follow Jax through to the main gate and find Abby, Bryn and my father waiting. My father is arguing with the guy guarding the gate, who twirls a nailed club lazily in front of him.

Abby is the first to spot me. A green bag hangs over her

shoulder, bulging with what I suspect are bandages and medic supplies. "Aleesha! How's the arm doing?"

I glance down at the bone healer wrapped around my arm. "Feels fine but the med woman won't look at it for another couple of days. It's hot though, and I'm pretty tempted just to whip it off myself." I look up and roll my eyes at Abby's worried frown. "Don't worry, I know what you're about to say. She knows what she's doing."

"You're lucky she was there. I'm not sure if Amber and I together could have saved your arm, from how Bryn described it. And internal bleeding too." She shakes her head. "You're lucky to be alive." She waves to a large box that Bryn's carrying. "I bought you some seedlings, if you've anywhere to put them?"

"We'll find somewhere." I smile and give Jax a nudge with my elbow. He steps forward and takes the box from Bryn, who looks relieved.

"Come on in. Can't offer you much in the way of drinks, I'm afraid. My friends were pretty thirsty."

I lead them past the rowdy hall and into the small room that Jay had used as an office. They sit down awkwardly around the table, Abby curiously, Bryn blandly, and my father with an expression of disgust.

He catches me looking at him and schools his face into a smile. "It's good to see you're still alive. Mika said you had an excellent constitution."

And what on earth is a constitution?

I give him a curt nod. "Saw you talking to Samson this morning."

He nods. "Yes. He's an interesting man." He looks up as a drunken couple throw open the door then retreat hastily, giggling, when they see us sitting there. "My offer's still open if you want to leave ..."

"What, and leave them?" I shake my head. "What kind of leader would that make me? Besides, we've got an opportunity to change things now. Make things better."

"Rousing speeches are all very well, but you'll need more than that to keep that lot in check."

I lean back in my chair, determined not to let my anger show. "I know that. But I figured if you really want to help me, and if you're serious about changing things in this city, we could come to a deal."

His eyes narrow. "A deal?"

"Sure. You help us, we help you."

I catch Bryn frowning at me. But my father just throws back his head and laughs. "Seems like you are my daughter, after all."

"So, Aleesha," Abby says, a little too brightly. "Did you get a chance to catch up with Trey?"

"A bit. He's hoping to be able to come back Outside tomorrow so we can talk properly. He's got to go and see Milicent tonight."

"Milicent?" My father frowns. "Our Milicent?"

I nod.

"At least he's got someone to help him Inside," Abby says. "And it seems to make him feel better knowing that working at that place is doing some good."

Bryn looks confused. "What do you mean?"

Abby frowns. "Don't you know? He's reporting anything he can find out about Coleman's back to Milicent. Is she not passing it back to you?"

Bryn and my father exchange a look. "No," my father says grimly.

I feel a flicker of apprehension. *What's Milicent's game? Is she making another ploy for leadership?*

"We're not exactly sure on her motives, after the last time she went off on one," he continues. "She doesn't always think of the bigger picture."

I look from my father to Bryn. There's something in the tone of his voice that worries me. "Why didn't you tell Trey this? Is he in trouble?"

Bryn looks grim. "We didn't tell him because we didn't know that she'd been speaking to him. But as long as he isn't drawing attention to himself at the factory, he shouldn't be in too much danger. Do you know what information she's been asking him to get?"

"He was talking about the food distribution centres," Abby says, her voice laced with concern. "Mentioned something about a drug, but I don't think he's told Milicent about that yet."

"And he's been finding out about the people in charge. The Coleman family," I add.

Bryn glances at my father, who narrows his eyes.

"What's going on?" My fingers dig into the tabletop.

"If she finds him, kills him …" Bryn mutters under his breath.

"It wouldn't be the worst thing in the world." My father shrugs.

I push my chair back and it clatters to the floor. "Kills who?" Panic shoots through me. "Trey?"

"No, not Trey," Bryn says, looking up. "Coleman. Or rather, one of the Coleman seniors."

I stare at them, confused. *What are they talking about?*

Bryn looks at my father, who nods. "Milicent's only son died in a rebellion. It was decades ago. Most people have forgotten about it. But not Milicent. She—"

Quick footsteps sound outside, a light patter on the flagstones, followed by knocking on the door. I move to open it and Tommy falls into the room. His eyes find mine and he shoves a small roll of film up at me.

"Message ... for ... you," he pants. "They said it was urgent."

My heart pounds as I unroll the piece of film and carefully read the words etched into it.

Trey is in trouble. The Metz have come for him. Meet me at Milicent's house. Ella.

Below her name is an address.

I read the message again, whispering the address under my breath.

Trey. The Metz. Not now, not when we were just ...

"Aleesha, what is it?" Bryn's voice breaks through my trance and I drop the film and run to the door.

"Aleesha, wait!" my father calls after me.

But I don't stop, not even when I hear Bryn's footsteps behind me. I'm faster than him, and he can't go through the Wall. Even if my father has contacts inside, they won't get there before me.

My arms pump and my lungs burn as I race through the streets, shoving people aside in my haste.

I'm coming, Trey. Hold on.

34

Trey

The smell of fresh rain on earth hits me as I walk up Milicent's front path. It reminds me of Wales and a wave of nostalgia rushes over me as I wonder if I'll ever return to our house there. I'd like to take Aleesha, show her that there's more to our country than just this city.

The door opens as I raise my hand to knock on it.

"Master Trey." The butler nods at me and waves me in. His expression is oddly strained.

Master Trey?

Milicent is standing in the hallway with her back to me, a light raincoat buttoned up to her neck. She turns as I approach. She's wearing makeup, but underneath it, her eyes are red-rimmed. Her painted lips curl into a smile. "Trey."

"Is now a good time? Or should I come back?" I ask, glancing down at her coat.

"No, I was just waiting for you. We will go out this evening." She glances over my shoulder and raises an eyebrow. "Is the taxi here yet?"

"Just arrived, ma'am."

Milicent's heels click across the floor to the door. I follow her, puzzled. She pauses in front of the butler, then reaches out and pats his arm. "You know what to do, Thomas."

He bows his head. "Yes, ma'am."

He keeps his head bowed as I pass, but as he straightens to close the door, I catch the glint of a tear on his cheek.

I jog a few paces to catch up with Milicent. "Where are we going?"

"You'll see."

I hesitate at the door of the pod. Something doesn't feel right about this. *Why would we go out?*

"Come on, Trey, we haven't got all night and I need to talk to you on the way there."

Where's there?

I step into the pod and sit down opposite her. The door closes and I feel the slightest of tremors as the pod lifts off the ground.

"Where are we going?"

Milicent turns to look at me. "Do you know how old I am, Trey? One hundred and twenty. When I was born, only one in a million people could hope to live to that age. And that was not counting the people who chose to die young so that their family line could continue. I could live for another twenty or thirty years, easily. We have invented treatments that prolong life far beyond what was once possible, beyond what nature intended for us. But we have still not been able to capture what makes life worthwhile."

She turns to stare at the window insert on the pod wall, which displays a static image of St Paul's Cathedral. "Tomorrow, it will be sixty years since William died. Sixty years and one week since my husband shot himself. He took the easy way out." Her voice is bitter.

"I didn't realize. I'm sorry."

It's not enough but I don't know what else to say.

A ghost of a smile flickers across her face. "Living loses its appeal after a while, you know."

I look down at my hands as I finally realize where we're going. "You're going to make the sacrifice."

It sounds awkward when I say it like that. But what else would I call it? Suicide? Euthanasia? So many words for such a simple thing.

Milicent nods. "Yes. I have lived too long. The fire that once burned in my veins has turned to ashes. Everything I once had, I have lost. My son. My husband. The woman who fought for justice, for her son's legacy. I can't remember when that woman died ... and this person took over my body."

She twists her hands, examining them as if she doesn't know them. I shift on my seat and tug at the collar of my suit, uncomfortable at her confession, at the intimacy she is forcing between us.

"Why do you want me here?"

Is this what all our meetings have been about? She just wants someone to talk to before she dies?

She jerks as if coming out of a trance and straightens her shoulders, placing her hands back in her lap. "Because, Trey, I have named you as my heir. Everything I have – all my money, the house, everything – will soon be yours to do with as you choose. I hope it will go some way to replacing what you have lost and help you forgive the mistakes of an old lady. I trust you to do some good with it." She hesitates. "I have no family. The people who know me best are my servants. I had hoped ... that you might accompany me, to the end."

The mask drops from her face for a moment and I have a rare glimpse of the woman underneath. Vulnerable, worn down by years of pain and loneliness, and yet fearful of taking this final step. "I don't know if I can face it alone," she whispers.

Empathy surges through me, and I reach forward and take her hand. "You don't have to."

Realization hits. *She's left me everything?* The house alone must be worth more than half the property in Area Four. And the money she has will be more than enough to pay for whatever treatment Mother needs.

Since I came back Inside, a weight has accumulated on my shoulders. The weight of my family's expectations, my mother's illness, Ella's worry. I hadn't realized how heavy it had become until now, when it's suddenly gone and I feel like I could float up from my seat, lighter than air.

"Thank you," I whisper, trying to control the grin that threatens to split my face.

Milicent gives me a small smile. "I hope it is worth it."

There's a bleep and the pod light flashes. We have arrived.

The crematorium looms over us, bathed red by the evening sun. Trepidation fills me as I look up at the stark white marble shot through with grey. Like the other side of the building, there's a Latin inscription above the door.

Amor vincit omnia.

Love conquers all.

It seems an odd phrase for a place of death.

I glance at the hedge separating the two sides of the crematorium and remember the conversation I'd overheard on the day of my father's funeral. The sacrifice is about love. Why else would you choose to give up your life for your family if it was not for love?

A man dressed in a black tailcoat suit greets us with a bow as we step inside the tiled foyer. Marble-columned doors lead off the large space and a giant chandelier hangs from the ceiling, hundreds of tiny lights casting a soft glow on the people below.

They seem to be expecting Milicent and we're taken through to a small room, furnished with soft chairs, a water fountain and pot plants. Gentle relaxation music plays in the background. In front of us is a plain wooden door.

"We will prepare the chamber for you, madam. It will take about fifteen minutes. Please relax here – if you need anything, just press that comm." The man points to a speaker on the wall and backs out of the room.

Milicent sinks into a chair. Her face is chalk white under her makeup and she wrings her hands over and over.

"Shall I take your coat?"

She nods and stands, taking something out of the pocket before unbuttoning the coat and letting me slide it from her shoulders. I stifle a gasp. Underneath the coat, she wears a dress that might have once been white, but the lace and silk has yellowed and stiffened with age. It hangs loosely on her frame, designed for the curves of a younger body, and her thin blue-veined legs are like matchsticks under the flared skirt.

Pink flushes her cheeks. "I know I look silly, but I just wanted to remember ..." She holds out an ancient photograph – an actual photograph, not a holo. The years have faded it and the edges are dog-eared, but the eyes of the young woman clutching her husband's arm outside a church still shine with excitement and love.

"You look beautiful," I say honestly.

"It was the second happiest day of my life. The happiest was when William was born. We loved each other very much, back then." Her voice is wistful.

I bite back the tears that spring to my eyes, wondering what it must be like to live alone for so many years, with just the memories of what it was like to love and be loved.

My hand trembles as I hang the coat on a rack by the door.

When I turn back, Milicent has her hands folded in front of her. "I ... I'm afraid I haven't been totally honest with you, Trey." Her fingers whiten on the photograph.

"About what?" I walk over and gently take her arm. "Would you like to sit down?"

"No. Thank you." She pauses. "You know what I felt when William died? Even more than grief? Anger. Anger that we lived in a society where one person was forbidden from loving another. Anger that we weren't even allowed to cremate our children with dignity. That they were written into the record books as criminals. I thought that other people would feel the same, that their anger over their children's deaths would make them rise up against the government. But when it came down to it, they still believed in what our society *was*. They favoured stability over change and didn't want to risk their positions, their wealth, the risk of a new society in which they may not end up with what they once had."

She pulls her arm from my grasp. "You never asked me what happened to the President – the man who ordered my son's death."

A sense of uneasiness washes over me. "What happened to him?"

Her face twists into a snarl. "Nothing," she spits. "Nothing. He stepped down from his position shortly after, on the grounds of ill-health. There was no trial. He was never brought to justice for the crimes he had ordered."

My mind races, wondering where this is going. Wondering what it has to do with me.

"Two years, I searched for him. Three times I nearly caught him, but always he slipped from the trap I'd created. For a year, I lived in a daze, barely eating, rarely sleeping, never leaving the house. I withdrew from society completely, going through the motions of living without really feeling alive. Sometimes I wondered what I was living for, but I was too scared of death to follow my husband into it.

"Then one day I realized that I had an opportunity. An opportunity to take up William's cause and try to create his dream. I had my family's wealth, plus that of my husband's, and I didn't need much to live on." She smiles, lost in a memory. "My first task was to dig that tunnel – the one you entered when you first came to my house with Bryn. Bella – the woman who owns the fabric shop – was an old school friend of mine. Her daughter was one of William's friends. I used to disguise myself and explore the areas Outside the Wall, to see for myself what William had seen. That's how I ended up getting involved with the Chain."

Her lips tighten into a thin line. "I believed in them. Dedicated myself to helping them for years. And for what? Nothing has changed!"

"It might now. Now the Leader is here. It feels as if things are changing …"

"I miss the optimism of youth." She sighs. "You do not have the same cynicism as those of my generation. You do not fear in the same way. You trust so freely … too freely, perhaps."

"What are you saying?"

"After our failure to get the data from the government headquarters, I almost gave up on everything. I thought if I had that, I would finally be able to find out where he was living, if he was still alive."

"Who? The President who killed your son?" I can hear the impatience in my voice. *When is she going to get to the point?*

"Yes." She looks straight at me. "Elmo Coleman."

My heart skips a beat. The pieces of the puzzle begin to come together in my mind.

"That was why you asked me to report back from the factory? Why you asked me to find out about Louis's grandfather? It was him?"

"Not him, his brother. Louis's great-uncle. They were twins. One ran the factory, the other ran the country. When you told me where they were living, I knew that he was still alive, and where to find him."

I feel a surge of anger. "And what about the other information – the distribution centres and the access codes – did any of that matter? Have you even been passing it back to the Chain?"

She shakes her head. "No. I couldn't risk them intervening. They've been trying to cut me out of things. All they want is my money, and the Leader has enough of his own to make me useless to them now."

I turn and walk over to the water fountain. The glass shakes in my hand as I fill it. "And I thought you were doing this for Outsiders. To build a better city." The bitterness in my voice mirrors her own.

"I was. For forty years I have tried to do that. But I have failed, Trey." I hear the hiss of her breath above the music. "I believe it is possible, but not by my hands. So all I had left was this one thing to do before I die. To finish what William died trying to do."

"Kill Coleman. Have your revenge."

"Not revenge. Justice. He murdered sixty-three of his own people so that he would not have to lose face. He never even apologized for it."

I take a sip of the water, hoping it will cool the burning in my stomach.

She used me. How did I not see it? I should never have trusted her, not after our first failed mission. I should have insisted on speaking to Bryn.

The water does not quench the anger inside me. But I know that I'm as angry at my own naivety as I am at her.

And I can still tell the Chain about the information I've uncovered. It won't be wasted. Whereas she will never get her family back.

There's a knock on the wooden door and a bald-headed man in a black suit steps into the room. "We are ready for you, madam."

He glances around, sensing the tension in the room, and takes a step back. "Or, I can give you a few more minutes if you're not quite ready."

I look at Milicent, her face ravaged with grief and anger, and the anger dies in me, to be replaced by pity. Pity for this woman who has lost so much and lived her whole life waiting for revenge.

"No, I think we're ready." I walk over to Milicent and take her arm, tugging her gently forward toward the doorway. "I can understand why you would do it. And now, it is done?"

"No, you don't understand, Trey, not everything." Tears shimmer in her eyes as she turns to me. "He wasn't there. When we got to the country mansion. He'd already escaped somewhere else."

"Well, perhaps it is better that way," I say soothingly. "He must be an old man, after all. He'll die soon anyway."

I lead her into a small, white room. The only furnishing is

what appears to be a bed in one corner, but when I look at it again, I realize that it has a retractable domed lid.

Like a coffin.

Milicent's hand is shaking as she reaches out for the edge of it and sits down. She still clutches the photographs in her hand.

"When you're ready, just lie down in the chamber." The man's voice is smooth and liquid.

Milicent turns a frightened face to him. "And it won't hurt?"

The man shakes his head and I suspect it's not the first time he's been asked that question. "You won't feel a thing. You'll just feel sleepy."

He steps back to give us some space.

Milicent swings her legs up and wriggles into position on the bed. "I did find him, in the end," she murmurs.

My hand freezes on her arm. She glances up at me. "I'm sorry, Trey. It was the only way I could find him. And even then, when I arrived, he was already dead. He had to take even that from me."

There's no bitterness in her voice any more, just sadness. She kisses the photograph of her son, then the photograph of her wedding day, and lies down on the bed.

The man moves forward to close the lid of the chamber, but I hold out a hand to stop him. "What do you mean, you're sorry?"

"I had to make a bargain with the President – it was the only way. He was the only person that I knew would know where Coleman was."

My heart begins to race as dread seeps through me. "What did you do? What did he want in return?"

Her eyes look at me sadly. "Can you not guess, Trey? He, too, was hurt long ago. He, too, lost someone. Everyone wants revenge for something."

She smiles at my puzzled look. “It’s all about love, at the end of the day. Everything comes down to love.”

I shake my head, still not sure what she’s talking about. What would the President want revenge for?

And then something Aleesha had said comes back to me. When the President had taken her captive, he’d told her that he’d known her mother. And he’d been desperate to find her father.

Because he was a wanted criminal ...

“You told him the Leader was here, in London? Where to find him?”

Milicent chuckles. “Oh, he already knew he was here. His spies told him that. No, I gave him the one thing that he could use against Richard. The one thing he could use to bring him to justice.”

My blood runs cold as I stagger back from the chamber, finally realizing what she been trying to tell me all this time. “No,” I whisper.

“I’m sorry, Trey. I didn’t want it to come to this. And I tried to warn you that helping us could hurt you.” Her eyes beg my forgiveness, my understanding. But I’m frozen, unable to move or even think.

“What have you done?” My feet unglue themselves from the floor and I run forward, wedging my shoulder under the lid of the chamber as it begins to close. The man in the suit makes a noise of irritation and asks me to step away, but I swat him back. “Where is she?”

There’s a hissing noise and something sweet-smelling is sprayed into the chamber.

“Sir, please step back now.” The man is tugging on my arm.

Milicent’s eyelids begin to close.

"Where is she?" I shout down at her.

Her eyelids flutter for a second, then close again. When she speaks, her words are slurred and broken. "The Metz are waiting ... At my house. Forgive me ..."

I pull back, feeling dizzy from the gas, and the chamber lid closes.

The man in the black suit stands with his hands crossed in front of him, his head bowed. "Her body is going into a deep sleep. In a minute, it will all be over."

I back away, then turn and yank open the door. I run through the waiting room and out into the foyer, ignoring the shouts that follow me. The evening air hits my face and I try and make sense of what Milicent was saying. She must have set a trap, baited Aleesha to come to her home. But if I can make it there before she arrives, perhaps I can warn her. Perhaps I can save her.

My lungs burn as I push my body to run faster. People turn to look at me, and I have to jump over a child who trips while trying to get out of my path. Streets pass in a blur and I find my way by instinct as much as knowledge. Finally, I get to a street I recognize, just around the corner from Milicent's house. The road is empty, the rich Insiders of this neighbourhood eating family dinners or relaxing in their virtual reality rooms behind the closed curtains and blinds of the houses I pass.

I round the corner and Milicent's house comes into view. On the street outside it is a familiar black and yellow striped pod.

No.

As I race toward it, it rises slowly up into the air.

Still, I run, black spots dancing at the corners of my vision as I strain to close the distance. But before I'm halfway up the street, it has gone, shooting off across the city.

I hug the lion-topped pillar, gasping for breath.

Perhaps she wasn't here. Aleesha's smart, she might have seen the trap for what it was.

Except she always comes to rescue you.

But I can't let go of the thread of hope that makes me believe she's waiting for me inside the house, or back at her gang headquarters. Perhaps I'll walk through the front door and she'll be there with Thomas, laughing at the fear on my face.

I trip up the stairs, my feet slipping on the smooth paving stones.

She will be there.

The door opens in front of me and the butler stands to one side to let me through.

"Is she here?" I gasp out. "Aleesha … Did they … take her?"

"The girl, sir?"

I nod, casting my eyes around for any sign that Aleesha was here. Is here.

"They took her, as the mistress requested."

I fall back against the door frame as my legs give way, and I sink to the ground.

I was too late.

"Welcome to your new home, Master Trey."

I was too late.

Find out how the story ends

Coming in 2019...

Liberators, the fourth and final book in The Wall Series.

If you'd like to receive an email when Liberators is available to pre-order, you can sign up for a one-time notification here: https://www.subscribepage.com/Liberators

Alternatively, you can join my Readers' Club for fortnightly updates on new releases, giveaways, free short stories and book recommendations. Sign up here: bit.ly/alisoningleby-outsider.

In the meantime, you can read my short story, *The Machinist's Daughter* (in the anthology, *On the Brink*), which tells the story of how Barnes and Samson first met...

Author's Note

When I first plotted out The Wall Series, I'd intended it to be a trilogy. The fact that it's now a four-book series probably tells you something about how rough that first plan was. (If you *really* want the truth, the synopsis for the third book was a single sentence on a rather spidery mind map of how I thought the series would go.)

Some wise person once said that no plan survives first contact with the enemy. I have found that the same is true when writing books. I can have a beautifully laid out plot but when I start writing, my characters stick their noses in, and poof! Everything changes.

Take Giles, who you may remember was first introduced very briefly in *Expendables*. That was the only part I'd planned for him to play. But he grew and developed in my mind, and I realised it would be a huge shame to sideline him. When it came to plotting *Infiltrators*, he just snuck right in there and weaved his own little story in. I'm sorry he didn't have more of a part to play in *Defenders*, but I promise his story isn't quite finished yet.

Anyway, back to the point of this note. I have one more book to write in this series. And while I've started writing it, it isn't ready yet. I don't have a definite release date for *Liberators* yet, but it's likely to be mid-2019.

I know there's nothing more frustrating than finishing a book and not being able to get the next one in the series. I did think about rushing to try and get it out in the next few months, especially given I've left you with that little cliff-hanger at the end. (Sorry about that!) But I felt my characters – and you, the reader – deserved more than that. My aim when writing is for every book to be better than the last. Which means *Liberators* will be the best book in The Wall Series. I just need a bit more time.

Do I know how Aleesha and Trey's story will finish? I have an idea. I even have a plot. (Kind of.) But I'm sure it will change as my characters grow, develop and make clear their own views of what their destinies should be.

But I can make you a promise: heads will roll, hearts will bleed, and London will never be the same again.

Until next time,

Alison

22 November 2018

Can you help me out?

As an independent author, reviews are really important to me. They help make my books visible to people who are browsing Amazon or other sites and they help readers decide whether they'll enjoy reading my books.

If you enjoyed reading *Defenders,* I'd really appreciate it if you could take five minutes to leave a review. You can jump straight to the pages using the links below.

Amazon: mybook.to/DefendersReview

Goodreads: http://bit.ly/DefendersGoodreads

Thank you!

Alison

Acknowledgements

With every book I write, I have more people to thank. This time, I have to say a huge thank you to my friend and fellow dystopian author, Clare Littlemore, for spending far too many hours listening to my writing woes and helping me figure out how *Defenders* should end. (Also, check out her books – they are great!)

Thanks as always go to my wonderful editor, Sophie Playle, and my cover designer, Meg Cowley. To my treasured beta readers: Anni, Isabel, Candy, Clare, William and Mum – you guys rock! Your feedback on my rambling drafts was invaluable, and I couldn't dream of having a better team to help me bring this book into the world.

To my first and most loved reader, Sam. Who always pushes me to write the next book, puts up with the ups and downs of writing life and is always there with a hug at the end of another long evening's work.

Last, and most importantly, thank you to you, my readers, for buying and reading this series. I hope you'll do me the honour of finishing the journey with me in *Liberators*.

About the Author

Alison Ingleby is a young adult fantasy and sci-fi author and disaster geek. She spends her days wondering what the future will be like and hoping it's not as bad as the worlds in her head.

When not writing, Alison loves reading, Yorkshire Tea and hiking in the mountains. Her dream is to live by the sea in a Scottish castle (preferably one with central heating and hot water).

You can find out more about Alison, sign up for her Readers' Club and get a free story by visiting her website: https://alisoningleby.com/

Alison's Books:

The Wall Series:

Outsider (prequel)
Expendables (Book One)
Infiltrators (Book Two)
Defenders (Book Three)
Liberators (Book Four)
The Machinist's Daughter – a short story available exclusively in *On the Brink: A Dystopian Anthology*

Cursed Lands:

The Shadow City Book 1 – launching May 2019 exclusively in *Cursed Lands.*

Cursed Lands is a collection of 22 exclusive, page-turning tales from today's bestselling and award-winning authors.

If you love dystopian, urban fantasy or paranormal romance fiction, pre-order *Cursed Lands* today for just 99c. cursedlands-boxedset.com

Short stories & novellas:

Red Sun Rising: A Story from the Alteruvium Expanse

The Climb, featured in *Future Visions: Volume 1*

25232970R00258

Printed in Great Britain
by Amazon